BEFORE THE REVOLUTION: THE VIETNAMESE
PEASANTS UNDER THE FRENCH

The MIT Press
Cambridge, Massachusetts, and London, England

BEFORE THE REVOLUTION: THE VIETNAMESE
PEASANTS UNDER THE FRENCH
Ngo Vinh Long

This book was set in Linotype Baskerville
by Wolf Composition Company, Inc.
printed on Decision Offset
by Vail-Ballou Press, Inc.
and bound in Columbia Milbank Vellum MBV-4932
by Vail-Ballou Press, Inc.
in the United States of America.

Library of Congress Cataloging in Publication Data

Ngo Vinh Long.
  Before the revolution.

    Translation (p.   ): —1. Phi Van. The peasants (Dan Que), chapters 2
    and 4.—2. Ngo Tat To. When the light's put out (Tat Den), chapters
    12 and 13. [etc.]
    Bibliography: p.
    1. Vietnam—Rural conditions—Addresses, essays, lectures. 2. Villages—
    Vietnam—Addresses, essays, lectures. I. Title.
  HN700.V5N43   309.1'597'03   73–5779
  ISBN 0–262–12065–8

Đã chẳng may giặc Pháp cầm quyền; lại cứ mực dã man quen thói.

Tội, tội, tội, đặt mâm xuống, khoai chất lan rẫu; khổ, khổ, khổ, rường đũa lên, cơm van không muối.

Ill fortune, indeed, for power has been seized by the French invaders, who are bent on barbarous deeds, as is their wont.

It's criminal, criminal, criminal to set out the food tray and find that one has nothing but roots and greens to eat;

it's misery, misery, misery to take up the chopsticks and have one's meal cry out beseechingly because of a lack of salt.

(From a popular chant in *Sở tuyển van thơ yêu nước và cách mạng, tập II, từ đầu thế kỷ XX đến 1930*.)

CONTENTS

For English-speaking readers, this book is likely to serve as a forceful, unpleasantly chilling introduction to some very representative Vietnamese views about what Vietnamese relations with the industrial West have meant to Vietnamese society over the past century. The actual subject under study is the social result, in rural areas, of the policies of French colonial administrators in Vietnam between the 1880s and 1945. But the implications of Mr. Long's translations, revealing as they do what was on the minds of many Vietnamese, spread well beyond this pivotal period of six or seven decades. The author would be the last to claim that this book, or any other book, was the last word on the subject.

In the work that follows, Mr. Long introduces a very small sample of the extremely rich legacy of writings on social change bequeathed posterity by Vietnamese writers in the 1920s and 1930s. Many of these writers were men in a hurry—prolific, tormented, and often short-lived. Hoang Dao, the lawyer, journalist, and nationalist politician who portrays the "mud and stagnant water" of decaying Vietnamese villages, also wrote novels, short stories, satirical reminiscences, and books of political theory; he died at the age of forty-one of a heart condition in Kwangtung. Another social novelist of the 1930s, one who does not appear in Mr. Long's book but with whom Western scholars should become acquainted, Vu Trong Phung, began his career as a secretary in a large French commercial firm in Hanoi. He wrote candid, devastating novels like *Ky nghe lay Tay* [The Industry of Marrying Frenchmen], *Giong to* [The Hurricane], and *Luc xi* [roughly, Loaded Dice, an examination of the relationship between colonialism and prostitution] and then died of tuberculosis at the age of only twenty-eight. Nguyen Cong Hoan, the former schoolmaster who looks in the following pages at the "dead end" of Vietnamese rural life, wrote at least eighty short stories in the first five years of his writing career (1930–1935), as well as a number of longer efforts. The pages of the Hanoi-centered journals for which these men wrote—*Tieu thuyet thu bay* [Saturday Novels], *Ngo Bao* [Midday Report], *Ich Huu* [Reliability and Friendship], and hosts of others—were, as Mr. Long testifies, often indirect but sophisticated platforms of opposition to French rule.

A very different Vietnamese periodical of the colonial period, *Thanh Nghi* [Clear Counsel], is one of Mr. Long's important sources. Appearing in the first half of the 1940s (1939–1945) as a monthly, a biweekly, and then a weekly, it was the organ of a new group of intellectual youth, French-influenced, most of whom had been to Paris and many of whom had had serious legal training. Such men were uncommon, outside the ranks of the civil service, before 1940—evidence of the sluggishness of colonial education. Their journal, whose title referred to the disinterested remonstrances given to the emperor by loyal, incorruptible mandarin intellectuals (*ching-i* in Chinese), covered politics, economics, history, and education with imagination, analytical dedication, and a more intensely indigenous perspective than any found in French-language surveys. Once again, Mr. Long points the way in showing Western scholars the importance of a basic East Asian historical document, long neglected in Vietnamese studies as well as in more general Western theoretical discussions of such problems as the culture of poverty and rural development.

Mr. Long himself is hardly a stranger to rural Vietnam. He came to the United States in 1964, graduated with an A.B. degree from Harvard College in 1968, and is currently (1971) in the History and Far Eastern Languages Ph.D. program at Harvard University. But he was born in Vinh Long province in the Mekong Delta and spent most of his boyhood in rural areas of southern Vietnam. After receiving a middle school education in Saigon, he reimmersed himself in the countryside, serving as a mapmaker in the early 1960s. With such a background he is qualified to be both a "chronicler of lowly and misery-stricken categories of people"—the title given to Nguyen Cong Hoan after the publication of his first collection of short stories in Hanoi in the 1930s—and a new upholder of the great Vietnamese tradition of the "investigation of things," economic and cultural, in the manner of a Le Qui Don or a Nguyen Van Sieu.

It is the hope of the Vietnamese Studies Project at the Harvard East Asian Research Center that this book will represent only the beginning of the conscientious exploration of previously unplumbed Vietnamese journals, newspapers, novels, and other twentieth-century or pre-twentieth-century writings by scholars in the West. To this end the project is directed.

Alexander Woodside
East Asian Research Center, Harvard University

In the past thirty years or so the determination and the resiliency of the Vietnamese peasantry in the struggle against the French colonizers and their American successors have demonstrated the truth in the oft-quoted Vietnamese saying that "in times of turmoil the peasants come first and the scholars second." But in spite of the crucial role they play in the recent history of their country, the Vietnamese peasants are seldom mentioned in English writings on Vietnam. Of the writers who mention them at all, the great majority simply ignore the question of their living conditions during the French colonial period. The assumption, oddly enough, seems to be that what happened to the peasants at that time has no bearing whatsoever on more recent events—a misconception of which the forces of the National Liberation Front, at least, have never been guilty. Nor is the treatment of those writers who do discuss living conditions under the French much more satisfactory. By and large they approach the matter from the point of view of the colonizers or the landlords. This is done either inadvertently, through uncritical use of French sources (that were usually written to justify French colonial policies), or intentionally, because of the need to rationalize the present American intervention. Instead of looking from the peasants' point of view at how much of their crops they could keep, in general these writers maintain that the French improved the rural situation in Vietnam because of French achievements in lengthening the mileage of canals, asphalt roads, and railroads, and in opening up new areas for cultivation, and that French failure was a case of not applying sufficient or appropriate technology to farming. This, presumably, can now be done by the Americans with their technological know-how and with their electric water pumps, mechanical plows, chemical fertilizers, and so on. The implication, of course, is that there is no need for social change, only a need for technological improvements. Thus American aid can

PREFACE

be of more help to the Vietnamese peasantry than a social revolution and its prophets.

These oversights have prompted this book. It is an attempt to begin the restoration of the peasantry to its rightful place in recent Vietnamese history.

Part One of the study briefly traces the peasants' living conditions during the high noon of the French colonial period (1900–1945). It details the impact upon the peasant of the French policy of land expropriation and free land concession; the resulting problems of tenant farming and sharecropping; and the roles of taxes, tax collection, usury, government agrarian credit programs, and industry and commerce in determining the peasants' living standards. The essay's aims are twofold. First, the essay seeks to demonstrate that the usual picture of the peasants' condition depicted in the published works of French and Vietnamese government officials, economists, agronomists, and others—as well as in the official records of the colonial administration—is contradicted by the very facts that these sources marshal to support their case. Second, the essay attempts to provide the reader with the historical background that forms the context of the translations in Part Two of the study.

As for the "complementary" translations, which comprise Part Two, they are offered principally in the hope that they will help the reader to get beyond the cold facts and statistics of Part One and enable him to gain a *feeling* for what it meant to be a peasant in colonial times.

Beyond this, the readings raise a historiographic issue of some importance. Under the French, all books and newspapers were censored. Most strictly censored of all were nonfictional essays (perhaps because the essay is usually the preferred vehicle of political commentary in Europe). Consequently, Vietnamese writers were driven to use the style and form of the novel and short story when they wanted to write about social, economic, or political issues; and some of the best documentation of the conditions of peasant life appeared in fictional disguise.* This fact is widely recognized in Vietnam; after their subjection both to the censorship of the colonial administration and to the scrutiny of a generation of the reading public, many of the "documentary fictions" (*phong su tieu thuyet*) and the essays in "realist literature" (*van chuong ta chan*) have come to be considered by Vietnamese the most informative and effective social commentaries of their time. Future historians of the colonial period will have to reckon with these Vietnamese sources that hitherto have been completely overlooked.

The materials chosen for translation comprise but a tiny sample of the great bulk of literature on rural life that appeared during the colonial period. Even so, because of the problem of space, generally only a few short chapters are selected from each work. While every attempt has been made to render the selections into readable English, the original style and figures of speech are maintained as much as possible. Perhaps students of the Vietnamese language can benefit by using these literal translations as a study aid in reading the original writings.

Finally, a word about my approach. It has become fashionable in recent years for studies of national peasantries to seek to defend or criticize some theory (or theories) about the peasants in general. All too often, these efforts tend to obscure the facts in the particular case. I have eschewed such theoretical exercises and sought only to present a straightforward account of the

---

* The difference in the attitude of the censors toward "nonfiction" and "fiction" was quite striking. While "Mud and Stagnant Water" (one of the readings) is quite conservative by the standards of the late 1930s, it was immediately banned upon publication because it was written in the essay style. In contrast, two other readings ("When the Light's Put Out" and "Dead End") that appeared as novels in the same year—and were much more devastating critiques of rural life—were allowed to circulate with the full blessing of the censor.

living conditions of the Vietnamese peasants under the French. I hope that the conclusions are clear for any who wish to draw them. In this study I have also avoided discussing peasant rebellions for the simple reason that I do not believe their living conditions were the only causes of rebellion. The various factors that led the Vietnamese peasants to rebellion and finally to revolution will be discussed in a separate study that is under way.

The writing of this book was accomplished mainly in the period 1968–1969. I am grateful to my father, Mr. Ngo Ngoc Tung, for having sent me most of the sources used for the writing of this book and hundreds more that are not cited here but that I hope to utilize in a future study of the Vietnamese peasantry. I also wish to express my sincere appreciation to the Harvard-Yenching Institute for the generous scholarships it has given me for my graduate studies at Harvard University, in connection with which I wrote the shorter paper from which this book grew.

Throughout the whole undertaking a number of scholars and friends have given me extremely valuable advice and comments. I am grateful to Mr. William R. Carter, an old friend and a classmate, and Dr. John L. Gliedman, another very good friend, for their warm encouragement and useful criticism. Mr. Carter helped me type the manuscript twice to allow me the necessary time for attending to my other projects. Sincere appreciation is extended to Professors John K. Fairbank and Alexander B. Woodside for their careful reading of the manuscript. Professor Woodside and Mrs. Olive Holmes of the Harvard East Asian Research Center Editorial Staff gave me extremely valuable editorial help with the final draft of the manuscript. Needless to say, no one but myself is responsible for the shortcomings.

Ngo Vinh Long

I ANALYSIS

1 LAND EXPROPRIATION AND LAND CONCESSION

Vietnam became a colony of France by stages during the second half of the nineteenth century. Cochinchina—the six southern provinces in the ambit of the city of Saigon—was seized by the French navy from the control of the Vietnamese court during the reign of the emperor Tu-duc in the period 1859–1867. Central and northern Vietnam succumbed to French military aggression in the 1880s, and by 1885 Vietnam had lost its political independence. Politicians and militarists of the French Third Republic spoke of fulfilling a "civilizing mission" (*la mission civilisatrice*) in a society that was, in fact, older than France itself, but they understood very little of the society they sought to improve. Frenchmen in Vietnam itself began by examining institutions, looking at them as if they were immovable objects or timeless sources of influence and drawing limited conclusions from them based on their own particular fields. Ethnologist administrators like J. Silvestre described the structure of the Vietnamese family, and novelists like Albert de Pouvoirville explained that filial piety was more important in Vietnam than romantic love. Little attention was paid to the Vietnamese peasantry; in particular, little attention was paid to the political and social processes of change among the peasants.

Indeed, at the time France conquered Vietnam, the peasantry had already been serving as the spearhead of the social upheavals that occurred repeatedly under the first four Nguyen emperors: Gia-long (1802–1820), Minh-mang (1820–1841), Thieu-tri (1841–1847), and Tu-duc (1847–1883).[1] These upheavals were precedents for the peasant politics of the colonial period, yet the French invaders of Vietnam were ignorant of them. Partly the upheavals were the result of the emperor Gia-long's cruel repression of his surviving adversaries from the civil wars of the late 1700s, the supporters of the Tay-son monarchy that had briefly unified Vietnam in the 1780s but then disintegrated in the 1790s.[2] Partly these social upheavals were the result of floods, droughts, crop failures,[3] and "bandit" invaders like the French,[4] all of which reduced the livelihood of the peasantry and created unmanageable political problems for the dynasty.

In spite of all its troubles and shortcomings, the Nguyen court's land policy nevertheless made some responses to the needs of the population. During the Nguyen as well as during earlier dynasties, all the land in the country belonged in theory to the king, and people paid him taxes for the privilege of working it.[5] Thus the king could grant to individuals a certain amount of land to be used as "private land" (*tu dien*) and grant to villages or groups certain areas to be used as "public land" (*cong dien*). In theory, the grants were conditional. The king had the right at any time to take back any land he wished without being obligated in any way to grant compensation.[6] However, in practice, whenever the king recovered lands, he estimated their value and compensated the farmers accordingly.[7]

During the Ming Chinese invasion (1407–1427), because of the social, economic, and political disruptions it brought about, Vietnamese land distribution had become extremely lopsided. Land tended to accumulate in the hands of collaborators and opportunists, who profited from the disorder brought on by the invasion. So some villagers had a lot of land to work, while others had none.[8]

After the Ming armies were driven from the country, Emperor Le Thai-to (1428–1433) adopted the *quan dien* ("equal field") land system in an attempt to put a limit on the amount of land an individual could own and to distribute land to those who did not have enough.[9] This system, which had its origin in China,[10] did not mean, however, that everybody would receive equal amounts of land. It only meant that people of the same rank and the same social status were supposed to receive equal amounts of land. For example, a duke received more land than a marquis, a marquis more than a count, a count more than a baron, and so on down the hierarchical ladder. A civil official received more than a military official of the same rank, court officials received more than local officials, and officials in general received more than common people. Among the common people, males between the ages of eighteen and sixty were to have more land than men over sixty; free men received more than bondsmen. Nobody, however, might own more than his legal share. In fact, the term for land granted to individuals was "personal share land" (*khau phan dien*). This land was to revert to the state for redistribution when the cultivator reached the age of sixty or upon his death. In China, under a similar system under the T'ang, this land was also supposed to be redistributed annually by the country magistrates to provide those who came of age their "personal shares." In Vietnam, under the Le, the "personal share land" was redistributed every four years in proportion to the increase or decrease of paddy laborers and the increase or decrease of the cultivated surface in a given area.[11]

In 1804, several years after he had proclaimed himself emperor, Gia-long again put into effect the Le land system, which was now also known as the "personal share land system" (*khau phan dien che*). Under this system, civil and military officials above rank 1A (that is, bureaucrats who had been given the noble titles of duke, marquis, and so forth) received eighteen parts, or shares (the size of a share varied with the locality).[12] Land was given in place of salary.

A bureaucrat with rank 1A received 15 parts (*phan*) of land, a 2A official received 14 parts, a 9B official, who was the lowest ranked, received 8 parts, and the most land a vigorous, tax-paying adult male peasant could expect to receive was 6½ parts.[13]

A peasant who was affected by long illnesses received 5½ parts;

old men above sixty years of age who were exempted from tax received 4½ parts each; old men who were seventy years of age or older received 5½ parts; tax-exempted young boys (that is, between sixteen and eighteen) and tax-exempt patients received 4 parts; orphans and widows received 3 parts.[14] Exactly how much land a part was equal to depended on the specific locality and period. In general, however, the most a vigorous peasant could receive was five *mau** and the least the lowest grade of commoner received was several *sao* (one-tenth of a *mau*).[15]

To make more land available to the commoners, the court switched policies in 1814 and began to pay its bureaucrats regular salaries:

In 1814 Gia-long granted all district magistrates serving in provinces from Quang Binh south a monthly salary of money and rice and a yearly sum of money for "spring clothes." In 1825 Minh-mang began to award exiguous stipends to sub-officials. The real turning point probably did not come until 1839, when a graduated salary system was devised which paid fixed salaries in money and rice to officials from 1A to 3B in bureaucratic rank twice a year, to those from 4A to 7B four times a year, and to those from 8A to 9B once a month. The yearly sum of money a 1A official received (400 *quan*) was more than 21 times the yearly salary of a ninth grade official (18 *quan*). It was only in 1839–40, significantly, that the court attempted to deny participation in the communal profits of the "public lands" in their neighborhoods to salaried bureaucrats and to reserve these profits exclusively for peasants and un-salaried sub-bureaucrats.[16]

From that time on, the only land that could be held by senior bureaucrats was "sacrificial land" (*te dien* or *tu dien*), land that was used for the purpose of maintaining ancestral graveyards and paying for the expenses of the ceremonies conducted in

* A *mau* of land was equal to 3,600 square meters (roughly nine-tenths of an acre).

honor of the ancestors. The maximum amount of land that could be held by a member of the royal family or by a court official bearing the noble title of *cong* (duke) was only ten *mau*. A *hau* (marquis) might own eight *mau*; a *ba* (count) six *mau*; a *tu* (baron) four *mau*; and a *nam* (earl) three *mau*.[17] Beginning in 1883, by the order of the court in Annam, meritorious officials who were given land for ancestor worship or for old age now had to return all their land to the state for distribution among the population. In place of the land they were paid forty *quan* per *mau* per year, which was equal to the price of the productivity of the average piece of land minus tax and production costs.[18]

Besides the *khau phan dien*, which was redistributed every three years in proportion to the increase or decrease of grantees and the increase or decrease of the cultivated surface in a given area,[19] land was given to the villages for various kinds of communal uses. The division of these lands followed a pattern traditional under the dynasties. The terminology varied from village to village and from period to period, but in general these lands consisted of: *luong dien* (or "salary land"), given to soldiers as part of their salaries; *tro suu dien* (or "tax assistance land"), used to help the poor pay their taxes; *hoc dien* (or "study land"), used for paying teachers and supplying students with educational materials; and *co nhi* and *qua phu dien* ("orphans' and widows' land"), which was for helping orphans and widows. The sale of these "public lands" (*cong dien*) was forbidden.[20] They could be rented to private cultivators, however, for a maximum of three years, if the rent money was devoted to village business. Before 1844 village chiefs (*xa truong*) had the power to decide whether such land could be rented for three years. After 1844 a law specified that written rental documents had to be signed by ten members of the village as well as by the village chief. In these documents the villagers had to explain the emergency that made it necessary for them to rent the lands and also which lands were being rented and what their values were.[21]

As in the case of the "personal share lands," the availability of the "public lands" differed from one region to another. The one exception to this was the "salary land" for soldiers. In 1809 the Nguyen court had measured out the available amount of the *luong dien* ("salary land") in the whole country and decided that soldiers would receive from eight *sao* to a *mau* of this land, depending on the individual's various military service. Besides the "salary land," all soldiers received equal parts of the "personal share land."[22] Beginning in 1820, the first year of Emperor Minh-mang's reign, guards of various types were given a *mau* of "salary land" each, as well as nine parts of "personal share land."[23] Beginning in 1833, soldiers were given land according to the different duties they performed. The most prestigious of the soldiers, the personal guards for the officials and the grade A military guards of palaces, received one *mau* of "salary land" and nine parts of "personal share land" each. The lowest-paid soldier, the road guard, received seven *sao* of "salary land" and seven parts of "personal share land."[24]

In China the "equal-field" land system had begun to break down in the first half of the eighth century because of population increases, corrupt officials, multiple grants to the same individuals (as rewards for meritorious services), and the registration of most of the holdings as permanent possessions.[25] Vietnam did not escape some of the same problems. They were most acute in the province of Binh Dinh.[26] There—owing to land usurpation and multiple grants—some landlords possessed estates from 100 to 200 *mau* before the land reform of 1839. The amount of private land comprised more than 70,000 *mau*, whereas public lands in the province totaled no more than 7,000 *mau*. Official corruption was yet another problem. In 1828, for example, Nguyen Cong Tru, a high official with extensive experience in the provinces, sent a memorial to Emperor Minh-mang saying that in many villages local officials were getting together to rent communal lands for private profit and, in order to pocket some of the land tax and head tax money, were sending in false reports on the amount of cultivated land and the number of males coming of age.[27]

Nonetheless, these problems generally did not get out of hand because the country was small enough for effective governmental enforcement and control. The 1839 land reforms, for example, not only were draconian on paper, but were actually enforced. As a result, in a single blow half of the private lands in Binh Dinh were converted back into village communal lands. All that one landowner was allowed to keep was five *mau*,[28] and the landlords were not compensated for the land confiscated by the government.[29] Also, officials, no matter how highly placed, who usurped the land of the people or rented communal land for private profit or beyond a certain authorized date were severely punished and dismissed from their posts.[30] (Any person who exposed such official misdemeanors would be given a *mau* of first-grade land as a reward for a three-year duration.[31])

The court's land system was not really as equitable as the term "equal-field" might suggest, but it at least had helped to keep land from becoming overly concentrated in the hands of a few.[32] The village communal land had also helped in the solving of various welfare problems. In fact, except for the difference in scale, the personal share land could be compared to the "private plot" or "5 percent land" and the village communal land to the "cooperatives" practiced today in North Vietnam.[33] In spite of its problems, the Nguyen land system worked reasonably well.[34]

The French take-over of Vietnam affected the ruler's supreme ownership of the land and the land policy of traditional Vietnamese courts. The changes introduced were not uniform, differing according to region.

In Cochinchina (Nam Ky), as a result of the occupation and of the treaties of June 5, 1862 (clause 3), and of March 15, 1874 (clause 5), the Vietnamese court ceded complete sovereignty to the French. The French colonizers in turn issued the decrees of January 20, 1862, of May 16, 1863, and of June 22, 1863, which attempted to rearrange the pattern of landownership in the Mekong Delta. The decree of January 1862 proclaimed that all land that did not belong to, or was not occupied by, the indigenous people would be confiscated.[35] The May 1863 decree set up statutes to protect and guarantee rights of ownership, particularly the "rights" of the French colonizers. The decree of June 1863 ordered that all Vietnamese peasants who had abandoned their native villages were to return to them before the middle of September of that year in order to claim their land and to continue working on it. Otherwise, after that date all lands not claimed in such a manner would be confiscated by the colonial administration.[36]

Behind this clinically precise decree lurked the vast ambitions of the activist naval officer who served as governor of Cochinchina from 1863 to 1868, Admiral De la Grandière. De la Grandière was determined to crush the various resistance movements that plagued the French rulers in southern Vietnam in the early 1860s and to govern the Vietnamese population in the south directly through the famous corps of French military officers, the "inspectors of native affairs," that he created. He was the pugnacious prophet of a Cochinchina that would be "forever French." To fulfill his own prophecy, he granted all the land in the Ky Hoa area in southern Cochinchina to French citizens (and at no cost to them). The French recipients of the admiral's largesse subdivided the land grants into lots of twenty to thirty hectares, which they then rented to Vietnamese. The fee was ten francs per hectare for the first five years and twenty francs per hectare annually for the following twenty years. Vietnamese could, in fact, buy certain of the lots outright, it is true, but only if they could meet the price set by the French: two hundred francs per hectare.[37] Many of the concessions the admiral's Saigon regime made to French citizens were larger than 30 hectares; some exceeded 4,000 hectares.[38] One Frenchman amassed an estate of more than 12,000 hectares, according to one report.[39]

But De la Grandière's aggressive vision of a "forever French" Mekong Delta did not rest entirely upon the artificial creation of an instant French landed gentry in Cochinchina. Vietnamese were part of the vision, too—Vietnamese who have been regarded by the Vietnamese nationalist tradition as "collaborators" for having allowed the French to win, or purchase, their loyalties. These persons—often Catholics, sometimes members of the new colonial militia, occasionally mandarins alienated from the Vietnamese court—also received hundreds of hectares of paddy lands free, by fiat of the French admiral in Saigon. Most of these lands belonged to people who had left their native villages when the French began to invade and occupy the country.[40] With the help of the French, the collaborators legalized their new ownership claims. The result was that when the original owners of these lands came back as ordered by the decree of June 1863—even if they managed to come back before the set deadline—they were often forced to become tenant farmers or sharecroppers on their own land.[41]

Tonkin (Bac Ky) and Annam (Trung Ky) were established as "protectorates" according to the treaty of June 6, 1884. The emperor, formally at least, retained his rights over administration and landownership in these two regions; yet, informally, the French gradually forced the court to give up most of its remaining powers. Thus, under the reign of Thanh-thai, an imperial decree was issued on October 3, 1888, which allowed French citizens and Vietnamese living under the French protectorate system to have rights of landownership in Tonkin and in the port areas of Annam, but only in accordance with French-made laws. In another imperial decree issued on September 27, 1897, however, the emperor wholly renounced his residual rights over the land, even in Annam (where the imperial capital of Hue was located). The decree allowed direct landownership by French citizens, as well as by Vietnamese under the French protectorate system, according to the regulations set up by the French Governor-General of Indochina.

Having obtained these imperial decrees, the French themselves issued the two decrees of August 18, 1896, and April 28, 1899, that readjusted the free land concessions to the further advantage of French citizens. The first decree canceled the 100-hectare limitation on French holdings that had been imposed by an earlier decree in 1888. Thus, all sorts of Frenchmen, engaged in a wide variety of occupations, were easily able to obtain paddy lands as large as 1,000 or even up to 30,000 hectares.[42] Perhaps owing in part to a certain degree of contempt in which some of these parvenu lower- and middle-class French landholders were held by the aristocratic French administrators, the second decree, three years later, limited the maximum amount of each free land concession to 500 hectares. All the same, this new limit was still nearly 150 times larger than the largest landholdings permitted by Vietnamese law after the Nguyen land reform of 1839—and more than six times larger than the largest landholdings before the land reform. Moreover, if a Frenchman wanted land for a specific purpose, or if he had already obtained one concession and had already cultivated four-fifths of it, the amount allowed him could be made higher. The same 500-hectare limitation for each concession was repeated in the decree of December 27, 1913; but fifteen years later, article 2 of the November 4, 1928, decree lowered the limitation to 300 hectares per concession.[43]

As a result of these policies, by 1930 the area of land concessions obtained by the French was 104,000 hectares in Tonkin, 168,400 hectares in Annam, and the still larger figure of 606,500 hectares in Cochinchina.[44] The statistics did not change appreciably afterward. For example, the area owned by French nationals in Tonkin in 1939 was 110,000 hectares.[45] As noted earlier, these concessions in Tonkin and Annam were drawn from land expropriated largely from farmers who had left their homes because of the insecurity brought about by banditry and by the French invasion.[46] A common technique used by the French was to exploit traditional Vietnamese court law in depriving the peasants of their rights of landownership and then to apply French laws to assert the rights of ownership of the colonists to the same lands.[47]

But a dry, complicated recitation of statistics and legislation does not really bring the reader close enough to the human realities and social tensions of colonial landholding manipulations. Nhat Linh, one of modern Vietnam's most famous writers, published a short story in 1927 entitled "Slavery" [No le]. In it he depicts one of the multitude of techniques by which Vietnamese supporters of the colonial government took lands from the peasantry.[48] A Vietnamese plantation owner, given permission to develop a coffee plantation in a certain location, had his agents fence off the desired concession area. Inside the fence lay plots of land belonging to the peasants of a nearby village. The peasants protested their threatened expropriation, but the plantation owner bribed the local village council of notables, offered employment to unemployed villagers, and convinced the peasant plot owners themselves that expropriation was not really expropriation: they could enter his plantation freely and continue to till their lands. In this way he skillfully muted local protest. Government land concession regulations stipulated that if local protest had not manifested itself within three months of the announcement of a concession, the land would become the permanent property of the grantee. But a few years later, when the coffee trees of the new plantation had matured, the plantation owner sternly reversed himself, forbidding the peasants to enter his plantation on the ground that their cattle would damage his coffee trees. If the colonial Land Concession Committee later sent one of its members to investigate, the owner showed him the plantation, wined him and dined him, and obtained legitimization for his now obscure act of theft. The expropriated peasants themselves ultimately became rootless workers on the owner's estate, on his terms. The importance of Nhat Linh's stinging sociological portrait of the disingenuous coffee plantation owner may be debated, but it suggests that colonial laws permitted greater polarization of Vietnamese rural society in practice than colonial lawmakers themselves intended.

The French tried to appropriate not only lands that had been worked on by individual families of peasants, who had therefore considered the land as their own, but also the communal lands that had been given to the villages by the court for welfare purposes and for meeting various village expenses, as mentioned earlier. In fact, the French colonial administration actively sought to reduce the area of communal land by permitting village officials to sell it.[49] According to one author, the total area of communal land plummeted as a result.[50]

According to Gourou, the total area of communal land in Tonkin represented 20 percent of the cultivated surface there. It was 26 percent in Annam, but not even as high as 2.5 percent in Cochinchina.[51] Official French sources in 1931 give the statistics of 20 percent, 25 percent, and 3 percent, respectively.[52] One of the reasons for the low level of communal land in Cochinchina, as given by Gourou, was usurpation of such land by rich landlords.[53] In some provinces in Tonkin, because of land usurpation and because of auction sale by village officials, communal land became almost nonexistent. But patterns in Tonkin were diverse. In provinces like Thai Binh and Nam Dinh, where usurpation and auctioning of the land were not yet extensive, the amount of communal land in many villages amounted to two-thirds and sometimes nine-tenths of the total cultivated area.[54] The relatively higher percentage of communal land in Annam, according to Gourou, was due to the determination and the wisdom of the "Annamite government" (meaning the Vietnamese court) in trying to maintain the communal lands. As a result, in certain areas in this region the total amount of cultivated surface was communal land. Registered inhabitants (that is, males from eighteen to sixty) in those areas could receive about one and one-fifth hectares each.[55]

Nguyen Van Vinh, in an important study, noted that in the villages on the borders of the Red River there still existed a remarkable predominance of communal land. For example, 59 percent of the total cultivated surface in the prefecture of Truc Ninh, and 77.5 percent of the cultivated area in the prefecture of Xuan-Truong in Nam Dinh province, was communal land. Vinh also stated that in Annam, in certain provinces like Thanh Hoa, Nghe An, Ha Tinh, Ninh Thuan, and Binh Thuan, there was very little communal land; in other provinces like Quang Tri, communal land represented the entire cultivated surface.[56] In other words, communal land tended to decrease in provinces more distant from the court in Hue. Also, if the amount of communal land in the provinces of Thai Binh and Nam Dinh in Tonkin and in certain areas in Annam was any indication of what the percentage of communal land had been before the arrival of the French, the area of communal land in the country as a whole had indeed been reduced substantially.

Besides the appropriation of lands that were already under cultivation when the French arrived, there was also widespread usurpation of virgin lands that the rural population was in the process of opening up for new settlement. A typical case, described by Gourou, was that of a farmer who went to open up a piece of virgin land and, while working on it, had to borrow money at high interest. After a while, so much interest on his debt had piled up that in the end he had to turn his land over to the usurer.[57] Another typical case, described by Nguyen Van Vinh, was that of the peasant who went to work on a piece of virgin land, hoping to become its owner. But when the first harvest came around, the land was confiscated because it happened to fall into a large land concession belonging to a "European" (meaning a Frenchman) or to a certain rich Vietnamese proprietor, who, of course, had the support of the French colonial administration.[58]

Yet another typical case is described by Phi Van in a book entitled *Dan Que* [The Peasantry]. French colonial authorities sent out notices stating that peasant families could clear up to ten hectares of virgin land each, with the stipulation that after the land was turned into paddy fields their names would be put down in the land registers as permanent owners. However, when the land at last was made into paddy fields, powerful village officials or landlords put in applications for free land concessions, claiming that those peasants who had been working on the land were merely their hired hands. The peasants then realized that they had been wasting their energy and resources for nothing, although there was not a thing that they could do to get their paddy fields back. Many did, in fact, make an effort to

sue the usurper but lost their lawsuits, depleting their resources in legal fees. Finally they were forced to give up; they
had to become tenants to the new owners.[59]

As a result of this land appropriation and free land concession, official French colonial sources listed the area of land
concessions in the hands of "European" individuals and companies as amounting to 872,000 hectares in 1932, 867,300 hectares in 1938, and 884,299 hectares in 1948; while the total
amount of land concessions held by Vietnamese landowners was
1,081,400 hectares in 1932, 1,227,500 hectares in 1938, and
1,403,863 hectares in 1948.[60] Thus, in round numbers, the total
area of land concessions held by both French and Vietnamese
amounted to 1,950,000 hectares in 1932; 2,100,000 hectares in
1938; and 2,300,000 hectares in 1948.

In 1931 the total surface of rice paddy for the country as a
whole was 4,300,000 hectares;[61] the total cultivated surface of
maize was from 130,000 to 145,000 hectares; while the cultivated surface of all other produce (including coffee and tea)
was less than 200,000 hectares.[62] These figures do not include
100,000 hectares in rubber plantations.[63] Even if one were to
include in the computation the cultivated area of all the industrial crops, the area of the land concessions still amounted to more
than two-fifths of the total cultivated surface. The statistics just
given concerning the total cultivated surface in Vietnam did not
change very much after 1931, since the official French statistics
for 1937 and also an updated and modified version by Gourou
in 1940 gave the figure of 6,000,000 hectares for the whole of
Indochina for all crops, including both agricultural produce
(that is, rice, maize, coffee, tea, tobacco, sugar cane, vegetables,
fruit, and greens) and industrial crops (rubber trees, jute,
ricinus, lacquer, rush, cotton, and so forth).[64] If one deducts the
1,000,000 hectares of cultivated surface in Cambodia alone from
the total area given for "Indochina," [65] then one can see that the

percentage of the land concessions in Vietnam still amounted to more than two-fifths of the total cultivated area.

These statistics do not account for the amounts of land that landlords controlled by other means (such as usury). The exact figures are unknown. However, as a result of land appropriation, land concession, and land usurpation, according to one investigation, in 1938 in Tonkin alone there were 968,000 peasant families who were completely without any land of their own.[66] Statistics given in 1952–1953 by "Le Bureau de Statistiques et de Recherches économiques du Gouvernement" showed that in Tonkin there were 1,303,700 landless peasant families (58 percent) as opposed to 944,000 families with land.[67] Another study in 1940 found that in the province of Hai Duong in Tonkin 36,000 out of 73,000 registered inhabitants (that is, men from eighteen to sixty years of age) of that province did not own any land at all.[68] These statistics, while revealing, cannot be regarded as absolutely accurate, since there were various additional complications.

For example, there might have been a large number of women who owned land, but as females they were not "registered inhabitants." On the other hand, while a peasant might nominally be a landowner, in fact he might only have been a sharecropper for some big landlord who did not want to put his own name down as the legal owner of the land, in order to avoid paying higher taxes. Henry admits that "in adding up figures by villages, perhaps we have counted the same landholder many times if he owns property in many villages. . . . Some large property owners register their land in the name of their wives."[69] Gourou also notes that large property owners usually hid their wealth by dispersing it in many villages under different names, particularly when they were mandarins in office or former mandarins, for they could be too easily accused of having taken advantage of their offices to enrich themselves.[70]

The most frequent case was one in which the land might be registered in the name of the peasants but was actually owned by creditors and usurers.[71] In spite of all these difficulties, let us look more closely at the distribution of landownership in the northern region of Tonkin, as it was estimated by the French.

In Tonkin, according to Gourou's estimate of 1939, there were 586,000 landowners who held less than a *mau** of cultivated land; 283,000 landowners who owned from one to five *mau*; 60,000 landowners who owned from five to ten *mau*; 20,000 who owned from ten to fifty *mau*; 800 who owned from fifty to one hundred *mau*; and 250 who owned more than one hundred *mau*.[72]

This estimate is not too far from the official one cited by Henry for the period 1930–1931: there were 882,000 small land-owners working on properties under five *mau* each; 81,000 persons whom he called "medium landowners," each with property of five to fifty *mau*; 815 "rich landowners," each with property of fifty to one hundred *mau*; and 252 "very rich" landowners, with more than one hundred *mau* each.[73]

Gourou notes that the small landowners (those with less than five *mau*) occupied 440,000 hectares (37 percent of the cultivated surface); what he defines as "medium landowners" (those with from five to ten *mau*) occupied 320,000 hectares (27 percent), and what he calls "big landowners" (those with more than ten *mau*) occupied 200,000 hectares (17 percent). The remaining 19 percent of the cultivated surface was still considered communal land.[74] But Gourou may have made a mistake when he categorized only those who owned from five to ten *mau* as "medium landowners." If one divides the 320,000

---

* A *mau*, in Cochinchina and in Tonkin, is 3,600 square meters or 0.36 hectare. It equals 10 *sao* (360 square meters each). In Annam, however, a *mau* is somewhat larger (about 5,000 square meters), perhaps owing to the poorer quality of the soil.

hectares of land that were supposed to be owned by the 60,000 persons in that category, one comes up with a little more than 5.3 hectares (about fifteen *mau*) per person, which is more than the maximum amount of land each of them is supposed to have in that category. The official classification given by Henry, listing as "medium landowners" those who owned from five to fifty *mau*, would make more sense. This would leave us, therefore, with less than 1,100 "rich and very rich" landowners (or about 0.1 percent of the total of some one million landowners) owning about 17 percent of the total cultivated surface of the region.

But the classifications made by Gourou and by the colonial government do not tell the whole story of the problem of landholding. First of all, the large landowners are certain to have had even more land than listed, although the exact figures are unavailable.

It is certain that the large landowners occupy more land than is accounted for in official figures; this is because large properties can be hidden under many forms; one should first combine all the properties which one single individual owns in different villages, but this kind of compilation is not done at this time; it is hard to do because the lands belonging to a single owner may be registered under different names. Besides, under certain forms of loan contract, the land used by the debtor as security can pass into the lands of the creditor yet may theoretically still be the property of the debtor; in reality, however, the debtor is now the creditor's tenant farmer. . . . In the province of Thai Binh, an unofficial survey shows that 122,000 landowners with less than 1 *mau* each together hold 61,000 *mau*; meanwhile, 254 big landowners directly own 28,000 *mau* and control 43,000 *mau* whose former owners still preserve their ownership in name but in fact have become tenant farmers on the latifundia.[75]

Second, the 586,000 small landowners who are supposed to have held less than a *mau* each may have owned on the average closer to half a *mau* or less, as is suggested by the preceding survey in the province of Thai Binh, and by the following one in Bac Ninh:

A precise survey conducted in certain villages of the province of Bac Ninh shows that the very small landowners are most numerous. Among the 1,672 landowners investigated, there are 1,528 small landowners (less than 3 *mau*), and among them 1,050 who own less than half a *mau* (0.18 hectares).[76]

Moreover, Gourou's own figures themselves suggest a somewhat similar value. For, recall that he says that the 586,000 landowners with less than one *mau* and the 283,000 landowners with one to five *mau* altogether accounted for only 440,000 hectares. Thus, even if the average holding of the one to five *mau* group was only one *mau*—which seems highly unlikely—there would only be 157,000 hectares left to be divided up among the half-million households owning less than one *mau,* or slightly more than three-forths of a *mau* (one-fourth of a hectare) per household. If it is supposed that the lands owned by these small landowners were all paddy fields and that they had not been taken over by rich landlords through usury, half a *mau* would give the owner only about 230 kilograms of paddy rice a year, or about 160 kilograms of milled rice (the conversion rate of milled rice to paddy rice being about 70:100).[77] The reason for this was that each hectare of paddy in Tonkin in the 1930s produced on the average 1,330 kilograms a year, as compared to 1,210 kilograms in Cochinchina and 1,170 kilograms in Annam.[78]

If on the average a person needed 337 kilograms of paddy rice (or 233 kilograms of milled rice) a year, as Henry states in his book,[79] then a landowner who owned half a *mau* could not produce enough for his own consumption, let alone his family's. Nor could he support, in addition, the burden of taxes and production costs. A landowner who had a family of four would thus need at least three *mau* (1.08 hectares) in order to produce enough food to feed his family. For this reason, the 586,000 small landholders who had less than a *mau* did not produce enough to eat; also many of the 283,000 persons who were supposed to own between one and five *mau* were in a similar situation. For, even if the peasants in the less than one *mau* group actually owned no land at all, the 283,000 households in the one to five *mau* group would still have only 440,000 hectares among them, or, *on the average*, only slightly more than 1½ hectares apiece.

At this point, it may be useful to compare at random the landholding patterns in Tonkin to those in China. Obviously, because of China's size and its vast regional discrepancies, such a comparison must be impressionistic. But even an impressionistic comparison can be enlightening: Tawney's statistics suggest that Tonkin—with more than half of its peasants landless—was worse off than much of China.

Whatever her rural problems may be, they are not complicated by the existence of a landless proletariat. The typical figure in Chinese country life is not the hired labourer, but the landholding peasant.

The conditions of his tenure vary widely from region to region, and even from village to village. According to the figures published by the Department of Agriculture and Commerce for 1918, about 50 per cent of the peasants were occupying owners, 30 per cent were tenants and 20 per cent owned part of their farm land while renting the remainder. A later inquiry, based on a sample investigation, gives a result which is substantially the same; the owners, it was found, formed 51.7 per cent, the tenants 22.6 per cent and the part owners 22.1 per cent.

The differences in the proportion of the three classes in different provinces were, in each case, striking. The proportion of owners was highest in the northern provinces, and least in the southern. In Shensi, Shansi, Hopei, Shantung and Honan, the first inquiry put it at 65 and the second at 69 per cent. In Kiangsi, Hunan and Kwangtung it was 31.8 per cent in the first and 27 per cent in the second.[80]

But it is, of course, misleading to compare the two areas in this way, since China is a large country with a diversity of staple crops (wheat, millet, and so forth) besides rice. A truer comparison should be made with areas in China where rice is the predominant agricultural product. This brings us in effect to the provinces of southern China where the landholding situation was also much worse than in the country as a whole. To do this we have to rely on case studies. The first case concerns Chekiang province, where "the acreage under rice is 67 per cent of the total crop area." [81]

Figures obtained from seventy-five villages in northwest Chekiang "show that 32.9 percent of the farmers were owners, 36.7 percent tenants, and 30.4 percent tenants and part owners." [82] Figures from sixty-eight villages in the same area also show that 38 percent of the landowning farmers had farms smaller than five *mow* each. Thirty-three percent worked from six to ten *mow*, 20.6 percent from eleven to fifteen *mow*, 6.6 percent from twenty-six to fifty *mow*, while the remaining 1.8 percent owned from fifty-one to 200 *mow* apiece.[83] The size of the *mow* used for the calculations was given as a fraction smaller than one-sixth of an acre.

In Tonkin, as we have seen, about a million peasants (or more than one-half) were completely landless. Of the nearly one million landowners (who were not all farmers, since most of the large landowners were absentee landlords), 600,000, or about 60 percent, held less than half an acre each, while in the area of Chekiang 62 percent of the landowners had more than five *mow* (five-sixths of an acre) apiece. While no statistics on average rice yields were given for Chekiang, the average yield of rice per acre in China as a whole is given as 2.7 times that of Indochina.[84] This means that these small landholders in Chekiang—and probably many of the tenants as well—were much better off than most of the so-called small landholders in Tonkin.

Another case for comparison is the area in the plain around Kunming, the capital of Yunnan province, which was studied by Fei Hsiao-tung and his colleagues during the period 1939–1943. In one of the localities studied, which was given the fictitious name of "Luts'un," the population density was about 900 persons per square mile,[85] or roughly comparable to the average of over 1,000 persons per square mile in the Tonkin Delta.[86] (However, in the plains of the highland regions in Tonkin where the terrain is similar to the area around Kunming, the highest density was only about 40 inhabitants per square mile.) [87] In Luts'un the distribution of landholding was approximately as follows:

The total land owned by individual families comprises about 1,800 kung, or 690 mow, which is an average of 5.7 mow, or 0.87 acre, per family. Thirty-one per cent of the households in the village, however, are landless. The 1,800 kung are owned as follows: 446 (25 per cent) by 35 per cent of the households with less than 16 kung each; 614 (34 per cent) by 19 per cent with 16–30 kung each; and 740 (40 per cent) by 15 per cent with 31–65 kung each.[88]

It can be seen that the percentage of completely landless households in Luts'un, as in the area cited in northwest Chekiang, was substantially lower than in Tonkin, which, as we have seen, had a percentage of more than 50 percent. In the relatively small area of Luts'un (where there were only about a thousand inhabitants), the concentration of landholding in the hands of a few, while evidenced to a certain degree, was not in any way comparable to the situation in Tonkin, where 0.1 percent of the landholders held 17 percent of the land. Of the

69 percent of the households in Luts'un who owned land, it can be seen that just over half possessed no more than sixteen *kung* (two-fifths of a hectare), which is roughly comparable to the statistics showing that 60 percent of the landowners in Tonkin possessed less than one Vietnamese *mau* (0.36 hectares). Nevertheless, the situation of the small landholders in Luts'un, as in neighboring localities of the Lake Tai region, seems to have been much better than that of the small landholders in Tonkin, since rice productivity there was substantially higher than in Tonkin.[89]

Besides the family holdings just cited, in Luts'un there was also collective land holdings by social groups like clans, clubs, and temples. Together such groups owned as much as "27 per cent of all the land owned by members of the village." [90] The collective holdings resembled the communal land in Vietnam in many respects. For example:

The largest property-holder of the village is the Temple of the Lord of the Earth, an institution which is found in almost every village in the region. . . . Specifically, its funds are spent for (1) the maintenance of the village temple, (2) part of the maintenance of the village school, (3) emergency restoration of the dam, (4) entertainment of soldiers passing through the village, (5) gifts at the marriages and burials of villagers, and (6) partial subsidization of the village government.[91]

Then there was the Confucian Club, which gave the income from its properties to the village school; the Imperial Teaching Society, which also assisted the poor in meeting burial expenses; the irrigation organization, which devoted its income to the maintenance of the dams and ditches; and the educational bureau, whose land provided the revenue to pay part of the expenses of the village school.[92] Besides their social welfare role, these group holdings also provided work for the landless in the village, although one can probably assume that they were tilled in part by individuals who owned some land of their own. These lands can therefore be equated with the communal lands in Vietnam insofar as they remained intact under the French.

Tonkin was just one region in Vietnam. What was the situation like in the other two regions? The landholding situation in Annam was similar to that in Tonkin, although the percentage of poor peasants was even greater. Statistics given in 1952–1953 by "Le Bureau de Statistiques et de Recherches économiques du Gouvernement" showed that in Annam there were 866,200 (53 percent) landless families, as opposed to 768,000 (47 percent) families with some land.[93] Using the same index number for the *mau* (in spite of the somewhat larger land area per *mau* in Annam)* to define the size of landholdings, Henry estimated that there were 615,000 "small landowners" (94 percent of the total number of landholders) working on an area of 293,000 hectares (37 percent of the cultivated land area); 40,000 "medium" and "rich" landowners (6 percent) who owned 174,000 hectares (22 percent of the cultivated land area); and 394 "very rich" landowners (considerably less than 0.1 percent) who occupied 133,000 hectares (17 percent of the cultivated land area).[94] The rest of the cultivated surface was considered public or communal land, thus making Annam the region with the highest percentage of public land in the whole country (some 24 percent).

As in the case of Tonkin, the majority of the 615,000 "small landowners" in Annam might actually own almost nothing at all. A minority among them might own about five *mau* each, which was the maximum size of holding for that category of landholders. Even if we were to assume that the 293,000 hectares owned by the "small landowners" were equally divided among these peasants, each of them would have owned less than

* Recall that one *mau* is 0.50 hectare in Annam as compared to 0.36 hectare in Tonkin and Cochinchina.

half a hectare. Since on the average a hectare of rice paddy in Annam produced 1,170 kilograms of paddy rice a year, the landowners in this category could theoretically produce on the average only 500 kilograms of paddy, or less than 350 kilograms of milled rice a year. Yet it seems that the landholders in this category may, in fact, have fared even worse. By 1932 in the whole of Annam there were 513,700 hectares of rice paddy producing only one crop per year and 246,400 hectares with two crops; in 1940 there were 560,000 hectares producing one crop out of a total cultivated surface of 807,000 hectares.[95] In all likelihood, those paddy fields producing two crops a year had fallen into the possession of the rich and the "very rich" landlords, since the low yields of the land with one crop might have been of less temptation to them.

As for Cochinchina, the estimate of Gourou, as well as that of Henry, was that in 1930 there were in the entire region only 255,000 landowners in a rural population of approximately 4,000,000 persons. The cultivated land area of Cochinchina was about 2,400,000 hectares.[96] Of the 255,000 landowners, 78 percent owned under five hectares each, 15 percent had from five to ten hectares each (that is, from about fifteen to thirty *mau*), 11 percent had from ten to fifty hectares, and 2.5 percent of the landowners (including a substantial number of Frenchmen) had more than fifty hectares each.[97] Gourou lumped the five to ten hectare category together with the ten to fifty hectare category as "medium landowners." He then went on to show that the small landowners occupied only 12 percent of the cultivated paddy surface, that the medium landowners occupied 43 percent, and that the big landowners occupied 45 percent.[98] In general, in the late 1930s, only one out of every four peasant adult males in the region was a landowner,[99] giving Cochinchina the highest percentage of landless peasants in the country. Because many Vietnamese were living in extended families with several adult males of different generations under the same roof, a slightly larger percentage of "households," namely, one out of three, was found to have at least one member who was legally an owner, even if he might also be a part-time tenant. This meant, however, that two out of three households were left completely landless; that is, all the adult members were either full-time tenants or wage laborers.[100] Statistics given for 1952–1953 by "Le Bureau de Statistiques et de Recherches économiques du Gouvernement" showed that in Cochinchina there were 1,111,600 (79 percent) landless families, as opposed to 295,000 (21 percent) families with land.[101]

If we look at the grouping of landholders given by Gourou, it seems at first that the small landowners in this southern region were better off than in Tonkin and Annam; if we divide equally the total amount of land owned by this category of landholders, then each of them could theoretically have had about one hectare each. But a closer look at the landholding situation at the provincial level shows that a great many of these landholders in reality owned almost nothing. For example, Gourou learned that in the province of My Tho there were 34,600 landowners, but among them 18,000 had less than a hectare each, "which is to say that 18,000 persons, at least, are barely above the condition of the landless."[102] The average yield per hectare in Cochinchina, as noted, was 1,210 kilograms of paddy rice a year, which was more than 100 kilograms lower than the average yield in Tonkin, though slightly higher than the average yield in Annam. With about 75 percent of the peasant population in Cochinchina landless, and with the majority of the "small landowners" (comprising nearly 80 percent of the total) owning almost nothing, the situation of the peasants in Cochinchina was indeed no brighter than that of their fellow peasants in the other two regions. A comparison of the Cochinchinese peasants' landholding situation with that of the Chinese peasants in either

Chekiang or Yunnan shows that the former were definitely much worse off.

There were more landless peasants in Cochinchina than in any other part of the country. From the figures cited we can also see that the degree of concentration of land in the hands of a few was greatest in Cochinchina.

French zeal in confiscating lands belonging to Vietnamese who fled the area during the early period of occupation was one cause, as noted. Another reason for such concentration was the fact that, despite the French boast of having increased the cultivated land area in the region, the Vietnamese peasants were effectively barred from owning any significant amount of land at all. The accompanying table, comparing land surface occupied by the various types of landowners in the central and western provinces of Cochinchina (still fairly unsettled at the time of the French arrival), illustrates this point.[103]

Land Distribution in Central and Western Provinces of Cochinchina (Percentages)

	0–5 hectares		5–10 hectares		10–50 hectares		50 or more hectares	
	area	land-holders	area	land-holders	area	land-holders	area	land-holders
My Tho (central)	27	80	16	12	26	7	33	1
Bac Lieu (western)	3	39	7	25	24	24	66	10

As we have seen, free land concessions to French citizens and to Vietnamese collaborators, as of 1948, amounted to 2,300,000 hectares out of the total of less than 5,000,000 hectares of cultivated land for the whole country. In Cochinchina, where land appropriations and concessions were most extensive, the French and their collaborators got most of the land, leaving the great majority of the peasants either landless or close to landless. This, plus the fact that there was no significant industry or commerce to draw the peasants out of the rural areas, produced a phenomenon that had previously been absent in Vietnamese history: tenant farming and sharecropping. While the role of industry and commerce will be discussed later, it is worthwhile to note at this point that the proportion of urban population was only 4.5 percent in 1931 in Tonkin,[104] 3.5 percent in Annam in 1940,[105] and about 14 percent in 1936 in Cochinchina.[106] The higher proportion of urban population in Cochinchina was due to the statistical practice of considering not only towns and cities but also rural areas with a population density exceeding 500 persons per square kilometer as urban centers.[107] Also it must be remembered that foreign nationals formed a significant portion of the population of the cities and towns. In 1910, for example, there were 70,000 persons in Saigon, and of these about 40,000 were Vietnamese; 20,000 were Chinese, Indians, and Cambodians; and 10,000 were French.[108] This percentage of foreign nationals in the urban areas rose somewhat from the 1920s on. In 1931 in the twin city of Saigon-Cholon there were 100,000 "legal" Chinese alone out of the total population of 250,000 inhabitants.[109]

Notes

1. According to the official Nguyen chronicles, the *Dai Nam thuc-luc chinh-bien* 大南寔錄正編 [Veritable Records of the Imperial Vietnamese Court] and the *Ban-trieu ban-nghich liet-truyen* 本朝叛逆列傳 [Biographies of Rebels against the National Realm], during the reign of the first Nguyen emperor Gia-long (1802–1819) there were 73 *khoi nghia* (literally, "uprisings for a righteous cause") against him; under Emperor

Minh-mang (1820–1840) these uprisings increased to a record number of 234; and under Thieu-tri (1841–1847) there were 58; under Emperor Tu-duc, that is, from 1848 to 1883 (the year that the French completed their conquest of Tonkin), there were over 100. The *Ban-trieu ban-nghich liet-truyen* (p. 9) records that "from the Minh-mang and Thieu-tri periods onward there were Chinese bandits, pirates, jungle bandits, and other small marauding groups; inside the country there were uprisings [against the imperial government] and from the outside there were so many enemies threatening that it is impossible to enumerate them all."

During the Tu-duc reign (1848–1883) the situation became especially critical:

There had never been a period in which there was so much unrest and banditry as the period in which he was king. . . . There were both foreign and native bandits, whom the mandarins and the armies were obliged to fight constantly. Inside the country, there were repeated disasters such as floods, broken dikes, and the like. In Hung Yen province [south of Hanoi], the Van-giang dikes collapsed eighteen years in succession, and the whole Van-giang district became a deserted sand dune. The inhabitants were hungry and miserable and unable to find employment, and as a consequence the number of people who turned to banditry increased daily.

See Tran Trong Kim, *Viet Nam Su Luoc* [A Short History of Vietnam] (Saigon: Tan Viet, 1964), pp. 500–501.

As for natural catastrophes, the *Chau Ban Trieu Nguyen* [Vermilion Books of the Nguyen Dynasty] record that destructive floods occurred approximately every three years, usually around the seventh or eighth month, but sometimes in the fourth and fifth months as well. Prolonged droughts proved even more disastrous to the crops, since they made irrigation impossible. In the province of Thanh Hoa, for example, serious droughts occurred in the years 1816, 1817, 1823, 1838, 1839, and so on, all through the Nguyen period. In addition, there were crop failures brought on by insects. An example cited by Tran Trong Kim (pp. 500–501) and also in *Ban-trieu ban-nghich liet-truyen* (p. 109) is the locust invasion that ruined 100 percent of the crops in the provinces of Son Tay and Bac Ninh in 1854.

2. Vietnamese historians argue that the overly severe and cruel revenge carried out against the Tay Son family was one of the main reasons for the widespread uprisings under Gia-long. For a detailed description of Gia-long's severe punishment of the Tay Son family see Pham van Son, *Viet Su Tan Bien: Tu Tay-Son Mat-Diep den Nguyen-So* [New Compilation of Vietnamese History (vol 4) : From the End of the Tay Son to the Early Period of the Nguyen] (Saigon: Tu Sach Su Hoc Viet Nam, 1961), pp. 233–249; and also Nguyen Phuong, *Viet Nam Thoi Banh Truong: Tay Son* [Vietnam during the Expansion Era: The Tay Son] (Saigon: Khai Tri,

1968), pp. 394–401. For an account of the Tay Son in English, see Truong Buu Lam's article in John K. Fairbank, ed., *The Chinese World Order: Traditional China's Foreign Relations* (Cambridge, Massachusetts: Harvard University Press, 1968).

3. In order to prevent floods, a Department of Dikes was established under Gia-long for the building and reparation of dikes and dams, and this required important money outlays. For example, in 1829 the construction and repair of dikes in the northern part alone cost the court up to 173,800 *quan* and 170 taels of silver. See *Chau Ban Trieu Nguyen: Minh-mang Ky,* 36: 313–324. Also see the following for a description of the courts' effort on the dike situation: E. Chassigneux, "L'Irrigation dans le Delta du Tonkin," *Revue de Geographie annuelle,* fasc. 1 (Paris, 1912) ; and J. Chesneaux, *Contribution à l'Histoire de la Nation Vietnamienne* (Paris: Editions Sociales, 1955), pp. 89–90. A tael of silver (thirty-eight grams) was equal to three *quan* under Gia-long and Minh-mang but was soon to rise up to four and five under Tu-duc and to six and seven under Thieu-tri. In the Gia-long reign, a *quan* was equal to about thirty kilograms of rice. From 1825 to 1848, however, the average price of rice in the thirty-one provinces under the Nguyen increased by 50 percent to 100 percent. (See the table of statistics on the price of rice compiled from the courts' records by Nguyen The Anh in *Bulletin de la Société des Études Indochinoises,* n.s. 42, nos. 1 and 2 (1967), p. 9.)

In times of crop failure and famine, the court also directed relief distributions. Figures taken from the *Chau Ban Trieu Nguyen* (see *Bulletin de la Société des Études Indochinoises,* n.s. 42, nos. 1 and 2 (1967) , pp. 19–20) show that from 1817 to 1842 the rice distributed in given provinces amounted to 15 million kilograms. What proportion these relief distributions bear to the total consumption of the population in those areas is difficult to know exactly since, although the court historiographies record the number of "registered inhabitants" (males from eighteen to sixty years of age) in the given areas (see *Bulletin de la Société des Études Indochinoises,* n.s. 42, nos. 1 and 2, p. 16) , there are no figures on the total population of most provinces. Many Vietnamese historians say that, depending upon the period and the specific locality, the ratio of registered inhabitants to total population varies from 1:3 to 1:8. According to a French source, in 1884, twenty years after the French took over the southern part of Vietnam (Cochinchina), the number of "registered inhabitants" there was 400,110 persons while the total population is said to have been 1,633,824 persons, giving a ratio of one to four. See A. Bouinais and A. Paulus, *L'Indochine Française Contemporaine* (Paris: A. Challamel, 1885) , pp. 160–166; also *Annuaire de la Cochinchine* (Paris, 1884), p. 402.

Perhaps more important was the fact that the court decreased or waived taxes for many provinces or for the whole country in times of trouble. A scale for tax exemptions was worked out as follows: for 50 percent crop failure, the tax reduction would be three-tenths; for 80 percent crop failure, the reduction would be five-tenths; and for crop failure above 80 percent, the peasants would be exempted completely. Moreover, in times of severe crop loss the court also exempted the peasants from tax debts left over from previous years. For example, in 1841 the inhabitants of Hung Yen province were exempted from taxes totaling 23,385 *quan* and 5,000 metric tons of rice. The inhabitants of Nam Dinh were similarly exempted from some 30,000 *quan* of currency and 6,000 metric tons of rice. (*Chau Ban Trieu Nguyen: Thieu-tri Ky*, 13: 16–17, 274.) The court would also supply rice from the granaries in exchange for other produce and products (*Chau Ban Trieu Nguyen: Minh-mang Ky*, 10: 125–126; 13: 160; 29: 69; 37: 20–21, 137–138, and so on).

As for droughts, however, the only recourse possible in the eyes of the provincial magistrates and local authorities was to install special altars for appealing to heaven. In 1829 Emperor Minh-mang had to reprimand the governor of Hai Duong province for having lengthened the duration of the appeal to some two months, which created unbudgeted expenses. On this same occasion, Minh-mang issued numerous other directives counseling against the further occurrence of such immoderate practices. (*Chau Ban Trieu Nguyen: Minh-mang Ky*, 35: 231–232.)

4. Breaks in the dikes, floods, droughts, and insects were thus the cause of successive crop failures, and as shown in the *Chau Ban Trieu Nguyen: Minh-mang Ky*, 6: 128–129; 8: 215–216; 19: 55–60, and so on, those periods of crop failures were precisely the periods in which the incidence of banditry increased. Of course, a lot of the "banditries" were revolts led by dissatisfied scholarly gentry because of the court's handling of their situation. Notable examples of these were the revolts led by the Governor of Thanh Hoa province in 1805 and the scholarly gentry Cao Ba Quat and Le Duy Cu in 1854–1855. In fact, many of the uprisings under Tu-duc were caused by the court's inability to deal with the French. For example, the court sent Phanh Thanh Gian and Lam Duy Hiep to sign a twelve-clause treaty with Admiral Bonnard in June 1862. (The contents recognized French ownership of the three Con Lon islands and the three southeastern provinces of Gia Dinh, Dinh Tuong, and Bien Hoa; stipulated freedom for the propagation of Christianity; and proposed freedom of commerce in certain port areas, a war indemnity to the French of 4 million Mexican dollars, the cessation of all fighting against the French, the extradition of Vietnamese natives of the three ceded provinces that had fought against the French, etc.) The population in the southern part of Vietnam was greatly angered by this treaty, and great numbers of Vietnamese, under

such slogans as *"Phan Lam mai quoc, trieu dinh khi dan"* [Phan and Lam sold the country out and the courts despise the people], *"binh tay, sat ta"* [Pacify the Westerners and kill the heretics (that is, Catholics)], and *"nhan dan tu ve"* [People's self-defense], resolved to take matters into their own hands by assassinating collaborators, attacking French forts, poisoning Frenchmen in their garrisons, denying them food, and so on. These people were thus branded bandits and rebels by both the French and the court. For a good summary of the various movements and their leaders, see Pham van Son, 5: 190–218; also see Truong ba Can et al., *Ky niem 100 nam ngay Phap chiem Nam Ky* [In Memory of the 100th Anniversary of the French Conquest of Cochinchina] (Saigon: Trinh Bay, 1967), pp. 166–180.

Banditry and revolts became so serious that the local magistrates were helpless against them. The Imperial Court thus had to send out the court generals as well as the ranks of the conscript soldiers to pursue them. At any given time, a great number of able-bodied peasants either were army conscripts fighting against the bandits and rebels or were themselves participants in the uprisings. This made for a shortage of people to take care of the fields and the dikes and dams. Consequently, there was growing hunger and famine, which in turn produced more uprisings and bandits.

The Nguyen court officials were thus never able to still the uprisings or to disperse the bandits completely. In the northern part of Vietnam, as late as the reign of Thanh-thai (1889–1907), after the French had already defeated the Nguyen court, bandits were still ravaging the countryside, worst of all the Chinese bandits. Julien Gauthier, *L'Indochine au Travail dans la Paix Française* (Paris: Eyrolles, Imp. de Laboureur, 1949), pp. 24–25. The situation was especially serious in the delta region of northern Vietnam (Tonkin), for example, the provinces of Son Tay, Hung Hoa, Tuyen Quang, Bac Ninh, and Bac Giang. The people in these provinces, who were squeezed between the bandits on the one hand and corrupt officials on the other (officials who were accusing them of cooperating with the bandits and who themselves had become collaborators with the French), had either to move to the cities for security's sake or else to depart for the highlands to join the ranks of the dissatisfied. See J. Borie, *Le Métayage et la Colonization Agricole au Tonkin* (Paris: Giard et Biere, 1906), p. 60. Thus, by 1893 whole villages in these provinces had moved away, and the abandoned paddies had turned into marshes and brush land. Charles Robequain. *L'Évolution Économique de l'Indochine Française* (Paris: Centre d'Études de Politique Étrangère, 1939), pp. 212–213.

5. Luong Duc Thiep, *Xa Hoi Viet Nam* [Vietnamese Society] (Hanoi: Han Thuyen, 1944), p. 121; also Dao Duy Anh, *Viet Nam Van Hoa Su Cuong* [A Cultural History of Vietnam] (Saigon: Xuat Ban Bon Phuong,

1951), p. 54. The percentage of taxes will be discussed later in Chapters 2 and 3.

6. Dao Duy Anh, idem. In 1839, for example, in a single stroke the court took away half of the land from the rich landowners and gave this land to the soldiers and the poor villagers in the canton of Binh Phu, the province of Binh Dinh. The owners were not compensated and were allowed to retain only five *mau* each (a *mau* was 3,600 square meters, or slightly smaller than an acre). The reason for this measure was due to the concentration of the lands in the hands of a few. *Kham Dinh Dai Nam Hoi Dien Su Le* [Official Compendium of Institutions and Usages of Imperial Vietnam] (Hue, 1842–1851), 37: 14a–b.

7. Dao Duy Anh, p. 55; Luong Duc Thiep, p. 23; and P. Pasquier, *L'Annam d'Autrefois* (Paris: A. Challamel, 1907), p. 233.

8. Tran Trong Kim, p. 237.

9. Ibid.; see also Phan Huy Chu, *Lich trieu hien-chuong loai-chi* [A Reference Book on the Institutions of Successive Dynasties], presented to Minh-mang in 1821. See original text with translation into modern Vietnamese by Luong than Cao Nai Quang published by Saigon University, 1957, p. 429.

10. For an excellent summary of the system in theory and in practice in China, especially under the T'ang, see D. C. Twitchett, *Financial Administration Under the T'ang Dynasty* (Cambridge: University Press, 1963), pp. 1–9.

11. For the basic provisions of the "equal field" land system in China, see D. C. Twitchett, pp. 4–5.

For the basic provisions of the system in Vietnam from the Le dynasty, see Phan Huy Chu, pp. 161–165, 181–183, 229–233, 237–241, 425–445. Also see *Kham Dinh Viet Su Thong Giam Cuong Muc* [Official General Summary of the Comprehensive Mirror of Vietnamese History] (Hue: Quoc-su Quan [Institute of National History], 1885), 23: 20–25, 33; Nguyen Thanh Nha, *Tableau Économique du Vietnam aux XVIIe et XVIIIe Siècles* (Paris: Éditions Cujas, 1970), pp. 61–64; and Le Kim Ngan, *To Chuc Chinh Quyen Trung Uong duoi Trieu Le Thanh Tong, 1460–1497* [The Organization of the Central Government under the Reign of Le Thanh Tong, 1460–1497] (Saigon: Bo Quoc Gia Giao Duc, 1963), pp. 148–151.

12. *Kham Dinh Dai Nam Hoi Dien Su Le*, 37: 16.

13. Alexander B. Woodside, *Vietnam and the Chinese Model: A Comparative Study of Nguyen and Ch'ing Civil Government in the First Half of the Nineteenth Century* (Cambridge, Massachusetts: Harvard University Press, 1971), p. 78.

14. *Kham Dinh Dai Nam Hoi Dien Su Le*, 37: 16b.

15. Nguyen The Anh, *Kinh-te va Xa-hoi Viet Nam duoi cac Vua trieu Nguyen* [Vietnamese Economy and Society under the Nguyen Rulers] (Saigon: Trinh Bay, 1968), p. 58.

16. Woodside, pp. 79–80. On p. 143 Mr. Woodside writes:

One mid-nineteenth-century source suggested that in 1803 there had been 57 prefectures, 47 sub-prefectures, 201 districts, 4,163 cantons, and 16,452 villages or village-typed settlements of one kind or another in Gia-long's Vietnam. . . . New districts were created regularly after 1802, however, often merely by elevating cantons to a higher status, as in 1813. By the 1840's it seems certain that Vietnam possessed a number of districts between 250 and 270, although a scholarly private source of the early Tu Duc period has claimed that there were 72 prefectures, 39 sub-prefectures, and as many as 283 districts.

We can thus safely assume that save for the subbureaucrats such as village officials, the total number of salaried bureaucrats was not in excess of 10,000 persons. The total population of Vietnam was 8 million or less by 1847 (Woodside, p. 143). As we will see later on, the small size of the bureaucracy made the tax problem a fairly light burden for the peasants.

17. André Dumarest, *La Formation de Classes Sociales en Pays Annamite* (Lyon: Imprimerie P. Ferreol, 1935), p. 28, gives the quota under Minhmang and Nguyen The Anh, p. 37, the quota under Thieu-tri.

18. Phan Khoang, "Xa Hoi Viet Nam truoc day co phai la Phong Kien khong?" [Was Premodern Vietnamese Society Feudal?], *Su Dia* [History and Geography], no. 6 (Saigon, 1967), p. 26; also Nguyen The Anh, p. 37.

19. Dao Duy Anh, p. 55; Luong Duc Thiep, p. 122; and *Kham Dinh Dai Nam Hoi Dien Su Le*, 37; 23b.

20. Dao Duy Anh, p. 55; Luong Duc Thiep, p. 122; and Nguyen The Anh, p. 55.

21. Woodside, p. 78; Nguyen The Anh, p. 60.

22. *Kham Dinh Dai Nam Hoi Dien Su Le*, 37: 18a.

23. Ibid., p. 18b.

24. Ibid., pp. 19b–20.

25. Edwin O. Reischauer and John K. Fairbank, *East Asia: The Great Tradition* (Boston: Houghton Mifflin Company, 1960), p. 163.

26. Woodside, p. 221.

27. Le Thuoc, *Nguyen Cong Tru* [Biography of a Famous Court Official under Minh-mang] (Hanoi: Le Van Tan, 1928), p. 136.

28. Woodside, p. 221; Nguyen The Anh, p. 64.

29. Nguyen The Anh, p. 61; *Kham Dinh Dai Nam Hoi Dien Su Le*, 37: 14b.

30. Nguyen The Anh, pp. 59–60.

31. Ibid.

32. According to Nguyen The Anh, p. 58, before the land reform of 1839, there were at most from three to five persons in each province who owned about 100 *mau* or more.

33. For a brief discussion of the land system in North Vietnam, see *Études Vietnamiennes, No. 13: Problèmes Agricoles* (Hanoi: Xunhasaba, 1967), pp. 80–135.

34. One problem the Nguyen court did not have to face was overpopulation. Until the early 1930s Vietnam was an expanding society, and increases in population were accommodated by increasing the amount of land under cultivation.

35. Borie, p. 51.

36. G. Taboulet, *La Geste Française en Indochine: Histoire par les Textes de la France en Indochine des Origines à 1914* (Paris: Adrien-Maisonneuve, 1956), pp. 536–537; also P. Cultru, *Histoire de la Cochinchine Française des Origines à 1883* (Paris: A. Challamel, 1910), p. 271.

37. Cultru, p. 272.

38. Nguyen Van Vinh, *Les Réformes Agraires au Vietnam* (Louvain: Universitaire de Louvain, Faculté des Sciences Économiques et Sociales, 1961), p. 36.

39. Truc Chi, *Viet Nam Kinh-te luoc-khao* [A Summary of the Vietnamese Economy] (Saigon: SAPI, 1949), p. 23.

40. Nguyen Van Vinh, p. 36.

41. Le Thanh Khoi, *Le Viet Nam: Histoire et Civilisation* (Paris: Éditions de Minuit, 1955) , p. 409.

42. Borie, p. 81; also see J. Morel, *Les Concessions de Terres au Tonkin* (Paris, 1912), p. 194.

43. Ly Binh Hue, *Le Régime des Concessions Domaniales en Indochine* (Paris: Les Éditions Domat-Montchrestien, 1931), p. 179.

44. Y. Henry, *Économie Agricole de l'Indochine* (Hanoi: Gouvernement Général, 1932) , p. 224.

45. Robequain, p. 211.

46. Vu Van Hien, *Le Propriété Communale au Tonkin* (Paris: Presses Modernes, 1939), p. 49.

47. Borie, pp. 103–104.

48. Nhat Linh, *Nguoi Quay To* [The Reeler of Silk] (Saigon: Doi Nay, 1962), pp. 13–17.

49. Morel, pp. 145, 201.

50. Vu Van Hien, p. 50.

51. Pierre Gourou, *L'Utilisation du Sol en Indochine* (Paris: Centre d'Études de Politique Étrangère, 1940), p. 276.

52. Nguyen Van Vinh, p. 34.

53. Ibid.

54. Henry, p. 33; also see Pierre Gourou, *Les Payans du Delta Tonkinois* (Paris: Éditions d'Art et d'Histoire, 1936) , pp. 365–367, for the amazingly high percentage of communal lands left in the provinces of Ha Nam, Kien An, Thai Binh, and Nam Dinh.

55. Gourou (1940), p. 235.

56. Nguyen Van Vinh, p. 34.

57. Gourou (1940), pp. 285–286.

58. Nguyen Van Vinh, p. 36. Also see Nguyen Tan Loi, *L'Économie Commerciale du Riz en Indochine* (Paris: F. Loviton, 1938); and P. Estèbe, *Le Problème du Riz en Indochine* (Toulouse: F. Boisseau, 1934) .

59. Phi Van, *Dan Que* [The Peasants] (Saigon: Nha Xuat Ban Tan Viet, 1949), pp. 5–10.

60. Quoted by Nguyen Van Vinh, p. 38, from *Bulletin Officiel du Sud Viet-Nam* (December 19, 1949), pp. 1160–1161. The slight dip in the land concessions held by Frenchmen at this time was due to the depression, when some land was left uncultivated. The land concessions were of two types, "definitive" and "provisional," the latter being revokable by the government if the lands were not being put to productive use.

61. Paul Bernard, *Le Problème Économique Indochinois* (Paris: Nouvelles Éditions Latines, 1934), p. 7.

62. Ibid., p. 9.

63. Ibid., p. 10.

64. Gourou (1940), pp. 15–17.

65. Ibid., p. 301.

66. G. Kherian, "Les Mefaits de la Surpopulation Deltaique," *Revue Indochinoise* (1938), 3: 476.

67. Michel Limbourg, *L'Économie Actuelle du Vietnam Démocratique* (Hanoi: Éditions en Langues Étrangères, 1956), p. 16; also Nguyen Van Vinh, p. 45.

68. Gourou (1940), pp. 228–229.

69. Henry, p. 112.

70. Pierre Gourou (1936) , p. 360.

71. Ibid., p. 356.

72. Gourou (1940), p. 229.

73. Henry, pp. 108–109.

74. Gourou (1940) , pp. 229–230.

75. Ibid., p. 230.

76. Ibid.

77. Gourou (1940), p. 241, gives a conversion ratio of 65:100.

78. Bernard, p. 6.

79. Henry, p. 332. Auguste Grandel, *Le Développement Économique de L'Indochine Française* (Saigon: Imprimerie C. Ardin, 1936), p. 51, also gives

337 kilograms of paddy rice as the average required per person.

80. R. H. Tawney, *Land and Labor in China* (London: Allen and Unwin, Ltd., 1932), pp. 34–35.
81. Ibid., p. 31.
82. Ibid., p. 35.
83. Ibid., p. 42.
84. Ibid., p. 49.
85. Hsiao-tung Fei and Chih-I Chang, *Earthbound China: A Study of Rural Economy in Yunnan* (Chicago: University of Chicago Press, 1945), p. 11.
86. Gourou (1936), p. 9; idem, p. 144.
87. Ibid., p. 156.
88. Hsiao-tung Fei and Chih-I Chang, pp. 53–54.
89. Incredibly high yields of 12,000, 17,500, and 24,000 kilograms of paddy rice per hectare per year can be deduced from the statistics given for the three localities studied in the work cited. See Hsiao-tung Fei and Chih-I Chang, pp. 50–51, 157, and 208. However, this writer believes that these figures must be in error, perhaps owing to an oversight in the definition of the units of measurement. In Luts'un, even if the stated yield of 17,500 kilograms per hectare were in error by a factor of ten, productivity would still have been greater than in Vietnam. For the sake of comparison, in the period 1958–1961, average yearly yields per hectare were approximately 4,700 kilograms in Japan, 3,700 kilograms in the United States, 3,000 kilograms in the People's Republic of China, 1,700 kilograms in Indonesia, and 1,400 kilograms in Thailand. See Georg Borgstrom, *The Hungry Planet* (New York: Collier Books, 1967), p. 143.
90. Hsiao-tung Fei, p. 54.
91. Ibid.
92. Ibid., pp. 55–56.
93. Nguyen Van Vinh, p. 45.
94. Henry, pp. 144–145.
95. Gourou (1940), p. 255.
96. Ibid., p. 272.
97. Ibid., p. 273.
98. Ibid., p. 274.
99. Ibid., p. 273.
100. Ibid.
101. Nguyen Van Vinh, p. 45.
102. Gourou (1940), p. 273.
103. Ibid., p. 274.
104. Ibid., p. 95.
105. Ibid., p. 128.
106. Ibid., pp. 129–130.

107. Ibid., p. 130.

108. Nguyen Vy, *Tuan Chang Trai Nuoc Viet* [Tuan, a Young Man of Vietnam] (Saigon, 1970), 1: 106.

109. Wang Wen-yuan, *Les Relations entre l'Indochine Française et la Chine* (Paris: Éditions Pierre Bossuet, 1937), p. 35.

2 TENANT FARMING AND SHARECROPPING

Inefficiency of tradition-bound agricultural techniques made significant access to land a condition of sustenance, and there were few alternate opportunities for employment for the peasants outside the rural areas. As a large portion of the country's land became concentrated in the hands of a few as a result of the colonial land appropriation and concession policy, the majority of the peasants were forced to become tenant farmers (*nguoi Iinh mau ruong*), sharecroppers (*ta dien*), and agricultural wage laborers (*tho gat cong, tho cay cong*, and so forth). Agricultural wage laborers were for the most part persons who did not own any land at all and who were at the same time unable to become tenants or sharecroppers. They hired out their labor on a daily, monthly, or yearly basis. The living conditions of these various types of landless peasants will be discussed in Chapter 6 of this account.

According to one Vietnamese author who was also an agronomist, sharecropping was a new phenomenon that appeared only after the arrival of the French.[1] In 1936, and again in 1940, Gourou maintained that in Tonkin some "medium landowners" who possessed from three to ten or fifteen *mau* "directly" (supervising their properties personally rather than by proxy) employed field laborers.[2] The big landholders and a large number of the medium ones were absentee landlords who used tenant farmers and sharecroppers.[3] By 1936 tenant farmers and sharecroppers worked about half of the cultivated surface in the Tonkin Delta.[4] The situation in Annam was not very much different from that in Tonkin, although the percentage of big landowners there was smaller than in Tonkin. In Cochinchina, as we have seen, the "medium landowners" (those who owned from five to fifty hectares each) and the "big landowners" (those who owned from fifty hectares up) owned 88 percent of the total paddy surface. Since some of the medium landowners cultivated their land through the use of wage laborers, the estimate by Gourou and others was that some 80 percent of the paddies, or 1,800,000 hectares, was worked by tenants and sharecroppers.[5]

Another way of investigating the degree to which tenants, sharecroppers, and agricultural laborers were used at this time would be by using man-day units of labor as a yardstick.* "One *mau* of paddy (0.36 ha.) demands about 70 man-days of work per growing season, or 200 man-day units of labor per hectare; and paddies with two crops or paddies on which a secondary crop is planted demand a double number of man-days of labor, or 400 man-days a year per hectare."[6] The work was not spread evenly throughout the year, of course, but was concentrated during a few months of the year. We can conclude that a hectare with two crops or with a secondary crop was the maximum amount of land a medium-size family (husband and wife and two or three young children) could work on without having to depend on outside aid. If this assumption is correct, then from the discussion of landownership in the preceding chapter we can estimate how many landlords were likely to have used tenant farmers, sharecroppers, or wage laborers. Any such estimate also reveals the overwhelming population pressures in Annam and Tonkin.

According to Gourou, in Tonkin there existed two types of tenant farming (*fermage* in French): "There is tenant farming with money payment (a sum of money paid in advance per *mau*) and tenant farming with payment in kind (a certain quantity of paddy rice, from a third to a half of the normal harvest, which did not vary with the actual crop yield; in case of a bad crop the tenant farmer still had to hand in the amount

* Each man-day unit is defined by Gourou (1940), p. 241, as ten hours.

agreed upon)." [7] The sharecropper (*métayer in French*) "gives to the landlord a part of his crop in increasing proportion to the fertility of the soil: the more fertile the soil, the greater the share of the owner. If the land yields two crops, the conditions for sharecropping can vary infinitely." [8]

Normally, the tenant farmers had to give the landlord "approximately half of the gross income and all the expenses of the cultivation are charged upon him [the tenant]." [9] The sharecropper, meanwhile, had to pay from 50 to 70 percent of his crops besides having to pay for all production costs. [10] Production costs included the purchase, maintenance, and renewal of farm tools, the rent of buffaloes, the purchase of seeds, and the hiring of extra farmhands during planting and harvesting time. [11] If a sharecropper or a tenant farmer rented a buffalo from his landlord to work on the paddy, he had to pay from 200 to 300 kilograms of rice for each buffalo, [12] that is, from 15 to 20 percent of his crop if he had a hectare of land to work on and if his land was of average productivity or above it. The high price of buffaloes forced many farmers and sharecroppers to hitch their wives and children to the plows in place of the buffaloes. A Vietnamese agronomist writing in 1943 makes the following observation:

Indeed, you must go to the poor villages and hamlets to be able to see this tragedy: a husband holds the plow while his wife, his son, his daughter-in-law, and his daughter act as buffaloes, pulling it. They hitch to their shoulders ropes padded with pieces of torn matting lest the ropes cut into their flesh. Because of the weight to be pulled, they are unable to keep their balance and must use a bamboo cane to lean on. [13]

As for seeds, normally from sixty to seventy-five kilograms of paddy rice were required per hectare, or about 5 to 6 percent of the crop. However, since this quantity of seed was more often than not borrowed from the landlord, the tenant farmer or sharecropper usually had to pay back about twice that amount, even though officially there was no interest on rice borrowed for sowing:

The estate owners [landlords] usually lend out about twenty to twenty-five kilos of rice to sow approximately one *sao* of rice sprouts, which in turn are used to plant about a *mau* of paddy. Although officially there is no interest on this rice, the landlords usually charge for it in cash corresponding to the very high prices of the fourth and fifth months, when the seeding begins. They make the sharecroppers pay in October when rice prices are very low. For example, at the time they borrow, the price of rice may be six piasters a can [approximately fifteen to twenty kilograms], but when they pay back, the price may be only three piasters a can. That is, they pay back the equivalent of two cans of rice for the one that has been borrowed. It is true that if those two cans of rice were to remain in the sharecroppers' house they would in any case surely have to sell them immediately, for six piasters, just in order to raise the money to spend on necessary items. But when this rice is put into the rice granaries of the landlords and the landladies, it can be stored until the spring of the following year, when rice is scarce, and when the same amount [two cans] can be sold for up to twelve or thirteen piasters.[14]

According to the author of this quotation, after paying for land rent, buffalo rent, seeds, and the maintenance of tools, the tenant farmer or sharecropper typically could retain only 10 to 25 percent of the total yield of the crop.[15] This percentage does not take into account the fact that "besides the dues agreed upon in the contract, they [the tenant farmers and sharecroppers] owe the landlords fairly expensive gifts and services." [16] Also, the tenant farmers and sharecroppers had to borrow rice for their daily consumption at exorbitant interest rates. (This problem will be discussed later in the chapter on usury and agrarian credits.)

The situation in Annam was not different from the one described in Tonkin.[17] However, in provinces like Quang Ngai, where there was an elaborate irrigation system and where water had to be bought from irrigation guilds, the landlords devised a system by which one-third of the crop went for the purchase of water, one-third to the landlords, and the remaining one-third to the tenants.[18]

In the case of Cochinchina, in spite of the sparse population and large land surface, the terms of tenancy were as bad as in the other regions. In fact, they were possibly worse. In Cochinchina there was relatively little sharecropping (*métayage*); tenancy, however, was a ubiquitous fact of life. Here the tenant had to provide his own lodgings, had either to bring along his own working animals or to rent them, had to pay for all supplementary labor on the paddies, and had to pay for his farm implements and seeds.[19]

In Cochinchina the basic paddy rent was about thirty to forty *gia* per hectare.[20] According to Gourou this amounted to about 40 percent of the gross yield of the crop, although more often than not the rent went up to about 50 percent of the crop yields.[21] But the reason for Gourou's statement that thirty to forty *gia* amounted to about 40 percent of the crop is that he equates a *gia*, which he says is forty liters,[22] to only twenty kilograms.[23] There is reason to believe, however, that this estimate is too low and that an estimate of twenty-eight to thirty kilograms per *gia* would be more accurate. An official French source of 1898 equates a *hoc* (a sixty-liter dry unit) of paddy rice to forty-four kilograms.[24] If one were to compute the rent of paddy fields according to the second estimate, this same rent would have amounted to 70 percent or more. Moreover, if a tenant farmer rented a buffalo from the landlord, the going rate was twenty to twenty-five *gia* (600 to 750 kilograms of rice) per buffalo per year.[25] The rent of a buffalo was thus about three times higher than in Tonkin, or more than half the total yield of an average hectare of paddy. This was likely to be prohibitively high—even if special arrangements could be made to rent a buffalo for only part of the year—for a farmer who worked a hectare or less. The majority of the tenants in Cochinchina had to rent about five hectares of paddy fields, as opposed to about one hectare in Tonkin and Annam, before they could hope to have anything at all left for themselves.[26] In Cochinchina, where the supply of landless agricultural wage laborers was greatest, even tenants typically relied on hired labor to a certain extent. Very few tenants ever rented more than five hectares, however, since above that limit the dependence on paid labor would begin to bring diminishing returns.[27]

Tenant farming and sharecropping were, in effect, forms of exploitation, and their adverse effects were legion. First of all, they decreased the fertility of the soil. Since the tenant farmer or sharecropper might pay more than 75 percent of the total crop yield to the landlord in rents and debt payment for production costs, and since it fell upon him to maintain and improve the soil, he was more than reluctant to buy fertilizers for the land. Were he to do so, his landlord would reap most of the benefit, while his own family remained hungry. For this reason, the land in many areas was used for periods of ten years or more without being fertilized.[28] The end result was that rice yields in Vietnam were among the lowest in the world.[29]

In order to appreciate the degree to which the land had deteriorated, let us look at some of the earliest French figures as well as some of the Nguyen records on the productivity of the land. According to a French official source published in 1899, the average yield of paddy rice in Cochinchina was 2,250 kilograms per hectare in first-grade paddy fields, 1,500 kilograms per hectare in second-grade paddy fields, and 800 kilograms per hectare in third-grade paddy fields.[30] First-class paddy fields occupied

57 percent of the cultivated surface, second-class paddy fields occupied 23 percent, and third-class paddy fields occupied 19 percent.[31] The average yield was given as 1,800 kilograms a hectare.[32] In 1899 it was reported that in the western part of Cochinchina an average yield of 3,000 kilograms per hectare was not infrequent, and in rarer cases yields of 4,000 kilograms per hectare were reported.[33] There is reason to believe, however, that the productivity of the land under the Nguyen was even higher than the 1899 statistics given by the French source. (The source admits that the problem of underreporting to evade taxes was widespread and usually amounted to one-half of the crop yield in regions outside Cochinchina.[34]) Trinh Hoai Duc, a precolonial Vietnamese governor-general of Gia Dinh, the region that later came to be called Cochinchina by the French, reported in an important gazetteer in the early part of the nineteenth century that each *hoc* (a sixty-liter dry unit) of seeds yielded from 100 to 300 *hoc* of paddy rice, depending on the specific region of Cochinchina.[35] In 1889 an official French source reported that it required sixty kilograms of rice to seed a hectare of paddy field in Cochinchina.[36] Gourou reported in 1936 that in Tonkin it took about 75,000 metric tons of seeds to produce 2,200,000 metric tons of paddy rice.[37] This is equal to 3.4 percent, or about fifty kilograms of seeds per hectare. Unless, under the Nguyen court, the peasants employed some different method of using less seeds per hectare, the productivity of the land under the Nguyen was about two and a half to five times higher than that under the French.

Also, as we have seen, the average price of the yield of a *mau* of paddy field was forty *quan* while the market price of thirty kilograms of rice was about one to one and a half *quan*. These figures mean that, on the average, a hectare must have yielded from 2,500 to 3,000 kilograms of paddy rice per hectare. One of the earliest official French reports on the yield in Tonkin published in 1898 seems to agree with this estimate. In the province of Nam Dinh, for example, first-class paddy fields occupied about 40 percent of the cultivated area and produced, on the average, more than 3,000 kilograms per hectare. About 80 percent of the second-class paddy fields, which occupied 30 percent of the total cultivated land, produced about 2,500 kilograms per hectare. The rest of the paddy fields, the third-class ones, yielded over a metric ton per hectare on the average.[38] According to the same source, for example, the average yield for Nam Dinh was considerably less than the average yields of the provinces of Thai Binh and Hai Phong.[39]

In contrast with the precolonial Nguyen era (1802–1885) and the early period of French colonization, in 1938 one author reported that the average yield per hectare was 1.2 metric tons in Indochina, as opposed to 1.5 in Java, 1.8 in Siam, and 3.4 in Japan.[40] Gourou, who thinks that the official estimate was low because of underreporting to evade tax (after at least fifty years of colonial scrutiny!), gives an adjusted estimate of 1.4 metric tons for Tonkin[41] and 1.34 metric tons for Cochinchina.[42] These figures are still much lower than the 1898 and 1899 official French estimates just cited, and also much lower than all the comparable figures given for Java, Siam, and Japan.

The system of tenant farming and sharecropping also engendered tension and distrust between landlords and tenants, and this atmosphere in turn inhibited agricultural production.

Often they [the tenants and sharecroppers] are looked on as permanent slaves who by their labor dig the soil and turn out the rice to enrich the landlords, but who, if lucky enough, may earn no more than a meal a day. It is precisely because of this that between the landlords and the sharecroppers there so often does not exist any spirit of willing cooperation or mutual aid. The landlords are only concerned that the sharecroppers deliver enough rice for rent and the repayment of debts. Usually when the harvest comes they claim payment impatiently. Most often the landlords force the sharecroppers to reap all the rice themselves, making them carry it to their residential estates to have it threshed and dried there. Then, from this total yield, the landlords first measure out for themselves the rice for rent and debts, and only then, if there is anything left, the sharecropper will be allowed to take it home. If, unluckily, there should be only enough to cover rent and debts, then the sharecroppers will have to go home empty-handed, and cannot but see their situation as one of working in the fields all year round just for their meals and not for payment. A worse situation is to have delivered all the rice and yet still to remain in debt to the landlords. Then the sharecroppers must sign a contract of debt with interest, promising to pay it in the coming year. . . .

Since there are greedy and merciless landlords, there are also dishonest sharecroppers as a result. Fearing that the landlords will collect the entire yield, they secretly reap a portion of the rice and hide it away. When the landlords cannot exact sufficient rice for rent and debts, the sharecroppers stall for time and try to leave for other estates. . . . There are some sharecroppers who insist on borrowing rice for seeding and for daily consumption, and also insist on renting buffaloes. When seeding time comes, they take the buffaloes to plow and harrow for wages on other people's fields, earning from 1.2 to 2.15 piasters a day. Only at the end of the planting season do they come back to the fields that their landlords have rented to them, to do a quick and sloppy job on them. Afterwards, the rice yield naturally turns out to be poor because of the poor harrowing and late planting, and so the sharecroppers try to avoid the landlords and are unwilling to deliver the full amount of rent in rice to them. If necessary, they will run away.[43]

It is interesting to note that at the present time in the province of Thai Binh, North Vietnam, the yield of paddy rice is from 5 to 5.5 metric tons per hectare per year.[44] Under the French, Thai Binh was one of the least productive provinces of Tonkin. In the province of Ha Tay, the average yield per hectare has recently been about 4 metric tons per crop.[45] By comparison, under the French the average yearly rice yield in Tonkin was only 1.4 metric tons of paddy per hectare, including fields that gave two rice crops per year. In South Vietnam, from 1955 to

1965 the annual yield per hectare was only 2.0 metric tons of paddy, as opposed to 1.2 to 1.4 metric tons under the French.[46] This increase in the South was due to the widespread use of fertilizer, which "enabled the soil to support a second crop" in many areas, "and varietal improvements [that] shortened the growing period for the first and second crops." [47] The difference in the yield of the same land during the two periods can thus be attributed to capital and labor inputs. The present-day difference in the productivity of the land in the north (where landlordism, tenant farming, and sharecropping have been eradicated) and in the south (where landlordism and tenant farming are still widespread) may serve as further support for the thesis that landlordism and sharecropping have a negative effect on rice yields: they slow the rate of capital and labor inputs into the land.

Then, too, the system of tenant farming and sharecropping encouraged landlords to regard the production of rice only for its commercial value and not for its food value. Whenever the price of rice decreased to a level that they considered as not bringing in enough profit, they would call a halt to production.[48] This was the situation during the depression of the 1930s, as will be described in Chapter 5 of this book. In normal times the land lords, instead of improving the land they already owned, would spend money to buy up cheap land from smaller landholders who were forced to sell because of high taxes and usury. Writing in a government-sponsored magazine in 1933, one author concluded that the rich landlords were interested only in making profits and paid no attention at all to the possibilities of progressive agricultural improvements or of social progress.[49]

Once again it may be useful to compare the tenant farming and sharecropping situation in Vietnam with that of China. On the whole the situation in much of China again seems to have been better. First of all, the percentage of tenant farmers and sharecroppers in Tonkin and Annam was about twice as high as in most provinces of China, while the percentage in Cochinchina was nearly three times as high. Second, the terms of tenancy were much better in China. There the landlords typically provided the sharecroppers "with part of their seed, manure, livestock, and equipment," while the rent was only about 50 percent.[50] Third, because the rice yields in China were generally more than twice as high as in Vietnam, the Chinese tenant farmers and sharecroppers enjoyed a much better return. In fact, in the Luts'un area of Yunnan, tenant farming was such that "the tenants can enjoy a profit even if they operate their rented land by hired labor.[51] Therefore, the peasants in that area tended to "expand the amount of land under their management through renting rather than through purchasing land."[52] Also in Luts'un "the rent on the collectively owned land is usually much lower than the normal rate. To be tenant of the collective owners is, in fact, a privilege. Those who are able to rent a piece of land from their clan are not far from acquiring a piece of land of their own."[53]

Before the arrival of the French, and French policies of land expropriation and free land concessions, the Vietnamese peasants never had to endure any kind of rent even approaching that of the Chinese level just cited. In spite of all the social upheavals and natural disasters that tended to dislocate the rural population, most of the Vietnamese peasants under the Nguyen emperors had lands to work on, lands that they considered to be their own. For this they had to pay only a very small tax. During the Gia-long period (1802–1820) this tax was twenty *thang* of rice for each *mau* of first-grade paddy, fifteen *thang* per *mau* of second-grade paddy, and ten *thang* per *mau* of third-grade paddy and of paddy with only one crop a year.[54] A Nguyen official court document states that there are forty-seven *thang* in a *hoc* (a sixty-liter dry measure).[55] Thus under Gia-long the Vietnamese peasants had to pay only about twenty-five liters of paddy rice per *mau* of first-class field, twenty liters per *mau* of second-class field, and thirteen liters per *mau* of third-class fields or fields with only one crop a year. Translated into the metric system, this would amount to about sixty-five liters, fifty liters, and thirty liters, or forty-eight kilograms, thirty-seven kilograms, and twenty kilograms of paddy rice per hectare of land in the respective category. Even if we take the low average yield of 1,800 kilograms per hectare given for Cochinchina in 1899 by the French source cited earlier, then the land tax under Gia-long amounted to less than 3 percent for each category.

Beginning in the Minh-mang period (1820–1841), because bureaucrats were now paid regular salaries, the land tax was slightly increased. Minh-mang divided the country into three regions for taxing purposes. In the first region, which included the prefectures of Quang Binh, Trieu Phong, Dien Ban, Thang Hoa, and the provinces of Quang Ngai, Qui Nhon, Phu Yen, Binh Hoa, and Dien Khanh, the tax was forty *thang* per *mau* of first-grade "personal share" (*khau phan dien*) or of communal paddy fields (*cong dien*), thirty *thang* per *mau* of second-grade paddy fields, and twenty *thang* per *mau* of third-grade paddy fields. In the second taxing region, which was composed of the provinces of Nghe An, Thanh Hoa, Son Tay, Kinh Bac, Hai Duong, Son-nam-thuong, and Son-nam-ha, the prefecture of Phung Thien, and the six protectorates (*tran*) of Quang Yen, Hung Hoa, Thai Nguyen, Lang Son, Tuyen Quang, and Cao Bang, personal share landowners had to pay twenty-six *thang* per *mau* for first-grade paddy and thirteen *thang* per *mau* for third-grade paddy; those in charge of communal lands had to pay eighty *thang* and thirty-three *thang*, respectively. In the third region, which included the provinces of Binh Thuan, Gia Dinh, Dinh Tuong, Long Xuyen, and Kien Giang, the tax on "deep paddy fields" (*ruong sau*) was twenty-six *thang* per *mau* regardless of whether it was personal share or communal land, while the tax on "shallow paddy fields" (*ruong can*) was twenty-three *thang* per *mau*.[56] (As under Gia-long, the tax on communal land was also, in effect, its "rent": no other taxes or rents were paid on crops raised on communal land.)

Translated into percentages of the estimate for rice yields in Cochinchina in 1899, these numbers are tiny. For the third region (known under the French as Cochinchina), the land taxes came to less than 4 percent of the estimated yield. In the second region (known in colonial times as Tonkin), taxes on the personal share lands were also less than 4 percent, and the tax rate on communal land was at most 12 percent of its estimated yield. Taxes on the personal share lands and communal lands ranged from 3 to 6 percent in the first region (later known as Annam). What all this meant was that, even if a healthy man could only cultivate a single *mau* (instead of his lawful share of the personal share lands, usually about five *mau*, plus his share of the village communal lands), he would still have retained after all taxes about 600 kilograms of paddy rice a year, or enough to feed two adults for a year.

The high rents of as much as 70 percent or more of the total crop yield during the French period were thus quite beyond any experience of the Vietnamese peasants up to that time. Indeed, they made even the French economist Pierre Gourou conclude in his study of the Vietnamese peasantry that the traditional system of communal land should be revived and the development of large properties eradicated.

Study of the land system leads us to conclude that in the interest of the peasant, it would be good to maintain and develop the communal lands and especially to eradicate the development of large properties. It would even be wholly desirable to use methods to be determined to limit the size of the large properties so that the peasants should not lose, through their rents, the best part of their income.[57]

Notes

1. *Thanh Nghi,* no. 55 (Hanoi, February 26, 1944), pp. 1–2.
2. Pierre Gourou, *Les Payans du Delta Tonkinois* (Paris: Éditions d'Art et d'Histoire, 1936), p. 376; idem, *L'Utilisation du Sol en Indochine* (Paris: Centre d'Études de Politique Étrangère, 1940), p. 233.
3. Gourou (1936), p. 376.
4. Ibid.
5. Gourou (1940), p. 282.
6. Ibid., p. 232.
7. Ibid., p. 234.
8. Ibid.
9. Ibid.
10. Nghiem Xuan Yem, "Nhung ta dien" [The Sharecroppers], *Thanh Nghi,* no. 55 (Hanoi, February 26, 1944), pp. 5–6.
11. Gourou (1940), p. 234; also *Thanh Nghi,* no. 55, pp. 4–5.
12. *Thanh Nghi,* no. 55, p. 4.
13. Nghiem Xuan Yem, "Canh ngheo thon que" [The Poverty Situation in the Countryside], *Thanh Nghi,* no. 47 (Hanoi, October 16, 1943).
14. *Thanh Nghi,* no. 55, pp. 4–5.
15. Ibid., pp. 5–6.
16. Gourou (1940), p. 234.
17. Ibid., p. 235.
18. Ibid., pp. 235–236.
19. Ibid., p. 282.
20. Ibid.
21. Ibid.
22. Gourou (1940), p. 398.
23. Ibid., pp. 281, 294.
24. *Bulletin Économique de l'Indochine,* no. 2 (Saigon: Governement Général de l'Indochine, Direction de l'Agriculture et du Commerce, August 1898), p. 45.
25. Gourou (1940), p. 282.
26. Ibid., p. 282.
27. Ibid., p. 283.
28. *Thanh Nghi,* no. 55, pp. 5–6.
29. R. H. Tawney, *Land and Labour in China* (London: George Allen and Unwin, Ltd., 1932), p. 49.
30. *Bulletin Économique de l'Indochine,* no. 17 (November 1899), p. 609.
31. Ibid., p. 608.

32. Ibid., p. 609.

33. Ibid., p. 609.

34. Ibid., p. 604.

35. G. Aubaret, *Histoire et Description de la Basse Cochinchine* [an edited translation of Trinh Hoai Duc's 鄭 懷 德 *Gia Dinh Thong Chi* 嘉 定 通 志] (Paris: Imprimerie Imperiale, 1864), p. 294; also see Ngueyn Thanh Nha, *Tableau Économique du Vietnam au XVIIe et XVIIIe Siècles* (Paris: Éditions Cujas, 1970), p. 48.

36. *Bulletin Économique de l'Indochine*, no. 17 (1899), p. 602.

37. Gourou (1936), p. 405.

38. *Bulletin Économique de l'Indochine*, no. 2 (August 1898), p. 45.

39. Ibid., p. 43.

40. Jean Goudal, *Labour Conditions in Indochina* (Geneva: International Labour Office, 1938), p. 204.

41. Gourou (1936), p. 405.

42. Gourou (1940), p. 294.

43. *Thanh Nghi*, no. 55, pp 6–7. Landlords usually had numerous devices to protect their own interests and to keep tenants from running away. One such device was to register their tenants and sharecroppers legally only as wage laborers. Thus, should the tenants run away with part of the crop, they would be considered thieves and would be sought by the authorities. See Phi Van, *Dong Que* [The Countryside], 2nd ed. (Hanoi: Xuat Ban Tan Viet, 1948), pp. 84–86.

44. Gerard Chaliand, *The Peasants of North Vietnam* (Baltimore: Penguin Books, Inc., 1969), p. 75.

45. Ibid., p. 198.

46. Robert L. Sansom, *The Economics of Insurgency in the Mekong Delta of Vietnam* (Cambridge, Massachusetts: The M.I.T. Press, 1970), p. 180.

47. Ibid., p. 77.

48. Pham Cao Duong, *Thuc trang cua gioi Nong Dan Viet Nam duoi thoi Phap thuoc* [The True Conditions of the Vietnamese Peasants during French Colonization] (Saigon: Khai Tri, 1966), p. 119.

49. Nguyen Trong Thuat, "Van de nong nghiep cua nuoc ta sau nay" [The Problems of Agriculture in Our Country in the Future], *Nam Phong Tap Chi*, no. 190 (Hanoi, November 1933).

50. Tawney, pp. 65–66.

51. Hsiao-tung Fei and Chih-I Chang, *Earthbound China: A Study of Rural Economy in Yunnan* (Chicago: University of Chicago Press, 1945), p. 77.

52. Ibid.

53. Ibid.

54. Pham Van Son, *Viet Su Tan Bien: Tu Tay-Son Mat-Diep den Nguyen-So* [New Compilation of Vietnamese History (vol. 4): From the End of the

Tay-Son to the Early Period of the Nguyen] (Saigon: Tu Sach Su Hoc Viet Nam, 1961), p. 259.

55. *Kham Dinh Dai Nam Hoi Dien Su Le* [Official Compendium of Institutions and Usages of Imperial Vietnam] (Hue) 37: 3b.
56. Nguyen The Anh, *Kinh-te va Xa-hoi Viet Nam duoi cac Vua trieu Nguyen* [Vietnamese Economy and Society under the Nguyen Rulers] (Saigon: Trinh Bay, 1968), pp. 56–57. In cases of bad harvest and difficult transportation routes, taxes could be paid by cash instead. As of 1839, the yearly regional rice tax sent to Hue from northern Vietnam was expected to be about 15,000 metric tons while the ten southern provinces from Quang Nam to Gia Dinh were expected to send 10,000 metric tons. See Alexander B. Woodside, *Vietnam and the Chinese Model: A Comparative Study of Nguyen and Ch'ing Government in the first half of the Nineteenth Century* (Cambridge, Massachusetts: Harvard University Press, 1971), p. 139. In 1836 the total amount of taxable land, or "registered land," was given as 4,063,900 *mau*. See Nguyen The Anh, p. 53; and Tran Trong Kim, *Viet Nam Su Luoc* [A Short History of Vietnam] (Saigon: Tan Viet, 1964), p. 437. The difference between the registered land and the real cultivated surface could be 30 percent or more.
57. Gourou (1940), p. 235.

3 TAXES AND TAX COLLECTION

In addition to high rents, the Vietnamese peasants also had to endure high taxes—the subject of an enormous number of Vietnamese books and stories, and even poems and folksongs, during the French colonial period.

Some of the colonial taxes that seemed most onerous to Vietnamese peasants were far from being modern innovations. They originated in the statecraft of the premodern Vietnamese polity. The poll or head tax—known to Vietnamese more specifically as the "body tax" (*thue than*)—is a good example. In the eighteenth century, Vietnam was divided for all practical purposes into two rival polities: one was centered in the Red River Delta and governed by overlords of the Trinh family, and the other, less traditional, was located in central Vietnam and governed by overlords of the Nguyen family. Both these competing authorities were overcome at the end of the 1700s by the Tay-son revolution (1771–1802) and by the Nguyen restoration (1802), which reunified the country. But during their quarrelsome existence they pioneered new forms of taxation in order to sustain their rancorous civil war, and in 1724 the Trinh overlord developed the forerunner of the colonial poll tax.

The Trinh poll tax specified that each man between the ages of eighteen and fifty-five had to pay one *quan* and two *tien* per year.[1] In the first half of the eighteenth century a picul of polished rice cost about two *quan*.[2] Since a picul at the time could range from sixty to seventy-five kilograms,[3] the Trinh tax amounted to about forty to fifty kilograms. Under the nineteenth-century Nguyen court, this body tax was called the "grown man tax" (*thue dinh*), and in theory only a permanent resident (*noi tich*) of a village had to pay it, while a temporary resident (*ngoai tich*) did not.[4] During the reigns of Gia-long and Minh-mang, before the French take-over, the "grown man tax," or head tax, was still one *quan* and two *tien*.[5] Expressed in terms of rice, however, this tax appears to have been less onerous than it was a century earlier, since during the period from 1825 to 1848 the price of rice in the thirty-one provinces under the Nguyen varied from a little under a *quan* to nearly two *quan* per thirty kilograms, depending on the location and the year.[6] This tax was never imposed personally upon individuals, however. The villages were taxed collectively, and since for tax purposes the court referred only to the villages' own registers, individual villages did not always register all of their young male inhabitants, thereby enabling the villagers to pay less heavily.[7] For example, in 1884, when the French had just established their "protectorate" over Tonkin and Annam, only one-third of the actual number of young men had their names entered in the village registers.[8]

Beginning in 1897 in Tonkin, the French increased the amount of the head tax from five *hao* (0.50 piaster) to 2.5 piasters.[9] The *ngoai tich* were required to pay 0.40 piaster,[10] yet all those who worked for or collaborated with the French were completely exempted from this tax.[11] Europeans in Indochina did not have to pay taxes either. This prompted the French Minister of Colonies, Messimy, to write in 1910 that "there is a peculiar attitude displayed by the 'whites' toward the 'yellows.' In contact with people of another race, to whom we have come as conquerors, most of the French regard themselves as members of a new privileged aristocracy. In the eyes of these Europeans, the main appendage [prerogative?] of this nobility rests upon tax exemption."[12]

The same tax policy was applied in Annam, beginning in 1908. It was replaced in Tonkin in 1920, and in Annam in 1928, by another policy that required nearly every male citizen to pay 2.5 piasters, regardless of whether he was previously a *noi tich* or a *ngoai tich*.[13] In Cochinchina, beginning in 1880, the body tax was set at three francs (2.25 piasters) for each male inhabitant,[14] but by the time of the tax revision of 1937 each male peasant, whether or not he owned any land, was required to pay 4.50 piasters.[15] In the same year in Annam a peasant had to pay a "personal tax" totaling 3.95 piasters. This was a deceitfully all-embracing tax formula that contained a number of charges: 2.75 piasters for the body tax, 1 piaster for *corvée* tax, and 0.20 piaster for the plot of land on which he lived.[16] Meanwhile, even the "miserable peasants in the province of Thai Binh" (Tonkin) had to pay 4.20 piasters each if they paid in money, or the equivalent of about 6 piasters each if they paid in kind.[17]

In 1937 in Cochinchina the price of paddy rice was from 4 to 5 piasters per 100 kilograms,[18] not too different from the 1934 price of 4 piasters per 100 kilograms.[19] Thus, for a tenant farmer or sharecropper in Tonkin or Annam who worked on a hectare of land and paid only one-half of his crop (a conservative estimate) in rent, the head tax took about 20 percent of his after-rent income. The head tax also took away about the same percentage from the income of the majority of the landholders in those two regions, who owned much less than a *mau* (0.36 hectare). In Cochinchina, for the fairly well-off tenants who usually rented about five hectares of paddy, the head tax would typically amount to about 10 percent of their income. This figure is based on the assumption that the tenant kept about 20 to 25 percent of the crop yield after rent and production costs. (See the second translation and Chapters 18 and 19 of the third translation for descriptions of what the head tax meant to the peasants and what might happen to them and their families if they did not have the money to pay their tax on time.)

Another important tax on the peasants was the rice wine tax (*thue ruou*). Under the Nguyen, only a few of the biggest distilleries had been required to pay an alcohol tax, and only a very light one at that. In the villages people were allowed to distill their own rice wine tax-free. Rice wine was very important to the Vietnamese for their religious rites and for various social ceremonies and festive occasions. The importance of rice wine to the Vietnamese is expressed in an oft-quoted Vietnamese saying: "a man without wine is like a flag without wind" (*nam vo tuu nhu ky vo phong*). As a French author rightly observed, the rice paddies in Vietnam "not only play the role of wheat fields but also the role of vineyards." [20]

In the immediate aftermath of their occupation of Cochinchina, the French established a consumption tax on alcohols of European origin, and a Chinese businessman was given the right to collect this tax. In 1871 the colonial government laid a tax on native alcohols. Another Chinese businessman was given a monopoly on importation, on wine manufacturing, and on the transport and sale of all liquor of Asiatic origin. The French also gave this Chinese businessman the right to prosecute all cases of infraction of his monopoly.[21] Beginning in 1902 the French colonial administration forced all Vietnamese distilleries throughout Vietnam to sell their rice wine to the government at a fixed price, and the government in turn sold it to the consumers (through Chinese intermediaries) at a much higher price.[22] A few years later, the French reserved the monopoly on wine distillation for a small number of Chinese and French companies.

It was reported by a French author in 1910 that about 15 million piasters' worth of rice alcohol consumed each year in Cochinchina was produced by a French company or by Chinese manufacturers. Both groups handed their portion of the wine over to the colonial administration, which helped them to distribute it to the retailers, who were almost always Chinese.[23] At approximately the same time, 100 kilograms of polished rice cost about eight francs, or three piasters, and lasted for about six months' individual consumption.[24] It can thus be seen, by comparison, that 15 million piasters' worth of alcohol represented a large portion of the income of the roughly 3 million people in Cochinchina. Meanwhile, in Tonkin and Annam the colonial administration reserved a monopoly on wine distillation for two French companies, the Indochinese and Tonkinese companies, and Vietnamese who distilled wine illegally were severely fined.[25] All the same, many villagers continued to make their own wine, both because the French product was distilled (the "chemical process" was thought to be harmful) and because the wine was considered to be "impure" and was thus unfit for religious rites.[26] Because of this resistance, the French administration used a system of informers—who were given liberal rewards—in order to discover violators of the wine monopoly laws. Needless to say, "justice" was not always served by this stratagem. Many innocent people were sentenced to hard labor or deprived of their properties because of it.[27] As the Resident-General of Tonkin put matters in a letter to the Governor-General of Indochina on March, 1912: "The number of informers has increased manyfold due to the appeal of the rewards. Even if there is no illegal distilling, these people can create an incident just by throwing a handful of fermented rice into the yard of a neighboring house, thus causing the whole family to be ruined economically."[28]

The following is an account by the famous Vietnamese poet, Nguyen Thuong Hien, written during the period of the First World War:

The wine companies, with the help of the French government, have no reason to be timid, and so they dispatch patrolmen to search the villages, the rooms of the houses, and even the individual inhabitants. The year round they are as fussy as though they were chasing after bandits. Whenever they catch somebody brewing rice wine illegally, even if it is only a single jug, they fine him up to three or four hundred piasters. If one is poor and unable to pay the fine, his relatives have to pay it for him. If the relatives cannot pay, then his hamlet or village must pay. . . . In the district of Quang Xuong, province of Thanh Hoa, there was a small hamlet with just a little over a hundred families, and yet the number of people found guilty of making wine illegally was up to about a hundred. . . . The French Resident sentenced the whole village along with the actual wine distillers, ordering the district chief to arrest the villagers and jail them for alternate periods throughout the year. Yet still they were unable to pay off all the fines. Finally the inhabitants of the hamlet had to go to the district magistrate and offer all of their lands and paddies in substitution for the fines, arrests and jailing. The district magistrate reported this to the Resident and the Resident ordered the sale of the lands, turning the sale money over to the wine companies. Thenceforth, this hamlet had only people but no land of its own.[29]

But this was not all. As soon as the French began to feel that they were not making as much money as anticipated from the wine monopolies, they devised new ways to enforce the purchase of their "factory wine" by the peasants. Each province was required to consume a fixed amount of wine per month or per year.[30] If a village did not buy a quantity proportionate to the number of its inhabitants, it would automatically be considered guilty of making illegal wine, and its officials would be severely punished.[31] Thus the officials, in order to protect themselves, had to buy a prescribed amount of wine and force it upon the poor farmers, regardless of whether they wished to drink wine. (See the third and fourth translations for descriptions of the impact of the wine tax on the rural population.)

Still another important tax levied on the Vietnamese peasants was the land tax. Those whom the land tax hurt most were the small landholding peasants. Hoang Dao, a famous Vietnamese writer (and a judge in French colonial courts) wrote the following in his work *Bun Lay Nuoc Dong* [Mud and Stagnant Water]:

On the average, for each *mau* of paddy they should [theoretically] pay from 1.40 to 1.50 piasters, but the peasants typically must pay about two piasters per *mau* since in taxing a given village the government puts a tax on everything, from fields and houses to wells, ponds, and roads. That is not to mention the extra sums one must pay to village chief administrators, and innumerable other payments. . . .

The land tax, which is as high as 20 percent of the peasants' harvest, cannot be considered low. Thus, in years of poor harvests, small landowners—who comprise the majority of the [landholding] peasant population—are forced to sell their land at very low prices. The result is that rich people who lend money at high interest are gradually taking over all the land in the village, forcing most of the peasants to become their servants, or, in effect, their slaves.[32]

Under the Nguyen, as we have seen, the tax on the peasants' personal share land came to only 3 to 6 percent of our rather conservative estimate of the average yield per hectare; and the tariff on communal land (in effect, its rent) was never higher than 12 percent.

The tax situation was further worsened by the problem of "squeeze" (bribe-taking) by the officials. Of course, this problem had existed under the Nguyen, too, but it had never been as bad as it was throughout the French colonial period. There are at least three reasons for this. First of all, before the French arrival, officials had been selected via an examination system on the basis of their strict Confucian moral training, which stressed the five virtues of humanity, righteousness, propriety, wisdom, and trustworthiness. Under the French, a majority of the Confucian scholars refused to collaborate with the French "impostors." As a result the people who became officials were very often unskilled and dishonest, as the French themselves admitted.[33] This significant decline in morality and expertise on the part of Vietnamese officials is pithily discussed in a letter written by Phan Chu Trinh (a famous Vietnamese advocate of scientific training and modernization), addressed to the French Governor-General of Indochina, Paul Beau, in 1906:

During the last 40 years or so, the national condition of Viet Nam has deteriorated, the regime has become corrupt, and all the talented people have hidden themselves away. Meanwhile, those in high positions exploit others in order to maintain their wealth and honor, and those in low positions sneak about with bribes in the hope of being appointed officials. . . . Those who have not yet reached officialdom bow their heads in waiting at the gates of authority; those who are already officials misuse their authority and are a plague upon the hamlets and villages. Besides eating and love-making, they are not adept at anything whatsoever. . . . These officials, who have come to realize that your Protectorate Government indeed "protects" them and will not in the least reprimand them, have become inured to their bad habits and regard them merely as a matter of routine. Before becoming officials they engaged in bribery to gain their positions; once having attained their positions they are assiduous in safeguarding them, along with their robes and tassels and their vehicles. When someone inquires about their rank they will boast, "I am a Great Councillor of the Vietnamese government! I am a great bureaucrat of a Vietnamese province!" But when they are questioned about the ordeals of the people and the affairs of the country, they appear muddled and dumb, proving that they don't know anything!

In speaking of the provinces and districts, all that this or that province chief is capable of doing is to urge the people to pay taxes and to welcome his superiors, for he knows nothing about the affairs of his province or district. As for harassing, robbing and exploiting the poor, an official of high position is no different from his inferiors. It is as if, in order to become an official, there were a set mold one must conform to. . . .

In the past, although Viet Nam had laws which were not always so very just, as far as the officials were concerned, it was never so bad as it is now. This is because the "Protectorate" Government has tolerated the behavior of their officials and bureaucrats, thus enabling them to continue behaving in the way they do.[34]

A second reason for the increased "squeeze" practiced by officials under the French lies in the fact that most of those who aspired to such posts as village chief (*ly truong*), deputy village chief (*pho ly*), village registration chief (*chuong ba*), and village patrol chief (*truong tuan*) had to borrow money in order to buy the post in question. Once they got their appointments, they again had to borrow money in order to celebrate their newly acquired "social promotion." [35] A French economist writing in 1931 stated that in order to become a minor village official, such as village patrol chief, registration chief, village treasurer, or secretary, one had to pay from 200 to 300 piasters. If one wanted to become a canton chief or a village chief, the price rose to 4,000 or 5,000 piasters.[36] These posts, however, were not remunerated by the government.[37] Therefore, in order to pay their debts as well as to compensate for the time and energy put into their jobs, village officials were tempted to resort to practices of "squeeze."

Before the arrival of the French—and the reforms of 1839 —village officials had not been paid by the Nguyen courts (although their personal share lands were larger than other villagers' shares), but there had nevertheless been various village incomes that the village officials could use to defray their "official" expenses. First of all, there had been revenue from the village communal land. As we have seen, these communal lands, which had formed a very significant portion of the total land under cultivation under the Nguyen, rapidly diminished under the French occupation. Second, since the courts imposed taxes on the villages collectively and not on individuals as such, village officials could make up for some of their official expenses by failing to report all the names of those in the tax-paying category. Under the French, however, strict records of village inhabitants had to be kept, and taxes were now imposed directly upon the individual and not upon the villages. Thus, in order to satisfy their French superiors while at the same time retaining some money to pay for their "official" expenses, village officials felt obliged to exact higher payments from their fellow villagers, the peasants.

The third reason for the increased "squeeze" under the French was the shocking circumstance that a majority of these officials, both high and low, were opium addicts.[38] In contrast, under the Nguyen, opium smokers were prohibited from holding any official post, however insignificant.[39] (During the French period, opium was a government monopoly,[40] and the excise taxes gained from opium and from the other two government monopolies of alcohol and salt together accounted for 70 percent of the colonial government's operating revenue.)[41] Because one tael (*luong*, that is, slightly over an ounce) of opium cost as much as eight piasters,[42] or an amount equivalent to 200 kilograms of rice, officials who became addicted to this drug had no choice but to be corrupt.

These corrupt officials were precisely what Governor-General Paul Doumer (1897–1902) called them, "contractors" for the French colonial effort.[43] They were successful not only in collecting revenue for the colonial government but also in expropriating communal lands, embezzling public funds, and overtaxing the peasants.[44]

When peasants failed to submit to high taxes and to the attitudes of officialdom, and gave voice to protest, the likely result was that still greater disasters would be inflicted upon them. The sufferings risked by villagers who pleaded with the colonial establishment for a lowering of taxes were described by the poet Nguyen thuong Hien, around 1914:

In Quang Nam, a province south of our capital, the inhabitants were so heavily taxed that they came to the Resident's Headquarters to ask him to exempt them from the new tax increase. The Resident did not listen to them, but instead ordered his soldiers to charge against them. Among those driven back into the river, three drowned. The inhabitants' anger was aroused, so they brought the three corpses before the Resident's Headquarters, and for a whole week several thousand people dressed in mourning garments sat on the ground surrounding the three corpses, shouting and wailing continuously. The Resident reported the matter to the Resident General, who came and inquired of the inhabitants: "Why are you people rebelling?" The inhabitants replied: "We do not have a single stick of iron in our hands, why do you say that we are rebelling? It is only because the taxes are too high and we are not able to pay them that we must voice our opinion together." The Resident General then said: "If you people are so poor that you cannot pay taxes to the government, then you might as well all be dead." When he finished saying this, the Resident General ordered his French soldiers to fire into the crowd. Only after several hundred persons had been killed, shedding their blood in puddles, did the crowd disperse.[45]

In their attempt to justify the high taxes imposed upon the Vietnamese peasantry, many French writers have pointed out the French achievements in Vietnam: lengthening the mileage of canals, introducing asphalt roads and railroads. and building schools and hospitals. Generally, these writers only mention how many kilometers of roads were laid and how many schools and hospitals were built. They never mention who benefited from these things.

While it is true that there were more canals and roads, the roads and canals (built through *corvée* or cheap forced labor) were only communications "infrastructures" for the quick transportation of taxes in kind and agricultural produce for exportation. Equally important was the obvious military purpose of these communications "infrastructures," which served the colonial need to quell indigenous uprisings more quickly. The real benefit to the peasants was hard to discover.

An economist, writing in 1951, noted that throughout the French period, although railroads and asphalt roads were constructed and automobiles, trains, and steamboats introduced, the modes of transport used at all times by the Vietnamese rural population were traditional ones. They carried their baggage by shoulder poles when on land and by sampan when on water.[46]

One of the reasons for this was the fact that transportation by the more modern methods was too expensive for the majority of the peasants. French sources calculated that 45 percent of the price of a kilogram of rice sold at the port of Saigon went to cover transportation costs, while the producer got less than 13 percent.[47] Since the peasants had to transport their loads on their own shoulders and on their small sampans, there was little or no occasion for them to use the asphalt roads or the deep, wide canals. Nevertheless, it was the Vietnamese peasants who had to pay for the roads and the canals through their taxes and their *corvée* labor. Rich Chinese merchants, the Vietnamese landlords, and the French, who used large junks, steamboats, and automobiles, were the ones who benefited from those "infrastructures."[48] Moreover, not only did the country's longest railroad line and asphalt road—which ran side by side along the coast—duplicate the cheaper sea route, but they also "did not primarily serve the economically most developed and densely populated regions of Vietnam but ran for hundreds of miles through country that was empty." [49] One French economist admits that although the peasants had to pay for them and build them, the expensive French roads and railroads were of no benefit to the native economy.[50]

In educational matters, before the French forced the Vietnamese to change from the traditional school system to the French system, there were 20,000 schools in Tonkin and Annam alone[51] (not including the private tutoring done in the villages by parents and relatives). Indeed, according to one Vietnamese researcher, there were at least two schools in every village, and the rural literacy rate was even higher than the urban one.[52] In contrast, during the first fifty years of their colonization the French paid little attention to educational efforts. All they cared about was the training of a handful of interpreters to help them communicate with their new subjects.[53] Not until after the turn of the century did the French start to pay serious attention to education in Vietnam. There were two reasons for this.

First, the scholarly gentry—after having been frustrated many times in their efforts at armed resistance—began to exert pressure for educational reforms. They did so because the Japanese victories over Russia and China convinced them of the merits of a Western-style education. Second, the colonial administrative machine became larger and more complex, and there arose a need to train Vietnamese to operate the less important parts of this machine.[54] But even so, in 1925 only 200,000 out of a total number of over 2 million children of school age in Indochina were allowed to enroll in the schools. In the most privileged areas, only one out of every twelve boys and one out of every hundred girls were admitted. In the same year, all over Vietnam there were only 187,000 students in the grade schools. They were divided as follows: 90,000 in the first year, 54,500 in the second year, 25,500 in the third year, and 17,000 in the fourth and fifth years.[55] This meant that only about 10 percent of the students could study for four to five years.

In 1926, in an attempt to "reform" the lower school system, the French established the *écoles primaires de penetration*, which were called "village schools" (*écoles communales*) in Tonkin and "intervillage schools" (*écoles intercommunales*) in Annam. The villages now had to pay all the expenses, except part of the teachers' salaries. However, because the peasants already had to pay very high taxes, the villages did not have enough money to establish the schools as planned by the French administration. As a result, in 1932 in the prefecture of Nam Sach in Tonkin, for example, out of 190 villages only four had their grade schools.[56] In 1930 in all of Tonkin there were only 853 village schools with an enrollment of 27,627 students.[57]

In order to continue his studies after passing through the

village school, a student from the rural areas of Vietnam had to go to the district or provincial towns where "preparatory primary schools" (*tieu hoc du bi*) were located. Usually he had to walk for miles to get to these schools.[58] Since most of the peasants' children had to help their parents in their agricultural work and since most of the students from the rural areas who could reach this level were already quite old and many already had their own families, this new school system naturally eliminated most of the students from the countryside and favored those who lived in the district or provincial towns.[59]

After the preparatory primary schools, in order to attend "superior primary schools" (*enseignement primaire supérieur*), a student from the countryside had to go to the big cities and pay room and board there. There were only three superior primary schools in Tonkin, and four each in Cochinchina and Annam. These schools were in the cities of Hanoi, Nam Dinh, Hai Phong, Vinh, Hue, Qui Nhon, Saigon, My Tho, and Can Tho.[60] While a student from the rural area going to the preparatory primary schools could manage to walk home every day and share his meals and lodging with his family, it was impossible for him to attend the superior primary schools without having to pay for his room and board. As a result, only rich landlords, magistrates, and government employees living in the cities could afford to send their children to the superior primary schools.

At first all the hospitals built by the French were devoted to the needs of French soldiers and civilians. In the 1920s and 1930s, although the number of hospitals and medical personnel increased, even the most basic elements of medical care, such as vaccination, were unknown to the majority of the population.[61] As late as 1949, a French writer admitted that all the hospitals were located in the big cities and provided enough beds for only some twenty thousand persons.[62] Needless to say, the Vietnamese peasants seldom had the privilege of benefiting from the services of those hospitals, except for near-death cases.[63] As for medical personnel, by 1942 there were only 90 European doctors, 54 Indochinese doctors, 92 European nurses, and 1,462 indigenous nurses for the total population of about 23 million people.[64] This meant one doctor for every 157,000 persons and one nurse for every 15,000 inhabitants.

Because of the lack of medical facilities and personnel to check the spread of disease and to teach the populace the basic principles of public hygiene, disease was rampant. As late as 1944 one study found that in many villages up to 90 percent of the inhabitants suffered from tuberculosis, malaria, and trachoma—malaria and trachoma being the most common.[65] Nationwide, the 1944 study estimated that about 5 million of Vietnam's 20 million suffered from malaria and could work at only 50 per cent efficiency. The study did not estimate the national incidence of trachoma, but the following investigation of an unusually prosperous Tonkinese village gives an idea of the magnitude of that problem. According to the Vietnamese doctor who conducted the study in 1944, 790 out of 908 persons examined in Khuong Ha (a village outside Hanoi) had trachoma, and 316 were partially blind. These results came from a total population of only 1,000 persons and in one of the richest and cleanest villages in Tonkin, one in which all the streets and yards were paved and most of the houses were clean, tall, well ventilated, and built of bricks.[66]

In short, the French achievement in the fields of medicine, education, and public works was of little or no benefit to the Vietnamese peasants. Therefore, it can hardly be used to justify the high taxes imposed. In the words of one Vietnamese writer, "Western civilization is only a thin coat of whitewash over a decaying wall." [67]

Notes

1. Nguyen Tuan, in his introduction to Ngo Tat To, *Tat Den* [When the Light's Put Out], 5th ed. (Hanoi: Van Hoa, 1962), p. 14.
2. Nguyen Thanh Nha, *Tableau Économique du Vietnam au XVIIe et XVIIIe Siècles* (Paris: Éditions Cujas, 1970), p. 159.
3. Ibid., p. 156.
4. Pham Cao Duong, *Thuc Trang cua gioi Nong Dan Viet Nam duoi thoi Phap thuoc* [The True Conditions of the Vietnamese Peasants during French Colonization] (Saigon: Khai Tri, 1966), pp. 143–144; and Hoang Dao, *Bun Lay Nuoc Dong* [Mud and Stagnant Water] (Saigon: Tu Do, 1959), pp. 57–60. First published by Doi Nay in 1938 in Hanoi.
5. Pham Van Son, *Viet Su Tan Bien: Tu Tay-Son Mat-Diep den Nguyen-So* [New Compilation of Vietnamese History (vol. 4): From the End of the Tay Son to the Early Period of the Nguyen] (Saigon: Tu Sach Su Hoc Viet Nam, 1961), pp. 259, 337.
6. *Bulletin de la Société des Études Indochinoises*, n.s. 12, nos. 1 and 2 (1967), pp. 9–12.
7. Pham Cao Duong, p. 144.
8. Ibid.
9. Ngo Tat To, p. 14.
10. Pham Cao Duong, p. 148.
11. Ibid., pp. 150–151.
12. Thomas E. Ennis, *French Policy and Development in Indochina* (Chicago: University of Chicago Press, 1936), pp. 64–65.
13. Pham Cao Duong, p. 148.
14. Ibid., p. 149.
15. Ibid., p. 153.
16. Pierre Gourou, *L'Utilisation du Sol en Indochine* (Paris: Centre d'Études de Politique Étrangère, 1940), p. 400.
17. Ibid., p. 412.
18. Ibid., p. 339.
19. Ibid., pp. 414–415.
20. L. Roubaud, *Viet Nam* (Paris: Librairie Valois, 1931), p. 198.
21. Nguyen Van Nghi, *Étude Économique sur la Cochinchine Française et l'Infiltration Chinoise* (Montpellier: Imprimerie Firmin et Montane, 1920), pp. 57–58. The reason for the French giving the Chinese this monopoly (as well as many others) was that they wanted the Chinese to become devoted compradors, as explained by a French author in 1910:

When the French administration was installed in Cochinchina, it discovered that the Chinese settled in the midst of the Annamese population were a priceless help in carrying out its colonization. Because of the strict attitude assumed by the kings of Annam to prevent their subjects from being in contact with foreigners, the native population kept away from us for a long time. In order to get in touch with them [the native population], to change their habits and ill-will, to educate them in the field of commerce, and *to make them take out of their earthen jars the piasters needed to sustain our administrative machine*, we needed an intermediary living side-by-side with them, speaking their language and marrying women of their race. That intermediary was the Chinese. The Chinese is flexible, skilful, without prejudice, and loves gain. (emphasis added)

See René Dubreuil, *De la Condition des Chinois et de leur Rôle Économique en Indochine* (Bar-sur-Seine: Imprimerie C. Caillard, 1910), p. 71.

22. Pham Cao Duong, p. 160.

23. Dubreuil, p. 72.

24. Nguyen Van Nghi, p. 35.

25. Pham Cao Duong, p. 160.

26. Ibid., p. 161.

27. Ibid., pp. 161–162; also Jean Marquet, *De la Rizière a la Montagne* (Paris: Moeurs annamite, 1920) . In this book the author describes in some detail the fate of those who were sent to hard labor in the mountain regions.

28. Pham Cao Duong, pp. 163–164.

29. Quoted by Nguyen Tuan in the introduction to Ngo Tat To, *Tat Den*, pp. 15–16.

30. Paul Isoart, *Le Phénomène National Vietnamien* (Paris: Librairie générale de droit et jurisprudence, 1961) p. 204.

31. Le Thanh Khoi, *Le Viet Nam: Histoire et Civilisation* (Paris: Éditions de Minuit, 1955), p. 199.

32. Hoang Dao, p. 60.

33. Milton E. Osborne, *The French Presence in Cochinchina and Cambodia* (Ithaca, New York: Cornell University Press, 1969), pp. 302–308.

34. The Nguyen, *Phan Chu Trinh* (Saigon: Tan Viet, 1956), pp. 84–86.

35. Vu Quoc Thuc, *L'Économie Communaliste du Viet Nam* (Hanoi: Presses Universitaire du Vietnam, 1951) p. 105.

36. Y. Henry, *Économie Agricole de l'Indochine* (Hanoi: Gouvernement Général, 1932), pp. 37–38.

37. Nguyen Van Vinh, *Les Réformes Agraires au Vietnam* (Louvain: Université de Louvain, Faculté des Sciences Économiques et Sociales, 1961), p. 39.

38. Hoang Dao, pp. 67–68; also Nguyen Cong Hoan, *Buoc Duong Cung*

[Dead End] (Saigon: Thieu Quang, 1967), pp. 148–160; and Ngo Tat To, pp. 76–111. The majority of the officials had become addicted to opium because of the forced purchase (hence consumption) of fixed quotas per village. See J. Buttinger, *Vietnam: A Dragon Embattled* (New York: Praeger Publishers, Inc., 1967), 1: 15–28.

39. *Nam Phong Tap Chi* [The Vietnamese Ethos], no. 104 (April 1926), p. 262.

40. Hoang Dao, pp. 67–68; and Paul Isoart, p. 202. According to Dubreuil (p. 73), from the time of the French conquest of Cochinchina up to 1881, the farming of opium taxes and the right to prosecute opium smugglers was given to the Chinese. As a result, "one could then see in almost every village houses kept by the Chinese which were opium, alcohol and gambling dens, all in the same place." In 1881, however,

the Colonial Council of Cochinchina became worried about the possible harm done to our influence and policy by letting the Chinese control the monopoly of such an important product. In 1883 the farming right was taken away [from the Chinese] and was replaced by direct collection (*régie directe*). The system of direct collection was administered by an organ called the Services of Indirect Contributions. It monopolized the importation of raw opium, the refining process and the sale. However, the personnel of this organ was exclusively recruited from among the former Chinese employees of the system of farming [of opium taxes]. This organ set up a plant in Saigon and put a Chinese in charge of preparing the refined opium. In the provinces, it established a number of private warehouse owners who were given the exclusive right of sale within a determined area. All these warehouse owners were also Chinese.   (Dubreuil, pp. 73–74)

With this arrangement the Chinese middlemen could collect a profit of over 300,000 piasters a year, since they were given 10 percent commission and the official sales of opium in Cochinchina amounted to about 3 million piasters a year, between 1883 to around the turn of the century (Dubreuil, p. 74; Nguyen Van Nghi, p. 59). The total benefits reaped by the Chinese amounted to much more than just 300,000 piasters, however, since "being in charge of the official opium, they could easily manage to sell all of their smuggled opium" (Dubreuil, p. 74). The sale of smuggled opium, according to a French author writing in 1900 and quoting from sources given by high officials, brought to the Chinese societies in Cholon several million dollars a year. See H. L. Jammes, *Souvenirs du Pays d'Annam* (Paris: A. Challamel, 1900), p. 119.

41. Isoart, p. 205.

42. *Nam Phong Tap Chi*, no. 104 (April 1926), p. 262.

43. Paul Doumer, *Situation de l'Indochine, 1897–1901* (Hanoi: F. H. Schneider, 1902), p. 90.

44. Nguyen Nhu Ngoc, "Ban gop ve van de cai luong huong chinh" [Suggestions on Rural Administrative Reforms], *Nam Phong Tap Chi*, no. 41 (November 1920), p. 406; also Marquet, pp. 182–185.

45. Quoted by Nguyen Tuan in his introduction to Ngo Tat To, *Tat Den*, p. 16.

46. Vu Quoc Thuc, pp. 95–96.

47. Nguyen Van Vinh, p. 39.

48. *Dai Viet Tap Chi*, no. 10 (March 1, 1943), p. 19.

49. Buttinger, vol. 1, p. 32.

50. P. Bernard, *Le Problème Économique Indochinois* (Paris: Nouvelles Éditions Latines, 1934), p. 90.

51. J. Boissière, *L'Indochine avec les Français* (Paris: Société des Editions, 1896), p. 72.

52. Nguyen Trong Thuat, "Van de giao duc o thon que hien nay," [The problem of education in the countryside at the present time], *Nam Phong Tap Chi*, no. 173 (June 1932), pp. 632–633.

53. J. Chesneaux, *Contribution à l'Histoire de la Nation Vietnamienne* (Paris: Librairie Générale de Droit, 1955) , pp. 195–198.

54. Ibid., p. 195.

55. P.L.R., "La diffusion de l'enseignement populaire en Indochine, 1924–1925," *Revue Indochinoise* (1925), 1: 257–265.

56. *Nam Phong Tap Chi*, no. 173 (June 1932), p. 633.

57. "Le service de l'intruction publique en Indochine en 1930," *Publication de la Direction générale de l'Instruction publique* (Hanoi: Exposition coloniale internationale, 1930), p. 55.

58. "L'enseignement dans les villages," *La Revue Indochinoise*, no. 33 (December 25, 1937), p. 4.

59. *Nam Phong Tap Chi*, no. 173 (June 1932), p. 633.

60. A. Rivoalen, "L'Œuvre française d'enseignement au Vietnam," *France-Asie*, nos. 125–127 (October–December, 1956), p. 405.

61. Chesneaux, p. 199.

62. J. F. Bayen, *Problèmes Medicaux et Sociaux de l'Indochine* (Saigon: Centre d'Études Indochinoises des Forces Maritimes d'Extrême Orient, 1949), p. 62.

63. Hoang Dao, pp. 104–105.

64. *Annuaire Statistique de l'Indochine* (1942).

65. Nguyen Trinh Co, "Muc dich va chuong trinh truyen ba ve sinh va pho thong y hoc o thon que" [The purpose and program for teaching hygiene and popularizing medical studies in the countryside], *Thanh Nghi*, no. 57 (March 11, 1944), pp. 13–18.

66. Vu Van Can, "Benh dau mat hot tai lang Khuong Ha" [The disease of trachoma in the village of Khuong Ha], *Thanh Nghi*, no. 63 (April 29, 1944), pp. 11–12.
67. Hoang Dao, p. 104.

4 USURY AND AGRARIAN CREDIT

Since the French policies of land expropriation and free land concession made the majority of the Vietnamese peasants landless and the majority of those who were still landholders nearly landless and since land rents and taxes were horrendously high, most Vietnamese peasants had to borrow. They had to borrow in order to pay for production costs and for the food to live on while working on the paddies.[1] Gourou states that in Cochinchina there was no case of a peasant who could begin the season's rice cultivation without having to borrow from the landlords first.[2] Another writer reported that often the Vietnamese peasants had to borrow each bowlful of rice for their daily consumption while waiting for the harvest or while waiting to market a piece of cloth they were weaving.[3] The peasants also had to borrow at times of sickness, childbirth, weddings, and funerals.

The peasants had no choice but to borrow to produce and to survive until the next season. For their part, landlords were at the same time generally eager to have the peasants borrow from them. Gourou reported that tenant farmers and sharecroppers who did not ask for loans would not be well treated by the landlords and actually risked being sent away.[4] Another writer described a typical case of how a certain landlord categorically refused to rent his land to a certain peasant unless the latter agreed to borrow a sum of money from him first.[5] Yet another writer described in some detail how a rich landlord typically connived with the officials to get landholding peasants with no immediate need for loans into trouble, so that the landlord could then extend loans to the victims for the express purpose of paying the officials to keep them out of jail.[6] This system of forced loans, according to many writers, grew from the fact that usury was the easiest, most secure, and most profitable way of making money[7] and from the fact that it was also the easiest and cheapest way for landlords to take over the peasants' paddies and to extend their estates.[8]

For the majority of the Vietnamese peasants who had nothing to mortgage or to offer as security, the usual type of loans obtainable were on a short-term basis. These short-term loans were often quite small, yet carried extremely high interest rates. The following quotation from Gourou regarding small short-term loans in Cochinchina described a situation also found in the other two regions of the country:

There are two methods of granting short-term loans. According to the first, which is called *bac gop* ("money collected daily"), a loan of 10 piasters is reimbursed by a daily installment of 0.40 piasters over 30 days. At the end of this period, the lender has gained 2 piasters, that is, disregarding calculation of compound interest, an interest rate of 240 percent a year. By the second method, which is called *vay bac ngay* or *vay cat co* ("daily loans" or "cut-throat loans"), a piaster borrowed in the morning is paid back the same afternoon with a supplement of 0.10 piaster: the annual interest is thus 3,650 percent.[9]

Short-term loans could also be paid in labor. If a peasant borrowed 1 piaster, he had to pay back 2.5 piasters' worth of labor; and if he borrowed 2.5 piasters, he had to render 5 piasters' worth of labor.[10]

Loans granted for periods extending over several months were considered long-term loans. According to Gourou, in Tonkin loans in kind ranged from 30 to 50 percent per rice season, or 60 to 100 percent a year.[11] In Cochinchina, however, if a tenant farmer borrowed rice or money from his landlord, he had to pay interest of 50 to 100 percent over a period of six months,[12] or from 100 to 200 percent a year. These loans were supposed to cover the production costs and food consumption of the tenant farmer and his family while they worked on the paddies. Thus the interest rates were made slightly lower than the going interest rates applied throughout Vietnam to loans for other purposes, which were from 10 to 20 percent per month, or 120 to 240 percent per year.[13] In Cochinchina, a 100-piaster loan, if paid back in paddy rice, usually amounted to between 80 and 100 *gia* (100 *gia* equaled about 3,000 kilograms of paddy, worth about 75 piasters at 1937 prices) per year for three successive years.[14]

In order to obtain the long-term loans, borrowers had to mortgage their property or offer other kinds of securities. For the landless tenant farmers and sharecroppers this could mean offering to the creditor the free services of their wives and children until the debt and interest were all paid, or it could mean turning over to the creditor their portion of the premature rice crop (*ban mau*) long before harvest time at very low prices.[15] For the small landowners it meant that they had to sign loan contracts in which they agreed to offer their properties as guarantees. These contracts comprised two general types of loans which were known as "pledged loans" and "conditional sale loans." [16] Pledged loans could be either real or nominal. "Real pledged loans" meant that the borrower had to turn his real estate (rice paddies and any additional land) over to his creditor. The yields, rents, and other incomes from the properties were the creditor's to collect as interest on his loan. Failure on the part of the debtor to pay back the principal by the date of maturity meant that the creditor could either keep the properties for good or dispose of them as he wished. "Nominal pledge loans" meant that the borrower had only to turn his ownership papers over to the creditor but could retain his paddies for cultivation and could gather the crop yields and any land rents, of course, having to pay all the taxes and all the production and maintenance costs. What the borrower had to do was to meet the dates of reimbursement and the interest rates specified in the contract; otherwise his property could be legally taken over.

In the case of the "conditional sale loan," there was an actual transfer of ownership, and the creditor's name was entered into the official land register. The debtor still had the option of buying the property back, provided that his payments could be made on time.

The signing of all contracts had to be witnessed and certified by the officials, with all the requisite formalities. As a result, in order to finalize their loans, borrowers always had to "pay a certain commission to the village officials, especially to the *chuong ba*, keeper of the land register, and to the *ly truong*, keeper of the communal seal."[17] The bigger the loan, or the more advantageous it was for the borrower, the higher went the commission. In this way, whatever favors might be granted by benevolent lenders (if there were any) did not profit their debtors in any way.[18] Besides the money commissions that were paid to the village officials, borrowers also had to bring "gifts" such as chickens' or pigs' heads to their creditors at the time they came to borrow the money or when the creditors held memorial celebrations for their ancestors. Debtors who did not conform to the convention would be automatically charged by their creditors for the expected gifts, anyway.[19]

Because of the kinds of loans just described, usury proved to have corrosive effects on the peasants and on the society as a whole. Those tenant farmers and sharecroppers who pawned their wives, their children, and their unharvested crops did so precisely because, after paying their rents, they did not have enough left for consumption and for the production costs of the next harvest or because they did not have enough to pay their taxes and their medical expenses. The consequence was that, once in debt, they were likely to sink still further into debt. The end result was that most of them became unpaid slaves to their landlords.[20]

The majority of the peasant landholders who had to borrow did so because, after paying taxes and production costs, they retained only enough rice for a few months' consumption,[21] or because they had become involved, perhaps involuntarily, in one kind of trouble or another. Even though they were forced to borrow while they still had their land and could reap its full benefit, once they had pawned their land in accordance with the "real pledged loan" or the "conditional sale loan" scheme, it became almost inevitable that they would lose it. The "nominal loan" method was somewhat better than the other two because the peasants could still cultivate their lands and reap the harvests, but the high interest rates on these loans and the problems of repayment before the date of maturity almost always meant that sooner or later the debtors would lose their land. As a result, a few usurers in many villages grasped all the land.[22] Peasants who could not pay their debts on time were likely to receive all kinds of sadistic harassments from hired hoodlums sent by the usurers.[23] Thus, in the words of one author, loans gave support to the peasant "in the same way that a rope gives support to a hanged man."[24]

Usury also contributed to the decrease in land productivity and land utilization, as well as to the lack of commercial or industrial activity and development.[25] The debt-burdened peasants did not have any resources to put back into the land in order to maintain or improve it. Moreover, they did not see why they should work hard or put money into the paddies to improve them under a system in which benefits accrued largely to the landlords and the usurers. Landlords and other moneylenders (most notably the Chinese and the Indian Chettis) meanwhile did not see why they should invest in improving the soil of the paddies or in commercial or industrial activities while usury was the easiest and most profitable way of making a return on their capital.

Next in importance to the Vietnamese landlords, as usurers, stood the Chinese moneylenders. Since they were also traders, the Chinese usually made greater profits than their Vietnamese counterparts by selling their goods at exorbitant prices on credit or on an installment basis, considered as a type of loan. The Chettis (short for the Indian word *Nattukottaichetty*) were the third most important kind of usurers. In this calling they were, it seems, extraordinarily skillful: "They conceal their merciless and illegal requirements under an appearance of honesty and straight convention. The interest is added on to the capital and the total is written on the receipt. This total is then divided into ten and it is agreed that the debt is to be paid in ten installments. Under these conditions the interest will easily amount to twice what the debtor thinks he is paying." [26]

Once again, a comparison between Vietnam and the rice-growing provinces of southern China—where usury was much worse than in the rest of China—may help place the Vietnamese situation in proper perspective. In Luts'un (in Yunnan), a community where profits made from loans were greater than land rents, because inflation forced the price of rice upward before 1939, the interest rate on loans in kind made the year before rose, in effect, to 112 percent, which was considered an unreasonable amount. (Cash interest did not exceed the 50 percent level, however.)[27] In another area in Yunnan called Yits'un, where there was a considerable amount of rural industry, the authors of *Earthbound China* reported that they "did not run into any loans where the interest charged was above the 40 per cent rate," both for cash loans and loans in kind.[28] In Kwangtung province, where the percentage of peasants who were in debt was more than 70 per cent,[29] an observer had this to say:

Usually in winter the peasants borrow grain for paying rent, or food for their own consumption; and in spring, at the time of sowing rice, they borrow cash. But the tendency of recent years indicates clearly that the debt is increasing in the form of money. In the villages of Kwangtung generally, the monthly interest on a cash loan is from 2 to 3 per cent, and the annual interest is about 20 per cent. Many districts, however, demand higher rates of interest. It is 4 or 5 per cent a month in many villages of Hwa-hsien, Meu-ming, Ta-pu, Kieh-yang, and Kao-ming. In Meu-ming, when a cash loan is of less than 20 yuan, the monthly interest rate is nearly always 5 per cent. In the Sha-ku of Pan-yu, a monthly interest of from 4 to 6 per cent is demanded. Again, in many places of the province the annual interest is above 20 per cent. For instance, 30 per cent is found in Ying-teh, 40 per cent and 60 per cent are found in Sin-hwei, 70 per cent is found in Sin-i; and in the village of Lai-tseng, in Wu-chwan, as much as 100 per cent is being charged. The usual interest charged on a loan in grain is 30 per cent for six months.[30]

In some cases, the interest rate on loans in kind could reach 200 percent a year; however, this was not a fixed interest rate, but rather "a total arrived at in devious ways."[31]

Even though interest rates on loans in the southern provinces of China were much lower than those in Vietnam, the Chinese peasants, like their Vietnamese counterparts, frequently did lose their lands because of debts. As in Vietnam, once their lands were mortgaged, there was very little chance of getting them back. One author describes the situation as follows:

But when a poor peasant in China mortgages his bit of land, he has practically no hope of ever getting it back. Everything conspires against him in his frantic effort to meet the interest charge, and eventually he loses not only the land but also this additional fruit of his labour. If he only knew, he would be far better off by selling outright at the start. . . . Of course, only a very few peasants would like to sell their lands; most of them prefer to mortgage in the hope of recovering them. But once the peasants have stepped into the sepulchre of usury, they are led to descend down the inescapable staircase with only a remote chance of coming out again. At least 70 or 80 per cent of the landless peasants in Kwangtung have lost some of their land possessions through mortgage.[32]

Since the interest rates on loans in Vietnam under the French were higher than those in China in the same period, and since as Gourou has stated, there was no case of a peasant who could begin the cultivation of his fields without having to borrow first, we can imagine the terrible impact of usury on the Vietnamese peasants.

To be sure, the French colonial government did attempt to combat usury, creating such institutions as Les Sociétés Indigenes de Credit Agricole Mutuel [S.I.C.A.M.] et le Service du Credit Populaire Agricole (1912–1933); L'Office Indochinois du Credit Agricole Mutuel [O.I.C.A.M.] et les Banques Provinciales de Credit Agricole Mutuel (1933–1940); and L'Office du Credit Populaire [O.C.P.] et les Banques Provinciales de Credit Agricole Mutuel (1942–1949). However, these institutions did not really help the peasant, as one author points out:

These state organizations function in almost the same way. . . . In order to obtain loans one has to be a cultivator and must be a member by paying a small fee. The loans are short-term (one year) or long-term (five years), with personal or real guarantee. At first sight the administrative formalities seem simple and everything seems to have been designed to improve the condition of the wretched peasants; but the reality is quite different: in effect, the small and poor cultivators have neither real guarantees (paddy fields) nor enough personal credit with the local authorities to get loans. Therefore they have to rely on the auspices of the average and the big landowners who meet all the required conditions. These landowners demand large commissions before agreeing to be their [the peasants'] guarantors, or else they lend them at a high interest rate the money which they receive at a low rate from those same credit institutions.[33]

Moreover, since most of the village authorities and notables were also large landlords, the government credit institutions in effect often lent out money at low interest rates to the very people who were exploiting the peasants:

All these establishments could in effect lend only to people offering sufficient guarantees; that is, to the landlord-notables. While these notables had no [basic] need to borrow, they borrowed [merely] to take advantage of the very low official rates (6 to 8 per cent per year.) They used these funds to lend at horrendous rates to their poverty-stricken co-villagers.[34]

A French economist, and a specialist on the economy of Indochina, had the following to say in 1937 about the agrarian credit system at the time:

The millions of piasters thus advanced to the members in order to fight usury have very often produced this paradoxical result: the usurers were thereby provided with new ammunition. In effect, members of the administrative councils of the S.I.C.A.M. have "royally" helped themselves, without forgetting their relatives and friends. Thus, having at their disposal sums of money which have been borrowed at an [interest] rate that is minimal for Indochina, they have in turn lent these out at enormous rates to their usual clientele. . . . The S.I.C.A.M. societies have above all assisted the large landlords to monopolize the lands of West Cochinchina.[35]

Since the official credit institutions benefited only the landlords and the moneylenders, the peasants had to rely on traditional means such as the mutual aid (*giap*) and mutual credit (*phuong*) organizations.[36] The *giap* was a subdivision of the village; members of the *giap* group were male inhabitants of the village who had come together for reasons of residential proximity, kinship, or friendship. The purpose of the *giap* was the concentration of community resources to meet the emergency needs of individual villagers. For example, upon the death of someone in the family of a *giap* member, all the members were obligated to come together to help dig the grave, build the coffin, make the mourning garments, and bake the cake. Their services helped their bereaved associate to avoid having to seek out loans at horrendous interest rates. The *phuong* was more limited in scope and was usually organized for a specific purpose. There were many kinds of *phuong*; the following kinds were the most common:

1. The *phuong hi*, or "wedding association," was formed by parents who had children of marriage age. If there were ten families in the association, and they decided that over a period of five years each of them might want to marry a son or a daughter off, they tried to arrange for two weddings a year. If they could not arrive at a definite timetable stating which families would marry their children off first, they would resort to lottery. For each wedding, the members of the association agreed in advance to pay a certain amount of money, perhaps 100 piasters each, to the family of the bride or the groom. In that way, instead of having to pay 1,000 piasters at one time for the wedding, each member family could spread the burden of this large sum over the period of five years.

2. The *phuong hieu*, or "filial piety association," was formed by those people whose parents or grandparents were already weakened by old age. It operated on the same principle as the wedding association, except that there was no specified duration, since they could not foresee when their elderly relatives would die and they would have the "filial" obligation of a large, expensive funeral thrust upon them. It was the costs of such funerals which inspired the association.

3. The *phuong lon*, or "pig association," was formed by families wanting to have a pig to offer to the spirits of their ancestors, or to feast their relatives and friends with, during the New Year Festival. If there were twelve members, each month a member had to save an amount equal to one-twelfth of the price of an average pig. At the beginning of each month the members gathered to draw lots for their priorities. The winner of each month's lottery would then gather the savings and buy himself a pig, which he raised for the New Year Festival.

4. The *phuong tien*, or "money association," also known as *ho* or *hoi* in the northern part of Vietnam, *hue* in the central part, and *hui* in the southern part, could be daily, weekly, or

monthly. The most common, however, was and is the monthly association, which usually had from ten to fifteen members. The association was usually started by an organizer known as the "mother" (*nha cai*) or "association master" (*chu hui*), and the members, or subscribers, were usually his friends, relatives, or neighbors who knew that he could be trusted. At the first meeting the value of the association and of each share (*chan*: literally, "foot") was decided. For example, if the value of the association was 1,200 piasters and its life was determined to be twelve months, then each share was 100 piasters. Each person could subscribe to one or more shares, or several persons could pool their resources and subscribe to one share. When all the shares were subscribed, the association was formed. At the first meeting, or a few days afterward, each member other than the "mother" deposited the full share value, or 100 piasters in this case, with the organizer. This first month was called the "mother month" (*thang cai*). The money deposited was regarded as a free loan to the organizer, in return for all his responsibilities; he had to pay it back, however, in monthly installments, at the full value. In some villages, the second month was regarded as the "mother month." However, if the first month was the "mother month," at the second meeting, a month later, the bidding process began. Two methods were used in the bidding. One was to bid for the sum the bidder wanted to receive from each member, and the other was to bid for the interest rate the bidder wanted to pay. The bidding was done in secret, either by writing a sum on a piece of paper and folding the paper up, or by putting sapekes in an overturned bowl. At this meeting, every member submitted a bid, except the organizer who had already received his 1,200 piasters. If the bidding followed the second method, the successful bidder received from every member, except the organizer, an amount equal to the share value minus the winning bid. The organizer had to pay the full share value since he had already received the loan. His share was now called the "dead foot" (*chan chet*). Each subsequent bidder received an amount equal to the share value minus the winning bid from every "living foot" (*chan song*), or member who had not submitted a winning bid, and the full share from every "dead foot." For example, if the winning bid of the sixth bidder was 25 piasters, then he would receive 75 piasters from each of the six members who had not submitted a winning bid and 100 piasters from each of the other five members who had. The total amount he would receive would be 970 piasters. The last member received the full share value from every member, since he did not have to bid.

The interest rate in such traditionalistic money associations tended to be highest during the first few months; then it decreased regularly until the association terminated. Around New Year's and during the harvest times, however, the interest rate tended to go up again; these were the times when cash was most needed. As a rule, those who submitted their winning bids during the first few months paid the highest interests, those who won their bids during the middle months came out either slightly worse off or slightly ahead, and those who got their money during the last few months made a profit. The interest rate, however, was very low compared with that demanded in regular moneylending. During the French colonial period, even the last beneficiary of the money association usually made a profit of not more than 10 percent of the capital, if the total monthly installments he deposited were compared with the amount of money he received at the very end of the association to which he belonged.[37] As for the first successful bidder, who had to pay the highest interest rate, during the French period the amount he usually received was from 80 to 85 percent of the nominal value of the association.[38] Since the interest rate that he had to pay was spread over a long time (at least twelve months), it amounted to only a fraction over 1 percent of the principal a month. This was very light, in contrast to the interest rates demanded by the moneylenders.

However, as it has been pointed out, the money association as a credit institution was not very widespread during the French colonial period because it had several inherent weaknesses.[39] First of all, it could bring together only people who had regular incomes and who were capable of saving. This ruled out participation for the majority of the Vietnamese peasants. Second, in the course of association transactions, if one partner was ruined financially, had to move, or died, the association suffered tremendous difficulties. Third, the only bond between the members of the association was the organizer. If he died or suffered financial difficulties, the association risked dissolution. Fourth, the association was based upon reciprocal trust and therefore was limited to friends and trusted neighbors living within the same villages. Lastly, it could not be extended beyond a certain limit. The maximum number of shares was thirty, and the maximum time duration was thirty months.

From this short discussion, we can see that the traditional institutions could not have been of much help to the Vietnamese peasants during the French colonial period. First of all, except for the *giap*, all the other institutions were too limited in scope and existed mainly for those who had some money to save. During the French period, however, saving was difficult, if not impossible, for the majority of the peasants, who were so poor that they could not even begin working on the fields without having to borrow money first for food and seeds. Under the precolonial Nguyen dynasty, saving was possible because the peasants could keep more of their crops. Taxes were light, and peasants could benefit both from their personal share lands and from the communal lands. Second, except for the *giap*, all the other institutions were designed to meet certain foreseeable needs, although one of the chief reasons for the peasants being forced into the hands of the usurers was unexpected misfortune, such as crop failure. During the Nguyen period, unexpected disasters were met partly by the state granaries and partly by the village granaries (*nghia thuong*). The village granaries were paddy banks in which a part of the communal land's yield, as well as contributions by village inhabitants, were deposited. The goal of the village granaries was to grant loans at low interest rates to the inhabitants when they were in need or in difficulties.[40] The state and village granaries were made possible because rice surplus was kept within the country and almost never exported. During the French period, as we will see in the next chapter, because of the exportation of the greater portion of the rice exacted from the peasants through the system of tenant farming and sharecropping and through usury, the residual availability of rice per capita was too little to meet even the lowest consumption requirement. Under such circumstances, no official or private organizations were ever created to provide any kind of social security. Thus, whenever the peasants met difficulties, they were wholly at the mercy of the usurers.

Notes

1. Nguyen Van Vinh, *Les Réformes Agraires au Vietnam* (Louvain: Universitaire de Louvain, Faculté des Sciences Économiques et Sociales, 1961), p. 38.
2. Pierre Gourou, *L'Utilisation du Sol en Indochine* (Paris: Centre d'Études de Politique Étrangère, 1940), p. 277.
3. Vu Dinh Hoe, "Van de di vay doi voi dan que" [The Problem of Usury and the Peasants], *Thanh Nghi*, no. 12 (May 1, 1942), p. 13.
4. Gourou (1940), p. 282.
5. Phi Van, *Dong Que* [The Countryside], 2nd ed. (Hanoi: Xuat Ban Tan Viet, 1948), pp. 85–86.
6. Nguyen Cong Hoan, *Buoc Duong Cung* [Dead End] (Saigon: Thien

Quang, 1967), pp. 48–97, 104–112. First published by Tan Dan in Hanoi in July 1938.

7. *Thanh Nghi*, no. 12 (1942), p. 15; also Gourou (1940), p. 270; and Nguyen Van Vinh, p. 41.

8. Pierre Melin, *L'Endettement Agraire et la Liquidation des Dettes Agricoles en Cochinchine* (Paris: Librairie Sociale et Économique, 1939), p. 53; also *Thanh Nghi*, no. 12, (May 1, 1942), p. 15.

9. Gourou (1940), p. 279. In *Thanh Nghi*, no. 12 (May 1, 1942), p. 13, another writer claims that the interest rate on the first type of loan was often from 360 to 720 percent a year.

10. Gourou (1940), p. 279.

11. Ibid., p. 231. Vu Dinh Hoe writes in *Thanh Nghi*, no. 12 (May 1, 1942), that the interest rates for loans in kind were, throughout the country, from 100 to 200 percent a year, depending on whether such loans were granted during the seasonal harvest time or the *chiem* harvest (usually the tenth month). The rate would be higher for loans granted during the seasonal harvest time, which usually comes in May.

12. Gourou (1940), p. 279.

13. *Thanh Nghi*, no. 12 (May 1, 1942), p. 13.

14. Gourou (1940), pp. 279–280.

15. *Thanh Nghi*, no. 12 (May 1, 1942), p. 15; also Gourou (1940), p. 279; and Vu Quoc Thuc, *L'Économie Communaliste du Viet Nam* (Hanoi: Presses Universitaires du Vietnam, 1951), p. 108.

16. Melin, pp. 49–51; also Nguyen Van Vinh, pp. 40–41.

17. Vu Quoc Thuc, p. 106.

18. Ibid.

19. *Thanh Nghi*, no. 12 (May 1, 1942), p. 15. Although this was the case, some present day writers choose to look at the situation from the point of view of the landlord. An example of this can be found in Robert L. Sansom, *The Economics of Insurgency in the Mekong Delta of Vietnam* (Cambridge, Massachusetts: The M.I.T. Press, 1970), pp. 29–31. Mr. Sansom attempted to learn about landlord-tenant relations under the French through interviews with present and former landlords. He came up with the following interpretation, which, although credited to one particularly large estate owner whose replies were more detailed than most, was nevertheless accepted as a general description of society-wide patterns (pp. 29–30) :

In the past, the relationship between the landlord and his tenants was paternalistic. The landlord considered the tenant as an inferior member of his extended family. When the tenant's father died, it was the duty of the landlord to give money to the tenant for the funeral; if his wife was pregnant, the landlord gave money for the birth, if he was in financial ruin the landlord gave assistance; therefore, the tenant *had* to behave as an inferior member of the extended family. The landlord enjoyed great prestige vis-à-vis the tenant. . . . The tenants considered their landlord as their protector and as a good father. (Italics in original.)

For details on how it was *never* the habit of the landlords to give their tenants anything at all, and how they neither enjoyed "great prestige vis-à-vis the tenant," nor were considered as protectors and as good fathers, read the following books: For Cochinchina, read Phi Van, *Dong Que* [The Countryside] (Saigon: Tan Viet, 1943); idem, *Dan Que* [The Peasants] (Saigon: Tan Viet, 1949) ; and Son Nam, *Hinh Bong Cu* [Portraits of Times Past] (Saigon: Phu Sa, 1964). For Annam, read Phan Du, *Hai Chau Lan To Tam* [Two Pots of Orchids] (Saigon: Cao Thom, 1969). For Tonkin, read Nguyen Cong Hoan, *Buoc Duong Cung* [Dead End] (Hanoi: Tan Dan, 1938).

20. *Thanh Nghi*, no. 55 (February 26, 1944), p. 6.

21. Nguyen Van Vinh, p. 38.

22. Ibid., p. 41.

23. *Thanh Nghi*, no. 12, (May 1, 1942), p. 14.

24. Nguyen Van Vinh, p. 41.

25. Ibid.; also Gourou (1940), pp. 277–278.

26. Nguyen Van Vinh, p. 40.

27. Hsiao-tung Fei and Chih-I Chang, *Earthbound China: A Study of Rural Economy in Yunnan* (Chicago: University of Chicago Press, 1945), p. 123.

28. Ibid., p. 200.

29. Chen Han-seng, *Agrarian Problems in Southernmost China* (Shanghai: Kelly & Walsh, Ltd., 1936), p. 88.

30. Ibid., p. 89.

31. Ibid., pp. 90–91.

32. Ibid., pp. 92–93.

33. Nguyen Van Vinh, pp. 42–43.

34. Vu Quoc Thuc, p. 107.

35. Quoted by Nguyen Van Vinh, p. 43, from G. Kherian, "Le Rôle de la Coopération dans l'Union Indochinoise," *Revue Indochinoise Juridique et Économique*, no. 1 (1937).

36. Vu Quoc Thuc, pp. 108–113.

37. Ibid., p. 112.

38. Ibid., p. 112.

39. Ibid., pp. 112–113.

40. Ibid., p. 113.

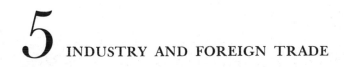

5 INDUSTRY AND FOREIGN TRADE

The impoverished peasants, plagued by the problems of excessive land rents, high taxes, and exorbitant interest rates on loans, might have fled the countryside in great numbers in search of industrial work. But this did not happen. There were at least two reasons.

First of all, the industrial establishments, which were almost all French-owned, were too small to employ any significant number of peasants as workers. The rubber plantations, which in 1937 comprised 98,000 hectares in Cochinchina and 1,700 hectares in Annam,[1] employed less than 40,000 workers at any given time. In all of Indochina mines employed only about 49,000 workers in 1937, a peak year.[2] Since 12 percent of the total production of mines came from Laos,[3] one can safely assume that at most the total number of mine workers in Vietnam was about 45,000 persons. "The workers employed in modern industry, exclusive of plantations and mines, were estimated at 86,000 in 1929, the peak before the crash. Probably their number is scarcely greater today." [4] The so-called modern industries were listed as the production of cement, ceramics, glass, wood, charcoal, paper, alcohol, soaps, soft drinks, sugar, tobacco, vegetable oils, buttons, explosives and assorted fireworks, paint and varnish, barges and small cargo boats, leather and rubber products, electricity, and so forth.[5] Since there were only 86,000 industrial workers in all of Indochina, the total number of Vietnamese engaged in all kinds of production outside of agriculture in the late 1930s may have amounted to only 150,000 persons.[6]

One way of appreciating the small scale of all industry is to compare the value of the two most important industrial products, rubber and coal, with that of rice. During the French period, all of the rubber produced in Indochina was exported, mainly to France.[7] Up to the mid-twenties, almost all of the coal produced in Vietnam was exported, while the local industries as well as the national railway had to use wood from the forests.[8] From the mid-twenties through the mid-thirties, less than one-fourth of the coal was left for use in Indochina.[9] ("Of the other mining products—zinc and tin, gold, gems, etc.—none remains in the country except for a few thousand tons of phosphate which are crushed on the spot.")[10]

Although all the raw rubber and most of the mineral products were exported, the total value of these products composed a small fraction of export income. The greatest part of the total revenues came from rice, maize, and other foodstuffs. The total value of raw rubber exported from Indochina, on the average, was only 5.5 percent of the total exports in the period 1922–1936, when rubber was first produced on a large scale.[11] (Only in 1906 did the French begin to experiment with planting rubber trees, and only in 1910, when about 1 million trees were planted, did they develop the first real plantations.)[12] The total value of all kinds of coal exported from Indochina, on the average, was only about 4 percent of the total export in the period from 1922 to 1936, when the production of coal was at its peak.[13] Before the development of the tin mines in lower Laos in the late 1930s, up to 98 percent of the total value of all mineral products in Indochina came from the coal mines in Tonkin.[14] In fact, when added together the total value of coal and rubber exported was considerably less than the value of corn, a secondary crop.[15]

While a large portion of the exported corn came from Cambodia, almost all of the rice came from Vietnam—and most of this from Cochinchina. Tonkin, which was second in Indochina in rice exports after Cochinchina, exported an average of only 200,000 metric tons of paddy a year,[16] as opposed to an average of about 2 million tons of paddy a year from Cochinchina.[17] According to the *Annuaire Statistique de l'Indochine*, rice and rice by-products exported from Vietnam formed, on the average, about 65 percent of the total value of all exports from Indochina during the period 1913 to 1940.[18] There was a marked dip in the percentage of the value of rice exported from 1931 onward. This dip does not, however, represent a fall in rice exports. They remained high while the world price plummeted. Indeed, the amount of rice and rice byproducts exported from Vietnam steadily increased after 1931.[19] In fact, in 1935 and 1936 Vietnam passed Thailand to become the second largest rice exporter in the world.[20]

However, the continued increase in rice exports did not mean that productivity increased or that more land was pressed into use. On the contrary, total rice acreage in Cochinchina—which supplied most of the rice for export—actually decreased about 10 percent during the 1931–1936 period.[21] Thus, the rise in exports during this period had the paradoxical result of throwing thousands of sharecroppers and tenant farmers out of work and causing those who retained their rented fields to be squeezed still harder by the big landlords. Even in relatively good times the French emphasis on rice exports left the population of Cochinchina with less rice than they needed. This in turn caused the population of the other two regions, who were unable to rely on imports from Cochinchina, to live in constant hunger and sometimes even face outright starvation. Needless to say, matters were even worse during the world depression. The fall in the world price for rice knocked the bottom out of the domestic rice market. Between April 1930 and November 1933, the Saigon wholesale price for rice fell from 13.1 piasters to 3.2 piasters.[22] Since most of the peasants had to borrow (at predepression rates) in order to survive between harvests and to cover production costs and since they had to pay their debts in cash or in paddy equivalents, the fall of the price of rice was a disaster of the first magnitude. Moreover, since taxes—which also remained at predepression levels—had to be paid in cash, the tax burden became all the more unbearable.

While rice exports did the peasants more harm than good, the greater part of the imported products never reached them.[23] As Bernard shows in some detail, 49 percent of the total imports (perfumes, opium, automobiles, etc.) were for the Europeans, the Chinese, and the rich Vietnamese; 9 percent of the imports (arms, armored ships and tanks, locomotives, etc.) were not for the direct consumption by any group; and the remaining 42 percent (consisting of such items as petroleum, medicines, paper, cotton yarn, and firecrackers) were for mass consumption.[24] These imported products, which were always about one-fifth to one-eighth of the exported products in tonnage, were nearly equal in value to the exports, except for the period from 1932 to 1936.[25]

Now let us return to the question with which we began this chapter: Why, given their miserable living conditions, did the Vietnamese peasants not flock to the industrial areas in search of work? We have already discussed one reason. The industrial sector was tiny, so there were very few jobs available. But there was another, equally important reason: the horrible working conditions, low pay, and outright maltreatment that industrial employees were almost sure to encounter. As a rule, the French writers on the French colonial period in Vietnam have shied away from these subjects in their writings. Instead, they have usually preferred to discuss the profits that the industries brought to their fellow Frenchmen and to the French colonial government. Of the few writers who attempted to show that they, too, were concerned with the workers' conditions, many, like Robequain, went only so far as to cite the regulations and the labor codes established by the French colonial government and remained silent about what the working conditions really were like.[26] Without questioning the reasons for such curious acts of omission, let us take a closer look at the actual working conditions of the workers in the rubber plantations and the mines.

These were the two largest French-owned industries in Vietnam, both in terms of monetary income and in terms of the number of workers employed.

Ninety-eight percent of all the rubber plantations in Vietnam were in Cochinchina, and yet the great majority of the workers were peasants from Tonkin and Annam.[27] This was not because the peasants in Cochinchina were much better off than their counterparts in Tonkin and Annam and therefore had no need to find work on the plantations, but rather because they lived near enough to the plantations to be well aware of the horrible working conditions there.

Since they were unable to get workers from the Cochinchina population, the French were compelled to carry out a very sophisticated recruitment campaign among the peasants of Tonkin and Annam, who were likely not to know much about the rubber plantations in the south. Well-dressed recruiters were sent to the villages in Tonkin and Annam with pictures of beautiful homes complete with beautiful garden plots in front and back, pictures of beautiful child-care centers, and pictures of healthy and well-dressed workers in the process of tapping the rubber trees. The recruiters then patiently explained to the peasants that if only they agreed to work or to sign a contract, they would be given the beautiful homes free once they got to the plantation; their babies and older children would be taken care of without charge at the child-care centers; they would be given free rice, free meat, and free fish; they would have a day off every week as well as on every holiday with full payment; besides the days off on holidays, feasts would be given by the plantation owners and everyone could eat and drink and gamble to his heart's desire; and the cost of living was so low in the south that much of their salaries would remain unspent, allowing them to help members of their families who were to remain behind, and to accumulate substantial savings for themselves.[28] To put the frosting on this imaginary cake, the recruiters waved handfuls of money, saying they would give advance wages to peasants who agreed to come at once. The rubber plantation recruiters even sang entertaining ditties, like the following:

Don dien cao su la thien dang ha gioi

Xu cao su la the gioi bac tien

Song cao su la song canh than tien

Cong tra man han chang buon hoi huong

The rubber plantations are heaven on earth

The world of rubber is the world of money

To live in the rubber world is to live in a fairyland scene

And when the contracts are expired, nobody will want to return to his native place.[29]

Peasants who agreed to become rubber workers soon found out that the reality was quite different. The following letter from a plantation worker to the publisher of *Echo Annamite* (a Saigon newspaper) in September 1928 describes it this way:

My name is Nguyen van Tho, a 46-year-old farmer from Quang Nam. I am a stranger among strangers here and therefore do not know to whom I can talk about the cruelties that are inflicted upon us at the plantations. I pray to the spirits of my ancestors that I can confide this in you.

Here is my story:

There was a certain person by the name of Xu-ba-Le who came to the central part of Vietnam [Annam], speaking in Vietnamese, to recruit workers for a plantation in the southern part. There were two Vietnamese accompanying him. The three of them bragged about the working conditions: daily salary of 80 cents, three bottles of polished rice, dried fish, steamed meat and fish sauce; decent lodging; good medical care when sick; the working location was only three stops from the Phan Thiet railway station, so that you could return to your native village any time you wished; good climate.

Lured by those promises, we volunteered to become coolies without signing any contract. There were 140 of us, 31 from my native place and the rest from Hue.

The group was loaded onto three trucks. The trucks sped away as if they were running away from something. Each person had been given 5 piasters in advance. After we had settled ourselves in the trucks, however, their masks were taken off. Instead of treating us nicely, they beat us with canes. We were guarded as carefully as if we were a herd of cattle. When we arrived in Nha-trang, we were transferred to four train cars. After we passed the Phan Thiet railway station, two of our fellow coolies jumped off the train in order to escape the miserable conditions awaiting them. What they had just experienced was only the beginning. I saw the two fall down unconscious on the ground. Whether they had died or had just been knocked unconscious, I did not know.

After the third station from Phan Thiet, another person jumped out of the train and lay there motionless. Two others were on the boarding steps about to jump when they were caught; and after being beaten until they were lifeless they were thrown out of the train. This cruel act made none of us dare to try to escape after that. The next afternoon we arrived in Bien Hoa. Three trucks came to take us to a place called Phu-rieng.

This is not a place where the climate is as good as we had pictured it, and neither was it only three stations from Phan Thiet. It is on the other hand an isolated place in the wilderness, about six hours by train or a day by automobile from Phan Thiet.

There were other disappointments, too. Instead of 80 cents [8/10 of a piaster] as we had been promised, our daily pay was decreased to 50 cents. That is not to mention other cuts due to a variety of trivial excuses. Also, instead of 3 liters of polished rice and fish sauce, we were given only a tiny amount of rice and a little bit of some sort of salty liquid just barely enough for subsistence.

At 5 o'clock in the morning, when it was still pitch dark, we had to file into lines for work. Those who got up a little late or were still sleeping were beaten with big canes as a reminder not to come late again.

Instead of comfortable lodgings as we had been promised, we were stuffed into thatched huts. Water leaked in everywhere. All night we had to squat on the floor, without any kind of light whatsoever, getting soaking wet and with the cold piercing our bones.

After a week in this kind of hell, I discovered a way to escape. But the next day I was caught again by some minority people who beat me, stripped off my clothes, and then turned me in to the plantation owner for a reward.

Then they had a boxing exhibition in which they used me as a punching bag in front of other fellow coolies. After that I was locked up: cold rice and feet in a cangue for eight days.[30]

What is described in the letter just cited seems to have been not an isolated case but representative of the situation in all the rubber plantations throughout the French colonial period. An author who had been in most of the rubber plantations during the 1930s and 1940s has described in considerable detail the horrible living and working conditions of the plantation workers. The following is a description of a normal workday on a typical plantation:

On all the rubber plantations, the workers had to get up at 4 o'clock in the morning. They hurriedly cooked their meals and prepared their tools for the day's work. Many people did not have time to eat their breakfast, yet when the gongs sounded at about 5 o'clock or a little after urging them out for the roll call all the workers had to be out in the yard by that time—for nobody was allowed to be late. The roll call took only about 20 minutes, but what a very nerve-racking twenty minutes this was! The workers' hearts thumped with fear since during roll call the supervisors and the French owners would try to find fault with them in order to have an excuse to scold them or beat them up. The workers were used to saying that a morning without enough time to eat breakfast was a morning for swallowing a beating. After the roll call, everybody had to go out to the rubber lots, although it was not light yet. Usually when one reached his work area he would still be unable to see the trunks of the rubber trees distinctly.

Many who visited the plantations for the first time would be highly surprised to see the workers shuffling their way to the rubber lots while it was still pitch dark. But they did not know that it was because of [sound principles of] private gain that the owners forced the workers to go out to tap the rubber that early in the morning and to work them to the limit to meet their daily prescribed requirement. One must tap that early in the morning in order to have enough time left for collecting the latex; that is not to say that by tapping early in the morning the rubber would necessarily come out more abundantly. If a worker was responsible for his quota in the morning, which usually meant from 280 to 350 trees to be tapped, he had to work non-stop from 5 o'clock in the morning to 12 noon before he could finish it. In the course of that seven hours he had to complete three main things: tap the latex, collect it, and hand it over to the owner. Then at 1 o'clock in the afternoon he again began work at such chores as weeding in the rubber lots, cleaning up the [managers'] residential area, etc., until 6 o'clock in the evening, when he could finally be let off.

Now a few words about the required number of trees that a worker had to tap from 5 o'clock to 10 o'clock in the morning. Since the rubber trees were planted 5 meters apart, in only one tapping the worker had to cover a distance of about 2,000 meters. On the average, in order to scrape the grooves clean, peel off the dried-up latex around the edges, pick up the rubber that had stuck to the spouts and the bowls, straighten up the supports for the bowls and make fresh incisions, each rubber tree takes up to about one minute. In that one minute one must work very fast. And yet one must make the incisions carefully, just the right depth into the bark, not too shallow and yet not too deep, lest it cut into the body of the tree. If the incision was either too shallow or too deep, the latex would come out too sparingly. If a worker made either of the above mistakes while tapping the rubber trees and if he were caught by the supervisors or the owners, his body would be beaten into a mess. For that reason, while tapping the latex the workers could not afford to be careless. They had to scrape without giving their hands a rest, as well as to be constantly on the run between one tree and the next. Their eyes also had to be quick since they had to pay attention to the bark of the trees in order to make good incisions, and at the same time they had to watch out for the supervisors and the owners. When the supervisors or the owners came around, the workers had to greet them in time, or otherwise they would be clubbed until they fell down unconscious at the feet of the rubber trees.

Even though they worked their breath away in this manner, many people still could not finish their tapping quota in time for the collecting of the latex. They then had to skip a number of trees on the sly, or else beg those foremen who still had any humanity left in them to help. Only a small number of people who were still strong and healthy could finish their quotas in time for the latex collection, or if possible ten minutes or so early so as to rest for a moment or take a smoke.

At about 10 o'clock the siren rang giving the signal for the latex collection to begin.

All the workers had to carry their cans and run about 2,000 meters all the way back through the rows of trees that they had incised in order to collect the latex that had dripped into the bowls. This is equally as demanding as the tapping of the trees itself. Especially when the more latex one collected, the heavier the cans would get; and the heavier the cans got, the slower one was constrained to walk. Also, by that time one was running very low on energy.

It took more than an hour to collect the latex. After that the workers had to carry the latex to the collecting stations in the middle of the lots so that trucks could come to take it to the main warehouses. Here the supervisors already stood waiting. They used a yardstick to measure each of the cans to see how much latex each worker was able to collect. This was another occasion for the supervisors to insult the workers or beat them up. . . .

If [instead of working at odd chores around the plantations] the workers had to tap latex in the afternoon as well, after leaning their backs to the rubber trees, panting like buffaloes, or after stretching out flat on the red soil to rest a little, they would hurriedly swallow the lunches that they had carried along with them since morning, gulp a few mouthfuls of water, draw a few times on their water pipes, and then come back to work on the afternoon quotas. The work was the same as it had been in the morning, although it was actually much harder since by afternoon their supply of energy was already just about exhausted.

Not until 6 o'clock in the evening, when the sun was going down beyond the rubber trees, did they get back to their compounds. . . . For the above reasons, on the rubber plantations people had a habit of saying that children did not have a chance to know their fathers, nor dogs their masters.[31]

In spite of the fact that they worked very hard and had little time even for eating their meals, the workers were constantly punished by the French plantation owners and managers for making deep incisions on the trees, for being late for the roll call, for pausing to rest, for not turning off the lights at a certain time, and so forth.[32] For these "infractions" violators could lawfully be punished:

On the rubber plantations, to be thrashed with a rod on the buttocks, to be beaten on the head with a club, to be punched, kneed, etc., were merely the most common forms of punishment. The following tortures were even more terrible:

They [the French owners and their labor supervisors] would make the workers lie down on the ground exposing the soles of their feet so that they could club them continuously for a count of about a hundred blows. When the blood began to ooze out, they would then proceed to make the workers stand up and jump on pebbles. . . . If it was not a matter of making the workers jump on pebbles, they would certainly be made to run around their living compounds, which was called "horse trotting" (*quan ngua*) . . . .

On some plantations the owners had a form of punishment which they called *up thung* (or "upside-down pot."). This form of punishment was especially reserved for pregnant female workers who committed mistakes. . . . On the earth foundation near the roll call yard they had a hole dug the size of a large pot. Then they made the female worker lie face down, with her stomach in the hole that they had dug so that she could lie down flat while they beat her. A rain of rods and clubs would then come down on her buttocks. A beating like that could knock a woman out more than once, and usually 8 out of 10 women would afterwards miscarry. But this was not all. There were yet many other kinds of punishment. . . .[33]

The plantations came therefore to be known by a phrase that translates as "hell on earth" (*dia nguc tran gian*) by the workers, and there were very few of them who ever made a successful escape from that hell. "The [French] planters had to guard against the desertion of the latter [Vietnamese workers]. The law permitted the local authorities to arrest deserters, who could be convicted and brought back under guard to their employer. The act of running off with a cash advance was regarded as embezzlement and severely punished." [34]

As described by Diep Lien Anh, punishment for workers who ran away was usually death by torture, hanging, stabbing, or some other form in order to make the "criminals" examples to the other workers. Because of this and because of sickness caused by overwork and lack of adequate food and housing, the mortality rate among the plantation workers was extremely high. Diep Lien Anh cites official records left behind by the rubber companies that show that in the period 1917–1944, out of a total of 45,000 workers of the Dau Tieng rubber plantation, an affiliate of the Michelin Company, 12,000 died there; 10,000 out of about 37,000 died at the Loc Ninh and Minh Thanh plantations belonging to the Cexo Company during the same period; and 22,000 out of a total of about 198,000 workers died at the plantations owned by the "Terres Rouges" Company from 1917 through 1945. The same author goes on to explain that the official records of the companies he cites included only contractual workers (*travailleurs engagés contractuels*) and not the so-called "free workers" (*coolies libres*). The latter did not sign any contracts; therefore the plantation owners had no legal obligation to record or report their deaths.[35]

The French planters blamed the high death rate on malaria, and many French writers uncritically picked up the story. Robequain, for example, who admitted that in 1927 the workers at the An Vieng plantation in Bien Hoa province suffered "the appalling losses of 27.4 per cent sick and 26.3 per cent deaths," said that after sanitation and drainage works were begun in 1929, by 1931 "only 8.7 per cent were sick and not a single death was recorded." He went on to say that in general the death rate among the plantation workers was reduced to only 2.8 per cent, which was about the same as the average rate for Cochinchina as a whole.[36] To blame the high death rate on malaria, and then to maintain that the death rate was suddenly and drastically reduced because of the French effort in sanitation and drainage works, was an attempt on the part of many Frenchmen to provide a convenient alibi for their maltreatment of the Vietnamese workers, as well as a rationalization for their "civilizing mission" (la mission civilisatrice). The truth, however, was quite different. A French writer, Paul Monet, wrote in 1931 (the year that Robequain said there was no death recorded at the An Vieng plantation) that plantation owners killed Vietnamese workers in groups of five and six persons as if the latter were simply animals like dogs or cats. Afterward, they would either have the whole thing hushed up or report it as "death from malaria." [37] A large body of folksongs left behind by the plantation workers also gives us an idea of the extent of the maltreatment and death inflicted upon them by the plantation owners.[38]

In this account we have generally not dealt with the situation after 1945 as far as the condition of the peasants was concerned. After that year, given the growing power of the League for the Independence of Vietnam (Viet Nam doc lap dong minh hoi, or Viet Minh for short), the French no longer controlled most of the countryside. In the case of the rubber plantations, however, the French were still in full control, even though most of their healthy workers had left to join the Viet Minh, leaving behind only the sick and the elderly. In a frantic attempt to find workers for their plantations, the French Army ordered its soldiers into the nearby villages to capture local residents. Prison labor was also utilized in plantation work. But these measures were simply not enough. On September 23, 1946, therefore, a law was passed and promulgated by the so-called Commissioner of the Republic of Cochinchina himself, ordering the police to arrest any Indochinese who did not have sufficient identity papers with him and to transport him to the rubber plantations in order to meet the plantations' requirement for 50,000 workers. As a result, illegal arrests became the rule of the day all over Cochinchina.[39] The French Army was used not only to abduct people to the plantations but also to prevent them from running away. In its January 13, 1946, issue, the French newspaper *Climats* publicly bragged that the most effective instrument for getting latex was the submachine gun.

Working conditions became even more deplorable than ever. The number of rubber trees each person had to tap in a day went up to 450 or 500, and if the rubber trees were young trees or recently grafted trees (*greffés*), the quota could be as high as 1,000 trees a day for each worker. Workers who expressed grievances in any form were branded as *Viet Minh* or communist and could be killed on the spot with the full sanction of the law. Thus, in order to meet their quotas or to earn a living at all, workers had to depend on their children for help. These children averaged five or six years of age, since ten-year-old children were given their own quotas to meet. The percentage of women workers also rose from less than 10 percent in 1944 to more than 60 percent in 1946. These women were frequently raped by the French supervisors and soldiers and often became pregnant as a result. But even pregnant women whose delivery time was near at hand nevertheless were forced to go out into the rubber lots to work. As a result, miscarriage, sudden delivery in the lots without any medical care, and death were commonplace. During this period the workers stopped calling the plantations "hells on earth," and substituted the new name of "slaughterhouses" (*lo sat sinh*).[40]

The history of the colonial mining industry presents a not too dissimilar picture of the bleakness of nonagrarian employment. In all of Indochina the mines employed about 50,000 workers during peak years. Before the development of the tin mines of Nam Patene in lower Laos, 98 percent of Indochina's total mineral production came from Tonkin, and most of this came from the coal mines in the Hon Gay region.[41] Most of the workers, both at the mines in Hon Gay and in Nam Patene, were Vietnamese from Tonkin and the northern part of Annam.[42] The mines employed a somewhat greater number of workers than the plantations, but working conditions were by no means any better. In fact, the Hon Gay region was again described as "hell," and the Nam Patene region as "death valley" by those who worked there.[43] The Vietnamese peasants, therefore, tried their best to stay away from the mines. As with the plantations, this gave rise to a labor shortage problem for the French. The solution was harsh: the mine owners razed to the ground village after village that happened to be on the thousands of hectares of land owned by the mining companies, in a deliberate strategy of depriving the peasants of all means of livelihood in order to force them to become workers in the mines.[44]

At the same time, whenever there were disasters of some kind that robbed the peasants of their crops, the French authorities would refuse to send relief. They intentionally left the population to starve, again in the hope that under such circumstances the peasants would find their way to the mines to become workers.[45] A mine supervisor by the name of Desrousseau sent a report to the Governor-General of Indochina as follows:

The *nhaque* [French derogatory use of the Vietnamese term *nha que*, meaning the peasants] will consent to leave their villages to work only when they are dying from starvation. Therefore we must come to the bizarre conclusion that the way to remedy the present difficulty [in getting enough workers to work the mines] is to impoverish the countryside.[46]

One of the many stratagems the French used to impoverish the countryside and drive the peasants into their mines and plantations was the destruction of the dikes and the flooding of the villages.[47] The following is a Frenchman's account of this:

The whole province of Vinh Yen was submerged under water. The Department of Public Works had closed an aqueduct about eight kilometers from the fortress of Phu Lo, creating a large pond of water, over ten square kilometers [*sic*], that submerged the whole area in its present miserable condition. Every day groups of peasant representatives went to Bac Ninh and even Hanoi, begging the government not to kill them, not to let the whole area be flooded, not to keep the aqueduct closed. But the government ignored them and cruelly looked on as the whole province was dying.[48]

Notes

1. Charles Robequain, *The Economic Development of French Indochina*, trans. I. A. Wood (Oxford: Oxford University Press, 1944), p. 207; also André Bourbon, *Le Redressement Économique de l'Indochine 1934–1937* (Lyon: Bose frères, M. & L. Riou, 1938), p. 93.
2. Robequain, p. 266.
3. Ibid., p. 252.
4. Ibid., p. 269.
5. Ibid., pp. 269–284.
6. "As late as 1937 the registers of the Labor Inspection of Indochina listed only 72,000 workers and employees (of whom approximately 50,000 were in mines and quarries); but this number was soon to expand to include about 150,000 salaried workers." Robequain, p. 79.
7. See Bourbon, p. 93, for the total amount of exports, and p. 108 for the total amount of production.
8. Roland Dorgelès, *Sur la Route Mandarine* (Paris: A. Michel, 1925), p. 93.
9. See Bourbon, p. 151, for the tonnage of coal exported, and p. 155 for the total tonnage of coal left for use in the whole of Indochina.
10. Robequain, p. 318.
11. André Touzet, *L'Économie Indochinoise et La Grande Crise Universelle* (Paris: M. Giard, 1934), p. 21, gives statistics from 1922 to 1932; Bourbon,

p. 116, gives statistics from 1930 to 1936. Bourbon, p. 264 and p. 280, gives statistics of the value of the total exports from Indochina.

12. Nguyen Van Nghi, *Étude Économique sur la Cochinchine Française et l'Infiltration Chinoise* (Monpellier: Imprimerie Firmin et Montane, 1920), pp. 40–41.

13. See Touzet, p. 69, for statistics from 1922 to 1932; and Bourbon, p. 272, for statistics from 1930 to 1936.

14. Robequain, pp. 252–257.

15. Ibid., p. 310.

16. P. Gourou, *Les Payans du Delta Tonkinois* (Paris: Éditions d'Art et d'Histoire, 1936), p. 405.

17. Paul Bernard, *Le Problème Économique Indochinois* (Paris: Nouvelles Éditions Latines, 1934), p. 94.

18. Nguyen Van Vinh, *Les Réformes Agraires au Vietnam* (Louvain, 1961), p. 19. Before the turn of the century, the value of the rice exported from Cochinchina amounted to around three-quarters of the value of the total exports from Indochina, or one-seventh of all the exports from all French colonial territories, including Algeria and Tunisia. See *Bulletin Économique de l'Indochine*, no. 17 (1899), pp. 610–611. It should be noted that not all the rice exported was actually carried out by the French colonizers as such. Rather, they used the Chinese as compradors. The French needed somebody who could go to the Vietnamese producers and get the rice for them. Here the Chinese were convenient not only because they had their contacts in the villages and because they owned most of the junks for rice transport but also because they were at the same time usurers who lent money to the Vietnamese peasants at oppressive rates and had, therefore, forced their debtors to mortgage most of their crops to them. See René Dubreuil, *De la Condition des Chinois et de leur Rôle Économique Indochine* (Bar-sur-Seine: Imprimerie C. Caillard, 1910), p. 102; and Wang Wen-yuan, *Les Relations entre L'Indochine Française et la Chine* (Paris: Éditions Pierre Bossuet, 1937), pp. 38–41. In 1910 Dubreuil (p. 102) wrote, "At the present time, the Chinese are the uncontested master of the rice market in Cochinchina." An official French source of 1906 stated that out of the total sum of 107,800,000 francs invested in commerce, mostly in the rice trade, the French controlled 41,400,000 francs, while the Chinese owned 66,400,000 francs. (*Rapport du Budget des Colonies au Senat—Exercise 1906—Journal officiel*, Senat, session ordinaire de 1906, Documents Parlementaires, Annexe no. 161, p. 510. Cited by Jean André Lafargue in *L'Immigration Chinoise en Indochine, sa réglementation, ses conséquences économiques et politiques* (Paris: Henri Jouve, 1909, pp. 289–290.) The Chinese predominance in trade, as noted by many authors, depended on favors given them by the French administration (Lafargue, p. 290; Dubreuil, p. 76, p. 109, and p. 114). From 1913 to 1935,

50 percent of all the rice exported went to China, and all these amounts went through the hands of the Chinese living in Vietnam (Wang Wen-yuan, pp. 133–137).

19. Touzet, p. 10; Bourbon, p. 271.

20. Bourbon, p. 62.

21. Ibid., p. 61.

22. Bernard, pp. 123–124.

23. Ibid., p. 33.

24. Ibid., pp. 32–33.

25. Bourbon, p. 264.

26. Robequain, p. 78.

27. Ibid., pp. 214, 217.

28. Diep Lien Anh, *Mau Trang—Mau Dao: Doi Song doa-day cua phu cao-su mien dat do* [Latex and Blood: The Wretched Life of the Rubber Plantation Workers in the Red-Earth Districts] (Saigon: Lao Dong Moi, 1965), pp. 35–40.

29. Ibid., p. 39.

30. Quoted in Nguyen Van Trung, *Chu Nghia thuc dan Phap o Viet Nam: Thuc chat va Huyen thoai* [The French Colonial Policy in Vietnam: Myth and Reality] (Hue: Nam Son, 1963), pp. 42–43. Original source: *Echo Annamite* (September 17, 1928).

31. Diep Lien Anh, pp. 56–58. French sources cited by Le Thanh Khoi, *Le Viet Nam: Histoire et Civilisation* (Paris: Éditions de Minuit, 1955), p. 426, show that some plantation workers had to get up at three o'clock in the morning and did not get back from work until it was already dark. They had to work an average of at least eleven and a half hours a day.

32. Diep Lien Anh, pp. 66–71.

33. Ibid., pp. 73–74.

34. Robequain, p. 215.

35. Diep Lien Anh, p. 23.

36. Robequain, p. 216.

37. Paul Monet, *Les Jauniers: Histoire Vraie* (Paris: Gallimard, 1931), p. 208. This whole book deals with the French recruitment and treatment of plantation workers.

38. Hoang Ngoc Phach and Huynh Ly, *So Tuyen van tho yeu nuoc va cach mang, Tap II, tu dau the ky XX den 1930* [A Collection of Patriotic and Revolutionary Literature and Poetry, (vol. 2) , From the Beginning of The Twentieth Century to 1930] (Hanoi: Nha Xuat Ban Giao Duc, 1959), pp. 253–256.

39. Diep Lien Anh, pp. 91–93.

40. Ibid., pp. 102–106.

41. Robequain, pp 252–257.

42. Ibid., p. 266.

43. Ibid., p. 267.

44. Dorgelès, p. 93.

45. René Dumont, *Révolution dans les Campagnes Chinoises* (Paris: Éditions du Seuil, 1957), p. 7.

46. *Témoinages et Documents Français Relatifs à la Colonisation Française au Vietnam* (Hanoi: Association Culturelle pour le Salut du Vietnam, 1945), 1: 10.

47. Diep Lien Anh, p. 35; also Nguyen Van Trung, p. 39.

48. Louis Bonnafond, *Trente Ans de Tonkin* (Paris, E. Figuière, 1924), p. 128.

6 HUNGER AND STARVATION

In 1945, the last year of the five-year Japanese occupation of Indochina, in an article entitled "The Crisis of a Hungry Population," an agronomist wrote:

All through the sixty years of French colonization our people have always been hungry [original italics]. They were not hungry to the degree that they had to starve in such numbers that their corpses were thrown up in piles as they are now. But they have always been hungry, so hungry that their bodies were scrawny and stunted; so hungry that no sooner had they finished with one meal than they started worrying about the next; and so hungry that the whole population had not a moment of free time to think of anything besides the problem of survival.[1]

One reason for this sorry state of affairs was the French policy of maximizing rice exports. Even in relatively good times the French emphasis on rice exports had a disastrous effect upon the rural population. This is clear even if one considers only the best years of French rule (1900–1930) and ignores both the depression years and the thirty years before the turn of the century when the French were trying to consolidate their control over the country.

Since most of the exported rice came from Cochinchina, let us begin with the situation in this region. The per capita availability of paddy rice for Cochinchina during this period was, on the average, some 250 kilograms.[2] This average is of course overly generous because it includes the amounts of rice used for seeding, for making alcohol, and so forth, as well as the usual loss in the production-consumption cycle. Together all these items may have amounted to 20 percent of the total productivity. However, even this generous estimate of 250 kilograms of paddy per capita does not suggest an amount large enough to have fed the population. Gourou maintained that even if the peasants were to eat a lot of potatoes, manioc, corn, and so on (which was not the case, since these products formed a very insignificant part of the Vietnamese agriculture), then even 0.76 kilograms of paddy rice a day, or 277 kilograms of paddy a year, would still have been too low.[3] Henry maintained that the average amount of rice per capita necessary for adequate nutrition should be 337 kilograms of paddy, or 223 kilograms of milled rice per year.[4] In an article entitled "The Alimentation of the Rubber Workers" published in the March 25, 1944, issue of *Thanh Nghi*, an author quoted a French doctor as saying that the 750 grams of rice given to each worker a day was not enough, and as a result workers had to purchase additional rice and other foodstuffs.[5] Since, as we have seen, the conversion index of milled rice to paddy rice is at most seven to ten, 750 grams of milled rice would equal about one kilogram of paddy. This means that each grown worker would have needed at least 360 kilograms of paddy a year, or 110 kilograms more than Bernard's generous estimate of per capita rice production.

This exportation of rice from Cochinchina not only left the population there with little to eat but also had a great impact on the other two regions of the country. The real average production of Tonkin, as cited by Bernard (1931), was 1,560,000 metric tons a year, while the real average production of Annam was 890,000 metric tons a year.[6] Statistics on the population in these regions as given by the *Annuaire Statistique de l'Indochine* indicate that in 1921 there were in Annam 4.9 million persons, in 1931 there were 5.1 million, and by 1936 there were 5.7 million; while there were 6.9 million, 8.1 million, and 8.7 million, respectively, in Tonkin.[7] Tonkin exported, on the average, about 200,000 tons of paddy per year through the port of Hai Phong, which meant that it had only about 170 kilograms left for each of its residents.[8] As for Annam, in the year 1931, for example, the availability of paddy rice per capita was about 175 kilograms.

This does not take into account seed requirements and rice used for making alcohol and other by-products. The amount of rice available for consumption by the population in these two regions was thus far below the average amount necessary per person. Indeed, so important was the export market to the French that, according to French sources, the total amount of paddy left in the country for individual consumption fell steadily during their rule: from 262 kilograms in 1900 to 226 kilograms in 1913 to 182 kilograms in 1937.[9]

But there were other reasons for the widespread hunger under French rule. The most important of these was the very low incomes of most of the peasants. According to the French economist Bernard, in the late 1920s (considered to be the best years of the French period) the average income of the "active members" of the "poor indigenous class" was 44 piasters in Tonkin, 47 piasters in Annam, and 55 piasters in Cochinchina. In contrast, the average income of French civilians and members of the "rich indigenous class" was from 100 to 125 times higher.[10]

The "poor indigenous class," as defined by Bernard, was "composed of all the salaried employees, the small landowners, the tenant farmers, and the sharecroppers working in large and medium properties." [11] The total population of the poor indigenous class in 1931 was given as 6.7 million in Tonkin, 4.7 million in Annam, and 2.3 million in Cochinchina, while the "active population" of this class was given as 3.7 million, 2.6 million, and 1.5 million, respectively.[12]

To show what the low income of the majority of the population meant in practice, Bernard cites a favorable case of a peasant family of five in west Cochinchina, the rice basket of the whole country. The family was able to rent five hectares of land to work on. This land was of relatively good productivity and yielded about 1,600 kilograms per hectare per year. After paying the landlord 50 percent of the crop, the tenant family still had 4,000 kilograms remaining, which at that time was worth about 128 piasters. This family of five was considered as 2.8 adult, or "active," members. The spending of this family, at 1931 prices, was 45 piasters for paddy rice; 33 piasters for meat and fish (to supplement the small amount of meat that they got from the animals they raised and the fish they could catch in their flooded paddies), salt and fish sauce; 25 piasters for tobacco, kerosene, betel, and tea; 12 piasters for clothing; 10 piasters for housing; 22 piasters for medicine, memorial celebrations for ancestors, and other miscellaneous items; 7 piasters for farm implements; and 10 piasters for direct taxes.[13] The total spending, therefore, was 165 piasters, or 38 piasters more than the income from the land. This spending, according to Bernard, was considered as "a strict minimum." [14] But Bernard never explains how this family of five made up the difference of 38 piasters. Presumably they had some other income from odd jobs or the like, or they had to borrow from the landlords. And they were a favorable case—not only because of the high productivity of their land but also because the landlord got only 50 percent of the crop as basic rent, or perhaps actually less (if we are to take the rest of the evidence at face value). It appears that the 50 percent cited also included production costs.

A more detailed study of the income of tenant farmers is given by Gourou. According to his investigation, a tenant who rented five hectares of land in west Cochinchina would, beginning in the fifth month, have to borrow from his landlord about 35 *gia* of paddy and 5 piasters in order to be able to start his cultivation at all. When the harvest came, he had to pay the landlord 70 *gia* for the loan in paddy and 12.5 *gia* for the loan of 5 piasters. The interest on the loan in kind was thus 100 percent, and on the 5 piasters 300 percent, since each *gia* of paddy was 40 liters (each liter being about 0.75 kilogram) and since the going price for 100 kilograms was 5 piasters. Besides having to pay for the loans, the tenant also had to pay the rent, which was equal to 150 *gia*, or 50 percent of the crop. All in all, therefore, the tenant had to pay 232.5 *gia* to the landlord and had only 67.5 *gia*, or a little over 20 percent of the crop, left for his family. This, according to Gourou, was not enough to live on.[15] Again, this seems to be a favorable case, since each hectare yielded on the average 2,500 liters, or 1,800 kilograms, of paddy rice a year, which is about 600 kilograms more than the average productivity of Cochinchina. Also, as Gourou points out, the majority of the tenants farmed less than five hectares.

According to Gourou, the living standard of the agricultural laborers in Cochinchina was much worse than that of the tenants. In west Cochinchina, for example, an agricultural laborer could get work during only seven months of the year (the first, second, sixth, seventh, eighth, eleventh, and twelfth), while he was usually unemployed for the rest of the time. From the eleventh month to the second month, which was harvest season, an agricultural laborer earned from 0.32 to 0.35 piaster a day in addition to his meals. His wife, who would be given somewhat less heavy labor, could earn only 0.20 to 0.25 piaster plus meals. As for the other months, the workers were hired to repair irrigation canals, embankments, and so forth, which paid much less.[16]

An agricultural laborer who was lucky enough to be employed on an annual basis might perhaps have a more stable, although not a very much better, life:

A wage laborer employed by the year may have a more stable but not a brighter life. For example, a laborer in the province of Ben Tre earns 36 piasters per year, besides his meals, betel, tobacco, and three pieces of cotton clothing; but his family can only make ends meet thanks to supplementary resources earned by the wife and the eldest son (in cotton-weaving, rice-planting, gleaning, etc.). Many of the families of these laborers live on the brink of starvation; during a slack period it might happen that they have no more food and not a cent left; even the humblest jobs, which earn them little, cannot always be found.[17]

Such was the situation in the more prosperous region of Cochinchina. The situation in Tonkin and Annam was much worse. One author describes the condition of a relatively fortunate peasant and his family in the following terms:

Besides himself and his wife, he has five children. The older children are only able to herd buffaloes and to cut grass, and the three younger children are scrawny and sickly. Their mother, too, is usually attacked by stomach ailments whenever the weather changes. This tenant farmer receives 8 *mau* of paddy, rents a buffalo, borrows 8 *noi** of rice for seeds, and 10 *noi* for food. The land rent is 5 *noi* per *mau*; and the buffalo rent is 10 *noi*. After every harvest, he has to pay the landlord a total of: 40 *noi* of paddy rice for land rent + 10 *noi* for buffalo rent + 8 *noi* for seeds + 10 *noi* for food = 68 *noi*. If the weather is good, the yield per *mau* is 12 *noi,* which means 96 *noi* in all. Therefore he can keep for himself 96 — 68 = 28 *noi.*

But during the planting season in the 5th month, he has already borrowed 30 piasters to hire rice planters for 5 *mau* of paddy, since his wife could plant only 3 *mau* herself during the whole planting period. When the 10th month comes around, he will have to pay back 40 piasters including the interest. When the harvest comes, although his family works all it can, he still has to hire 35 [man-day] units of labor, which cost about 30 piasters [*sic*]. Thus, in order to pay these two sums of money, he has to sell at least 15 *noi* of rice. After half a year of hard work, this farmer has only 13 *noi* left to put into his storage basket. To understand it more clearly, let us convert these 13 *noi* of paddy rice into metric measure, which gives about 300 kilos, or 200 kilos of milled rice. A family of seven persons, large and small, eating two meals a day, will require at least 2 kilos of rice daily.

* According to the author, a *noi* is a unit of weight that varies from twenty to twenty-five kilograms according to the locality.

Therefore, the 200 kilos of rice will enable them to have their stomachs tolerably full from the 10th month until Tet.* But we have only looked at their food consumption. Besides, there are clothes for the cold winter, medicine for the stomach ailments of the wife and the ailments of the children, contributions to the patrilineage anniversaries, interest on funeral debts caused by the deaths of parents and grandparents—all of which should be paid before the 30th of Tet [i.e., the end of the twelfth month]. In order to pay for these, the husband and wife and children cannot of course heedlessly sit down to eat their fill to the extent we assumed above. They have to tighten their belts and eat one meal of rice mixed with roots and one meal of gruel a day, or else eat only one meal a day, in the hope of saving 5 to 7 *noi* of rice to pay the above-mentioned expenses. And then, from Tet until the *chiem* season in the 5th month, or, if there is no *chiem* harvest, all the way until the 10th month of the following year, what shall the family of this tenant farmer survive on? On labor wages, which they can earn some of the time and some of the time cannot, and on roots. . . .

 . . . When the next rice planting season comes around, in order to [continue to] receive land from the estate owner, this tenant farmer will be required to borrow 10 *noi* of rice to eat, 40 to 50 piasters to pay for extra labor in rice-planting, etc. . . . By borrowing so much, he will have to sell almost all his rice just to pay his debts when the 10th month arrives. In the end, this tenant farmer only lives within a vicious circle of debts, and "making a buffalo of himself" he works his spine off just to pay his debts, then to get into debt once again, around and around. Nevertheless, this tenant farmer has had the [rare] good fortune to have come across a landlord who extracts a fair amount in rent, and who lends rice without interest. The great majority of the peasants who come to the estates to get work as tenants have to pay much higher rents: for example, 8 *noi* per *mau*. And sometimes, during the harvest season, the owners force the tenants to transport all the harvested grain up to the yard of the estate house where the owners take everything, leaving the tenants with only whatever rice is still clinging to the rice stalks [after threshing], and only when the harvest season is at an end

* The tenth month falls around the Western month of November, and Tet falls around the end of January or early February.

will the owners finally give each tenant from 10 to 15 *noi,* just enough [in effect] for paying the labor of reaping the grain.[18]

As for the wage laborers in Tonkin and Annam, their situations were even more deplorable. Usually it was very difficult for them to provide for their families. As the author just cited goes on to say:

A peasant who works as a wage laborer receives 12 piasters a month, and his meals. If he complains to us that, during the single season that he works for an estate owner, he runs a deficit of a set of clothes, we may be somewhat surprised. But the truth is that during each crop season there are two months of plowing and harrowing: the 5th month and the 6th month, during which time the laborer gets 24 piasters for his wage. After about 60 days of soaking himself in the rain and exposing himself to the wind, naturally he will wear out his set of clothes. Being soaked in seven or eight layers of sweat each day—there being nothing else for the laborer to change into—no cloth can stand the wear and tear. Therefore, after a single season, the laborer has in effect sacrificed a set of clothes in exchange for 24 piasters. Since the peasants have to pay about 10 piasters for a meter of cloth, the 24 piasters are not even enough for a short pair of pants and a short-sleeved shirt, since this takes at least three meters of material.[19]

In fact, according to Gourou, in Tonkin not long after the harvest the majority of the peasants would again be reduced to eating a meal of rice and a meal of rice gruel a day, and by two months after the harvest many of these people could only afford one meal a day. While a number of peasants might manage to have enough for two meals a day, usually their food was a mixture of roots, corn, and bran.[20] In 1937 an author related these words of a bran vendor:

These people who come to buy bran are buying it not for their pigs but for their own consumption. Rice is very expensive and corn and potatoes are also expensive, so many country people must eat bran. They don't care, so long as it fills their bellies. Also, you must know that there are three kinds of bran eaters: One kind may get together a few cents a day to buy bran, so as to cook it for eating, together with a few greens—the sort of thing eaten by the pigs that belong to well-to-do families. Another kind are those who can earn only about two cents a day; they can still buy their bran, but only have water to mix it with. And so they eat in the same way as the pigs that belong to the less-well-off families. The third kind are like the ones that you have just seen. That is to say, they earn nothing the whole day long, and so twice a day they go through the rows of bran vendors pretending to bargain on prices while managing to put a bit of it into their mouths as though they were sampling the quality. In this way, after going through the rows they just about get their bellies filled.[21]

The situation in Annam was equally bad, or worse.[22] Many Vietnamese writers, such as Phan Du, have very vividly described the problem of hunger there in their stories.[23]

But while the Vietnamese peasants were always hungry even in normal times, in times of crop failure or disasters of one kind or another they starved. As we have seen, disasters such as floodings were frequently caused by the French authorities themselves.

Perhaps the worst of these man-made catastrophes originated with the policy of rice collection during the years 1943 to 1945, which caused 2 million people to die in Tonkin alone during the few months from the end of 1944 to the early part of 1945. (See the fifth translation for a description of the great famine on a day-to-day, human level.)

Beginning in late 1942, largely because of the Japanese demand for rice,[24] the French colonial administration imposed upon the population the forced sale of given quotas of rice, depending on the area of land cultivated. In 1943, on the average, the peasants were forced to sell from 200 to 250 kilograms per *mau*, depending on the classification of the paddies they owned.[25] In 1943 the amount of rice an independent peasant producer (small landholder) had to render in forced sales went up to as high as three-fourths of his income.[26] In many individual cases it exceeded the total amount of paddy a peasant could harvest. A luckless peasant of this kind was forced to buy rice at the market price of 200 piasters per hundred kilograms in order to have enough to resell to the administration for 25 piasters.[27] According to another source, by 1944 the French had already collected so much rice that the black market price for 100 kilograms of paddy rose to 350 to 400 piasters. But still the peasant could get only 25 piasters per 100 kilograms when he sold his rice to the government.[28] In 1945 the Japanese increased the official price to 53 piasters per 100 kilograms, but in the meanwhile, in Tonkin, the price of 100 kilograms on the black market had already increased to 700 or 800 piasters.[29]

During the same period, in Cochinchina, the French and the Japanese burned rice and maize in place of fuel in the factories,[30] and the French in particular made it difficult for people to transport rice from the south to the north. During that time, there were junks available that could have carried large amounts of rice from Cochinchina to Tonkin. French colonial regulations discouraged their use, however: the French Administration would take three-fourths of the total amount of rice reaching the north and allow the junk operators only 20 piasters per 100 kilograms as transportation fees.[31] For this reason, although in 1941, 186,000 tons of milled rice reached Tonkin from Cochinchina, by 1944 the amount had dropped to only about 7,000 tons. [32]

The practice of burning rice as fuel in Cochinchina, as well as the use of rice to make alcohol for running machines elsewhere, was one of the major causes of the death from starvation of 2 million people in Tonkin alone and the utter misery of the people in other regions. Another was the French storage of about 500,000 tons of rice from 1943 to the beginning of 1945[33] and the export to Japan through the Mitsui Bussan Company of 1,000,000 metric tons in 1942, 1,000,000 in 1943, 500,000 in 1944, and 40,000 in the early part of 1945.[34] Of course, there were other factors contributing to this starvation. They included the export of 300,000 tons of maize to Japan from 1942 to early 1945[35] and the French and Japanese demands that the peasants uproot their rice stalks and convert their fields to growing hemp, peanuts, and castor beans.[36]

The starvation in Tonkin led a Vietnamese writer to make the following observation:

According to a recent investigation, we found out that in the village of Thuong Cam, in the district of Thai Ninh and the province of Nam Dinh, last year there were 900 grown men, but by May 20 of this year, only 400 men were still alive; males and females, young and old, the village used to have four thousand persons, but more than two thousand of them have died from starvation. The total area under cultivation in the village was 1,000 *mau*, but now more than 500 *mau* have been abandoned.[37]

In an article published in the April 28, 1945, issue of *Viet-Nam Tan Bao,* a Hanoi newspaper, another author had this to write:

Old men of 80 to 90 years of age that we have talked with all told us that they had never before seen a famine as terrible as this one. When we passed through areas that once had seen rice and potatoes growing in abundance and had been thriving with activity, now all we could see were dry paddy fields and people who were weak and tired.

Why was there this desolation?
   Because no sooner did the population grow the crops than the government took most of it away.
   Because the population had been so hungry that their strength had wasted away and they could not continue working.

When we entered market places we seldom saw foods like rice or potatoes. If there was any rice, the rice was full of husks, and if there were any potatoes, the potatoes looked not much bigger than the circumference of a chopstick. . . .

When we entered the villages we saw the peasants miserably dressed. Many of them had only a piece of mat to cover their bodies. They wandered about aimlessly in the streets like skeletons with skin, without any strength left, without any thoughts. and totally resigned to the ghosts of starvation and disease. Their rice had all been taken away from them by the government. They did not have any potatoes or corn. They were forced to eat everything, whether poisonous or not, they did not care. They had eaten up all the vegetation around them. They ate even those plants that had been formerly reserved for animals. A family which still had a little bran to eat considered it a heavenly blessing. When a dog or a rat died, it was the occasion for the whole village to come around to prepare it and parcel it out among themselves. . . .[38]

This situation led a certain French colonial officer, by the name of Vespy, to jot down the following words in one of his reports:

They walk in unending lines together with their whole families. There are old people and there are children; there are men and women, shrunken under the weight of their poverty and suffering. Their bodies are nearly or all naked and the bones jut out, shaking. Even girls who have already reached puberty and whom one might expect to show some embarrassment, are in the same condition. Now and again they stop to close the eyes of those who fall never to rise again, or to strip off any pieces of rag (I do not know what to call it exactly) which are left behind on their bodies. From looking at these bodies, which are more ugly than the ugliest of animals, and at these corpses, which are shrivelled up on the roadsides with only a handful of straw for clothes as well as for their burial garment, one feels ashamed of being a human.[39]

Notes

1. Nghiem Xuan Yem, "Nan dan doi" [The Starvation Crisis of the People], *Thanh Nghi,* no. 107 (May 5, 1945), p. 18.
2. P. Bernard, *Le Problème Économique Indochinois* (Paris: Nouvelles Éditions Latines, 1934), p. 94.

3. Pierre Gourou, *Les Payans du Delta Tonkinois* (Paris: Éditions d'Art et d'Histoire, 1936), p. 406.

4. Y. Henry, *Économie Agricole de l'Indochine* (Hanoi: Gouvernement Général, 1932), p. 332.

5. *Thanh Nghi*, no. 59 (March 25, 1944).

6. Bernard, p. 6.

7. A. Bourbon, *Le Redressement Économique de l'Indochine 1934–1937* (Lyon: Bosc frères, M. & L. Riou, 1938), p. 35. Hoang Van Duc, *Comment la Révolution a triomphé de la Famine* (Hanoi, 1946), pp. 5–6, says that in 1932 Tonkin produced 1.6 million metric tons of paddy rice for a population of 8 million people, and in 1943 it produced 1.5 million metric tons for a population of about 10 million. The rice in 1932 and 1943 were thus far below the per capita requirement. Of course, the figures just cited also included the amount of rice exported and the amounts used by the French to make alcohol for running their cars and other machinery.

8. Pierre Gourou, *L'Utilisation du Sol en Indochine* (Paris: Centre d'Études de Politique Étrangère, 1940), p. 255, gives a breakdown for seed, alcohol, and export to neighboring countries above and beyond the 200,000 metric tons exported through Hai Phong. Other exports: 30,000 metric tons. Seeds: 75,000 metric tons. Distilleries: 50,000 metric tons. This means that there were only 1,245,000 metric tons left for consumption, or only 155 kilograms per capita. Jean Goudal, *Labour Conditions in Indochina* (Geneva: International Labour Office, 1938), p. 218, estimates that per capita consumption of paddy rice in Tonkin was only 136 kilograms.

9. Le Thanh Khoi, p. 421.

10. Bernard, pp. 20–21. Bernard also gives the average annual income of European civilians in Vietnam as 5,000 piasters: 600 piasters for European military personnel; 6,000 piasters for the "rich indigenous class" for Tonkin, Annam, and Cochinchina. The "indigenous middle class," which is defined as people who owned from five to fifty hectares of paddy, specialists, functionaries, tradesmen, and so on, had an average annual income of 160 piasters for Tonkin and Annam and 180 in Cochinchina.

11. Ibid., p. 20.

12. Ibid., p. 21. Bernard appears to be in error when claiming that the "poor indigenous class" in Cochinchina totaled only 2.3 million. Since the members of this class were defined as those owning less than five hectares, they would indeed comprise the vast majority of the population.

13. Ibid., pp. 21–22.

14. Ibid., p. 23.

15. Gourou (1940), pp. 403–404.

16. Ibid., pp. 401–402.

17. Ibid.

18. Nghiem Xuan Yem, "Canh Ngheo o thon que" [The Poverty Situation in the Countryside], *Thanh Nghi*, no. 47 (October 16, 1943), pp. 3–4.

19. Ibid., pp. 4–5.

20. Gourou (1936), p. 573.

21. Lang Nhan, "Loi nguoi ban cam" [The Words of a Bran Vendor], *Dong Duong Tap Chi* [Indochina Magazine], no. 27 (November 13, 1937), p. 10.

22. Gourou (1940), pp. 407–409.

23. Phan Du, *Hai Chau Lan To Tam* [Two Pots of Orchids] (Saigon: Cao thom, 1965), a collection of short stories on the subject of poverty in Annam.

24. According to Joseph Buttinger, in 1941–1942 Japan took 80 percent of Indochina's rice exports, although Japan had taken relatively little before 1940. During the war years Japanese troops alone annually consumed 1 million metric tons of rice from Indochina, or approximately one-fifth to one-sixth of the total production. See Joseph Buttinger, *Vietnam: A Dragon Embattled* (New York: Praeger Publishers, Inc., 1967), 1: 239.

25. Tran Huy Lieu, *Xa Hoi Viet Nam duoi thoi Phap-Nhat, 1939–1945* [Vietnamese Society during the French-Japanese Period, 1939–1945] (Hanoi: Van Su Dia, 1957) , 2: 76. Also: *Trung Bac chu nhat*, no. 172 (August 29, 1943).

26. Tran Huy Lieu, 2: 77. Also *Thanh Nghi*, no. 110 (May 24, 1945), p. 7.

27. Tran Huy Lieu, 2: 91–92. Also *Thanh Nghi*, no. 110 (May 24, 1945), p. 7.

28. Tran Huy Lieu, 2: 77. Also *Trung Bac chu nhat*, no. 251 (July 1, 1945).

29. Tran Huy Lieu, 2: 77. Also *Trung Bac chu nhat*, no. 251 (July 1, 1945).

30. Tran Huy Lieu, 1: 140.

31. Nghiem Xuan Yem, "Nan dan doi" [The Starvation Crisis of the People], *Thanh Nghi*, no. 107 (May 5, 1945), pp. 19–20.

32. *Bulletin Économique de L'Indochine* (1944), 3 & 4: p. 163.

33. J. Decoux, *A la Barre de L'Indochine* (Paris: Plon, 1949), p. 449.

34. J. Gauthier, *L'Indochine au Travail dans la Paix Française* (Paris: Imp. de Laboureur, 1949), p. 283.

35. *Annuaire Statistique 1939–1946*, J: 166. Also Tran Huy Lieu, 1: 79.

36. Tran Van Giau, *Giai Cap Cong Nhan Viet Nam* [The Vietnamese Working Class] (Hanoi: Van Su Dia, 1962), 3: 221.

37. Tran Huy Lieu, 2: 96. Also *Thanh Nghi*, no. 110 (May 26, 1945).

38. *Viet Nam Tan Bao* (Hanoi, April 28, 1945).

39. *Témoignages et Documents Français Relatifs à la Colonisation Française au Viet Nam* (Hanoi: Association Culturelle pour le Salut du Vietnam, 1945), 1: 15.

7 CONCLUSION

Prior to the French arrival, the land system of the Vietnamese court was fairly responsive to the needs of the peasants. Every peasant was guaranteed his "personal share," for which he had to pay only a very small tax amounting, perhaps, to at most 6 percent. Besides the personal share lands, there were also village communal lands. These helped to pay for communal expenses and also contributed to the solution of various welfare problems. After the French took over the country, however, owing to their policies of land expropriation and free land concession, nearly half of the total cultivated areas in Vietnam was given to French citizens and to Vietnamese and Chinese supporters of the colonial regime. In addition, as the traditional order broke down, an unknown amount of land was usurped by landlords and merchants through usury and other devious means. As a result, the majority of the Vietnamese peasants became landless and were thus forced to work as agricultural laborers or as sharecroppers and tenant farmers.

Since there arose an excess of landless peasants competing with one another for work on the landlords' properties, the terms of tenant farming and sharecropping during the French period were extremely harsh. Often tenant farmers and sharecroppers had to pay half of their crops in rents, as well as having to pay for all production costs. Together, these charges may have amounted to 70 percent of their crops or more. The system of tenant farming and sharecropping under the French not only robbed the peasants of the better part of their crops but also had the effect of lowering the productivity of the land and also of the producers. The tenant farmers and sharecroppers did not have any resources left, after paying rents and production costs, to make agricultural investments, although it was supposed to be their responsibility to maintain and improve their lands. Furthermore, they were given no incentive to put extra money and energy into the land, under a system in which the profits would be largely taken by the landlords. The landlords, for their part, lacked incentives to put money into their land to maintain or improve it; usury remained the quickest, easiest, and most profitable way of investing their capital. As a result, the land was cultivated for years without being scientifically fertilized, or even well fertilized by old-fashioned means. It may well have deteriorated to about half of its former productivity. In the 1920s and 1930s, per hectare productivity in Vietnam was only about two-thirds as much as that of Siam, half as much as that of China, and one-third as much as that of Japan.

The exceptionally high rents and low yields during the French period forced the majority of the Vietnamese peasants to borrow for their food in order to survive from harvest to harvest, and also for their production costs in order to begin their agricultural work. The interest rates on loans from the landlords were horrendous: the rates on short-term loans could be as much as 3,600 percent a year, and those of long-term loans were usually above the 100 per cent level a year. Such high interest rates forced the peasants to become virtual slaves to the landlords once they got into debt. If they had any land of their own at all, they were sure to lose it to their usurers.

The peasants' situation was further worsened by the problem of high taxes. The head tax alone took away from 10 to 20 percent of the tenant farmers' and sharecroppers' incomes after rents. The situation of the agricultural laborers, whose incomes were less than those of the tenant farmers and sharecroppers, was even worse. High taxation tended to be exacerbated by official corruption. The French did not use their tax money to improve the livelihood or environment of the peasants. The roads and railways that they built were used mainly for the quick transport of their taxes in kind and for bringing the agricultural products that they squeezed from the peasants to the various seaports for exportation. The schools and hospitals that they built were too few and were designed for the urban population. The real benefits to the peasants were nil.

The French, and the Vietnamese landlords who prospered in the colonial period, did not invest much of the money they exacted from the peasants in industry. Industries that were developed remained very small throughout the French period. The total number of workers in all of Vietnam, even late in the 1930s, was only about 200,000 persons out of a total population of over 20 million. Even then, the working conditions of the laborers were so bad that many preferred escape, at the risk of getting beaten or killed, to remaining in the French-owned plantations and mines, which deservedly came to be known as "hells" and "slaughterhouses." Furthermore, the income from the results of the workers' labor did not serve to generate many significant new internal economic opportunities but instead went mostly into the pockets of the French and then flowed abroad. The costs of the few industries operated by the French were still largely borne by the agricultural sector of the economy.

The lack of investment in industries stemmed from the fact that loans to the peasants were the most profitable, quickest, and easiest way for the landlords to invest their money. Usury had become the most profitable way of making money because, of course, of the impoverishment of the peasants through the harsh system of tenant farming and sharecropping and through high taxation. Usury also inhibited commercial activities because the landlords and other wealthy people could always earn more through moneylending. Commercial activities were restricted largely to the exportation of agricultural products exacted from the peasants and the importation of products to be enjoyed by the French and the "indigenous rich."

The lack of industrial and commercial activities meant that there were few employment opportunities outside the agricultural areas. Thus, although the rural population increased rapidly, it was not absorbed by the urban areas. The urban population of Tonkin and Annam remained constantly under 4 percent on the average. In Cochinchina, where a large portion of the inhabitants in the few true urban centers were foreigners, the total "urban population" was at most 14 percent, even when one accepts Gourou's classification of rural areas with more than 500 persons per square kilometer as genuine urban centers. Yet while the rural population increased rapidly, the cultivated surface in Tonkin and Annam did not increase in any substantial amount. In Cochinchina, although the cultivated surface did increase in proportion to the population increase, more than half of the rice produced was exported. The money gained from it did not benefit the peasants in any comprehensive way.

Because of the increase of the rural population and the concentration of a large part of the cultivated surface in the hands of a few through the policies of land expropriation and free land concessions and through usury, even the luckiest tenant farmer could work only a few hectares of land at most. Meanwhile, the productivity of the land decreased, and land rents increased, so the peasants were left with little for themselves. Worse yet, rice cultivation was now manipulated by French ambitions to sell on the world market and was not destined solely for feeding the population as it had been before the French arrival. The monetization of the rural crops induced the landlords to export as much as they could when the world price of rice was high and to abandon cultivation of a large amount of land when the world price was low. Either way, it was the peasants who suffered most. Under the French, the convergence of all these factors did not just bring hunger, misery, and starvation to the peasants. Because of the way they were institutionalized, they dealt Vietnam's economic and social fabric a blow from which, as the history of the last twenty years shows, it has not yet recovered.

II TRANSLATIONS

1 Phi Van
THE PEASANTS
(*DAN QUE*)

Phi Van, whose real name is Lam The Nhon, was born in 1917 to a middle-class family in Camau, the southernmost province of Vietnam. As a writer, his speciality is "reportage and documentary fiction" on the livelihood and living conditions of the peasants in the Mekong Delta during the French occupation. From 1943 to 1949 Phi Van published four books that describe not only the condition of the peasants but also their changing attitudes toward their own situation. The first book, entitled *Dong Que* [The Countryside], is a compilation of true stories written in newspaper style. It "shows us the customs of the countryside, the beliefs and superstitions of the peasants. It tells us of the relationships and the conflicts between the landlords and the sharecroppers, the naive character of the latter and the power and influence of the former. . . . There is perhaps a profound moral lesson which the author does not point out explicitly, but leaves us to understand by inference, thus letting us become better able to empathize with the hard-working peasants who lead a simple and industrious life, but who, until their fate's end, must be the victims of the rich and influential."* Indeed, in the face of all the landlords' exploitation and tyranny, the only satisfaction for the peasants was the taking of personal revenge, which only got them into deeper trouble.

In Phi Van's second book, entitled *Tinh Que* [Love of the Countryside], the peasants had begun to learn how to band together and fight, but they did so only because of the foreign French presence and the local uprisings by the Cambodian minority and not because of any political or ideological consciousness of their social and economic position. In the third book, entitled *Dan Que* [The Peasants], the people were begin-

* Quoted from a speech given by Professor Nguyen Van Kiet at the Thu Khoa Nghia literary award ceremony in 1943, when the book was awarded first prize. See Phi Van, *Dong Que* (Hanoi: Xuat Ban Tan Viet, 1948) pp. 8–11.

ning to gain political awareness. They had begun to understand the reasons behind their miserable condition at the time, their mistreatment at the hands of officials, and their merciless exploitation by the landlords. Most important of all, they had begun to understand that they had invincible power if only they knew how to cooperate with one another against social injustices. But still they did not take any effective action. It was only in the fourth book, *Co Gai Que* [The Country Girl], that the peasants began to wake from their slumber and inactivity and began to participate actively in the revolution.

In other words, Phi Van's works give us in most graphic detail a comprehensive view of the peasants' evolution from colonization to revolution, from political unawareness to political responsiveness. Students of the Vietnamese revolution will find these works most helpful in giving them an understanding of the social basis for the revolution, as well as an understanding of the changing attitudes of the peasants on the many determining issues that led them into that revolution. Students of the peasants' conditions will find in every one of the books just mentioned graphic descriptions of exploitation and collusion by landlords and officials against the peasants.

During the war against the French, Phi Van also wrote two manuscripts of personal reminiscences about the peasantry entitled *Nha Que trong Khoi Lua* [The Countryside in Smoke and Flame] and *Hon Que* [Soul of the Countryside], which depict the peasants' struggle and wartime morale. Although these manuscripts were unfortunately lost during the war, Phi Van still hopes that he may someday retrieve them in order to publish them along with a new edition of the four works previously cited.

The following translation, consisting of two very short chapters (Chapters 2 and 4) from *The Peasants*, will serve to illustrate some of the things the peasants had to face. This book was

published in only one limited edition in 1949 by the Tan Viet
Publishing House in Saigon and is now difficult to find there.
The author himself, who is currently a reporter for numerous
newspapers and magazines in Saigon, including *Cap Tien*,
kindly provided a copy of the Vietnamese text for this English-
language translation.

Chapter 2 The Hamlet of Binh Thanh

Binh Thanh is the largest hamlet in the village of Long Son. The hamlet is over ten kilometers from the district headquarters of Thanh Binh. To reach this village one has to follow the winding and twisting waterways, since there is absolutely no road going there.

The village of Long Son is composed of four hamlets. In each hamlet there is a deputy village security chief who heads the local administration under the direction of the village council. The responsibility of the deputy village security chief is undoubtedly heavy: to guard the hamlet from thieves and robbers, to collect taxes, to transmit court summons, and so on.

Therefore, in each hamlet the deputy village security chief is equally as powerful as the village security chief himself. The inhabitants of the hamlet all attempt to flatter him by calling him "master security chief." It is not easy to become a deputy village security chief. One must climb the ladder step by step: from the position of deputy hamlet chief or headman to that of village patrol squad leader or village patrol chief. Then, to be appointed, one must first have some property and also must have all the members of the village council examine his background and file a report.

The deputy village security chief of Binh Thanh is named Thanh. People call him Deputy Village Security Chief Thanh. He is a rude person and knows how to read only a few words of *quoc ngu*.* His appointment depended largely on his skillfulness and persistence in toadying to the village security chief.

In the village of Binh Thanh there are several ex-village officials and a number of rich families, including a former "area representative" (*hoi dong dia hat*)† whose name is known above all the others. The rest are poor and illiterate peasants.

---

* Modern Vietnamese in Latin script.
† This was an honorary title usually bought by rich people.

The reason why Mr. The, the "representative," is so well known is that he is a big landlord whose paddy fields occupy most of the cultivated area in the hamlet.

The soil in Binh Thanh is very fertile, and the harvests are usually very good. For this reason many peasants come here to be tenant farmers of the representative.

The representative lives in a huge tile-roofed residence in the middle of the hamlet. His guests are a noisy, boisterous bunch. But he has lots of cattle and lots of boats, so everybody must show him polite respect.

Although his property is very extensive, so far as "posterity" is concerned, the representative is rather poorly endowed since he has begotten only two daughters. The elder is married to a provincial clerk, and the younger has just turned seventeen years old. Last year, when she was in her fifth year of the [six-year] provincial school, Mrs. Representative became severely ill and so she had to leave school and come home. Mrs. Representative was sick for a month and then died.

Mr. Representative did not want to be alone, so he forbade his daughter to return to school and kept her home to manage the account books in connection with the tenant farmers and the collection of rice.

This younger daughter differs from her older sister in that she has not used her wealth as an excuse for regarding those under her as mere trash. The older daughter, while she was still a schoolgirl in a French girls' school in Saigon, jabbered constantly in French whenever she was back home to visit her parents. She criticized her father for being backward, her mother for being backward, and all the inhabitants of the hamlet for being totally backward. She wore glasses for nearsightedness. Sometimes during her trips home, she even went out to inspect the paddy fields. She made the representative buy her a horse to ride. Each morning she slung a velvet cape over her and, carrying a horse-whip in one hand, jumped onto the horse's back and then galloped along the dirt paths into the paddy fields. Children and grown-ups alike were all afraid of her because of her hot temper. Whenever she was dissatisfied with anything, she immediately spat out the words *bet xa lu*.*

Only a few months after [getting her horse] rain began to pour from the sky. She complained that the countryside was dirty and damp and full of mosquitoes and insects. So, squeamishly she insisted that she should be sent to the provincial town to live with an uncle, and it was there that she married the clerk.

After Mrs. Representative died, Mr. Representative asked his daughter and her husband to come back to the village to help him out in supervising the paddy fields in return for a share of the property. But after discussing it with her husband, she vehemently refused. She claimed that it was degrading to stay in a village supervising paddy fields, because such work did not carry the same status as the more exhilarating life of the spouse of an interpreter or clerk in the provincial town.

The younger daughter is different. She is a kind and modest person. After her mother died, she put up with all the difficult circumstances [in the countryside] in order to help her father. She never dresses lavishly, nor has she ever insulted the servants and the tenants as her sister did. Moreover, she has compassion for them and often speaks up for them whenever the representative explodes in anger. For this reason, all have become attached to her, though they despise her father.

The representative is well known for his wealth, his influence, and his cruelty. He regards the tenants as worthless trash. Every-

* Popular Vietnamese transliteration of the French swearwords *merde* and *salaud*.

body knows that the reason he managed to acquire so much land —so much, in fact, that "the herons must fly with their wings outstretched" [in the hope of flying across it from one side to the other]—is that he at one time or another stole these lands from the poor peasants.

Formerly, the land in Binh Thanh was uncultivated brushland, so the government decreed that each person was entitled to ten hectares to clear and cultivate. After the land was transformed into paddy fields, the government was to give that land to them permanently for cultivation, and they would be given ownership papers so that the land would be registered as their permanent property.

At that time the representative was chairman of the village council. He waited until a group of peasants had nearly finished clearing some land and put it under cultivation; then he filed an application asking for a land grant. He claimed that those peasants [who had cleared the land and put it under cultivation] were his hired hands and that he himself had paid them and fed them in the meantime. Nobody knew how he did it, but only after he had already successfully gotten his name into the land register [as the legal owner] did the peasants find out that they had all along been only unpaid slaves to him. For that reason, many people hated him, but there was nothing they could do about it. Some tried to bring lawsuits against him, only to lose all their property [because of legal expenses], so they had to give up and in the end become his tenants.

There was only one person who dared to oppose him until the end. This was the schoolmaster Thien. Formerly he had taught school in the village, but because the director of education in the provincial capital made it difficult for him, he resigned and came to the hamlet to clear a plot of land and put it under cultivation. He managed to have about ten hectares of this land registered. This land was adjacent to the paddy fields owned by the representative, and the representative was constantly ranting about his intention of taking over this area also.

At one time a government land surveyor came to map out the boundaries [of landownership in the hamlet]. The representative bribed the surveyor and had him annex to his own properties the land that belonged to the schoolmaster, Mr. Thien.

Schoolmaster Thien took the representative to court and presented all the documentation and proofs in his favor. In the end, the representative lost the case and as a result has ever since been all the more full of hate and revenge.

Schoolmaster Thien has a brother-in-law, a very poor carpenter, who is known as Carpenter Tam. Because the schoolmaster's wife had died some time ago, the schoolmaster asked Carpenter Tam and his wife to come and live with him. He also hired some public land for the two to till.

Once the district police came into the village to search for moonshine. No one knew who had called them in, but they went straight to the schoolmaster's house and found by the side of the house a big basin full of alcohol residue.

The police and the soldiers then charged into the house, shackled the schoolmaster, and escorted him to the district headquarters. The schoolmaster knew that he had been falsely accused, but there was nothing he could do since the evidence was against him.

At that time moonshine was severely forbidden. Any person caught [either for making illegal alcohol or for having any trace of it on his property] would have to sell all his property and still have no assurance that he would have enough money to pay the fine or that, even after paying the fine, he would not have to sit in jail in any case.

Carpenter Tam simply could not endure having his brother-in-law suffer this misfortune, which could ruin his whole career. So he filed a paper saying that he himself was responsible for the whole thing. Even so, the schoolmaster was imprisoned for half a month before he was released. As for Carpenter Tam, he was convicted, and since he did not have money to pay the fine, he was sent to the provincial prison instead.

From that day on, things got more heated between the representative and the schoolmaster.

The schoolmaster knew very well that it was the representative who had tried to do him in, but since he himself was in a powerless position, he had to give the whole thing up and instead pay attention to cultivating his paddy fields, to looking after his son who was going to school, and to protecting his younger sister, who for his sake had been forced to endure a solitary existence away from her husband.

Days and months passed. Tensions kept building between the representative and the schoolmaster, but there was nothing they could do to each other except mutually to stand guard.

In the meantime, the hamlet of Binh Thanh continued on its normal course just like any other hamlet. . . .

Chapter 4 Influence

While everybody was watching Madame Dich-thien-Kim rant and rave on stage, all of a sudden from outside the temple there arose a commotion. Deputy Security Chief Thanh charged in, knocking aside the children (who tumbled down on all fours), pushed his way up to the front row of seats, and then, placing his mouth close to the representative's ear, he murmured in a panting voice [the following words], which Tam [the schoolmaster's son] could nevertheless hear very clearly: "The village security chief has just arrived, and he is raising hell out there. When he learned that there was gambling going on, he said he was going to clamp my head in the stocks. Now what are we going to do?"

The representative shot up abruptly from his seat. "All right. Let me take care of it. Don't you worry, deputy."

Then, carrying his cane, the representative walked outside. A moment later, smiling and chattering and locking arms with the security chief, he again entered the building.

Not until then did people begin to whisper and to cast stealthy glances at the awe-inspiring presence of the village security chief.

The two walked together to the front seats. Before sitting down, the village security chief clasped his hands behind his buttocks and took a look around just like a general looking over his soldiers.

In the meantime, the deputy security chief, who had lost his apprehensive look, was leading by the hand Village Patrol Chief Quoi, who carried a double-barreled shotgun. They went to the second row of seats in anticipation of further instructions.

The representative waved his hand to catch the attention of the manager of the troupe, who was at the time nervously peeking out from behind the curtain. Then he blustered; "Hey, the village security chief is here to watch the show! Tell the actors and actresses to pour out all the talent they've got, and make it something special. I'll have some money to reward you with."

The security chief took another look around. Suddenly his eyes came to rest right at the spot where Tam was standing with his aunt. He called Deputy Thanh to his side and asked in a lowered voice; "Who is that woman standing there behind the seats who looks very much like the wife of that carpenter who's in jail."

The deputy village security chief also looked behind him. "Yes, sir, that's Carpenter Tam's wife, Schoolmaster Thien's sister."

"Is she still living with him?"

"Yes, sir."

"Has the carpenter come back home at all?"

"No, sir, I heard that he's still in jail."

"That's all."

The representative, on hearing the village security chief firing those questions at deputy Thanh, also looked back, glued his eyes on Carpenter Tam's wife for a while, and then turned around to the village security chief. "Mother! Is that girl Carpenter Tam's wife? Why didn't I know this before?"

The village security chief also turned around, "What are you saying that for? Aren't you living in the same hamlet? Didn't you meet her when she went to the village office to sign the confession?"

"I didn't pay any attention!" said the representative, who looked back again to take another look as he smacked his lips in appreciation. "She's still awfully young and attractive, you know!"

The village security chief chuckled as he teased, "Don't tell me you've already got yourself hooked? Come, admit it now: maybe I can lend my good offices. Your wife has been dead for some time now, so surely you must be lonely!"

The representative whispered in his ear, "My daughter is sitting nearby. So don't be too loud, or she'll hear and will feel bad! But why are you so particular in asking me all this?"

The village security chief then became secretive, "This is a confidential matter. It's just between you and me, and don't tell anybody else, OK? I have been asked by the district chief to search for . . ."

During this time, Carpenter Tam's wife had become aware of the fact that the representative and the village security chief were now and again eyeing her, then whispering into each other's ear. Feeling very ill at ease, she pulled at her nephew's arm, saying, "Let's go home."

Tam pulled away. "But the show isn't half over yet, why are we going home so early?"

She whispered to him, "But don't you see how the representative keeps looking at us and then saying something to the village security chief? Maybe he's trying to cause us trouble again. Let's go. I just can't stand this any longer."

Thus reminded of the old family feud, Tam was inflamed with anger, "Damn them! Just don't pay any attention to them; let's go on watching the show. There is no reason to be afraid of them. Let's stay, and we'll just see what they can do to us."

"But I want to go. If you don't want to take me, I'll go home by myself."

Seeing that his aunt was determined, Tam took one last angry glance at the front row, then agreed to leave the building.

At the same time, the representative turned and said to his daughter, "Let me get somebody to take you home, all right? Tell Tu Lu and his wife to go over to Sau Quen's house to catch the black dog and have it drowned and cooked at once. In a little while the village security chief and I will come home for a drink."

After his daughter had left, the representative turned to the security chief and cackled; "It's difficult to talk business with the girl around. I sent her on home to get some food ready. Let's watch the show for a little while and then go home for a drink."

With this he came back to the old subject, "I never knew Carpenter Tam's wife was still so young and attractive." In a hushed voice he continued, "Help me out, will you? I'll do anything to pay you back, right away."

The village security chief smiled. "There is nothing difficult about this. But you must tell me how you're going to pay me back."

The representative said at once; "What else? Among my tenants there are women and young girls. Whoever you want, just tell me and I will arrange it for you."

The representative made it all sound so easy, but the security chief still was not quite convinced. "You make it sound very easy, but in case they scream and won't go along, won't it be a big embarrassment?"

"Don't you worry about it! On my estate, who dares to oppose my will? I have already tried it many times myself! Can't you see that my wife has been dead for over a year now, and yet I never think of taking another wife?"

The village security chief laughed out loud, his eyes partially closed. But he still had some doubts:

"All right, but . . . its's kind of difficult to say this. I am afraid you may be inconvenienced."

"What inconvenience? I have promised to satisfy you in any way, haven't I?"

The security chief scratched his head, "Remember what you have just said, all right? I am not going to hide it from you any longer. For some time now, I have had my eyes on the wife of your estate manager, Lanh. Can you help me to be satisfied in this?"

Hearing this, the representative was startled and said, "My this is going to be difficult. My estate manager, Lanh, is my trusted hand, how can I . . ." But after thinking it over for a few more minutes, he smiled, "OK, don't you worry about it. But there is no need to hurry since it may spoil the whole thing. Wait until tomorrow, after I have thought the whole thing over. Now, if you like, let's tackle the easy problems first!"

"What do you mean?"

"Don't you see my overall design? My tenants are busy

gambling* and are so absorbed in the desire to win that they've left their wives and children to look after their homes. Tonight you and I will walk freely in there and 'stir up our own wind and our own rain.†"

When he finished saying this, the representative stood up, "Let's go to my house now. It's about time."

The village security chief, feeling more cheerful, beckoned the village patrol chief to his side and said, "Tell the deputy village security chief and the patrol squad leaders to look after the theater troupe and the gambling parties. You come along with me to the representative's house. If I should be in need of the rest of them, I'll have somebody sent to tell them."

That night, after they had had their fill of liquor, the representative and the village security chief, with the escort of the village patrol chief, made their tour of the estate.

It was also the same night that many poor people who could not protect themselves and had nobody else to protect them once more had to put up with their disgrace, since they could neither resist nor yell for help. All they could do was to grit their teeth and nurse their hatred amid the paddy fields. . . .

* It was explained in Chapter 3 that the representative had purposely set up illegal gambling parties with the ulterior motives both of increasing the dependence of his tenants (since the losers would have to ask him for loans at usurious interest rates) and of drawing them away from their homes all night so that he could freely molest their wives and daughters.
† Do anything we please.

2 Ngo Tat To
WHEN THE LIGHT'S PUT OUT
(*TAT DEN*)

When the Light's Put Out, which was first published in 1939, speaks of the multiple problems thrust upon the Vietnamese peasants during the French colonial era: the behavior of official-dom and the landlords, and the various forms of taxes, of which the worst was the head tax, or, as translated literally from the Vietnamese, the "body tax" (*thue than*) or "man tax" (*thue dinh*), which was applied to adult males from the age of eighteen. More specifically, it describes the plight of a woman named Mrs. Dau, whose husband was arrested because he could not pay his body tax on time. She was consequently forced to sell her dogs, her provisions, and even her own child in order to meet the official bail set for her husband's release. She went on to experience a multitude of other misfortunes. Of the book's thirty-six chapters, two short chapters (Chapters 12 and 13) are presented here. Although the Foreign Languages Publishing House in Hanoi has already published a full translation of this work, the present translation, done independently, is included here for the reader's comparison.

The author, Mr. Ngo Tat To (1892–1954), was a Confucian scholar turned modern writer and is best known for his "reportage and documentary fiction" (*phong su va tieu thuyet phong su*).

Chapter 12

The afternoon sunlight printed its yellow rays on the tops of the bamboo. A flock of sparrows twittered among the branches of a carambola, and a few thrushes chattered to each other in the upper reaches of the areca nut tree.

Representative Que, his bearded chin thrust upward, stood in his brick-paved yard looking on as a pair of pigeons cooed to each other in front of their roost holes. When he saw Mrs. Dau and her daughter poking their heads into the yard, he addressed them curtly; "What took you so long getting here—making other people wait for hours like this? Getting involved with you people is just a big nuisance. None of your kind will ever learn how to keep an appointment!"

The mother and daughter bowed their heads politely. "Venerable sir, my husband is tied up at the communal house. It took me forever just to persuade the officials to untie him long enough to sign the contract here. Moreover, it is quite a long way, so I couldn't help being late. Please forgive me!"

"Madame is in the guest house. Take yourselves over there and speak with her!" Then he called across the yard, "One of you guys in there, come out and keep the dogs out of their way."

Like a clown waiting for his cue, the cook drawled out a long "ye-e-es," took up a rod to hold back the household dogs, and led Mrs. Dau and her daughter, together with their bitch and her puppies, up to the house.

Madame Representative commenced in a petulant voice, "I told you to bring something along to cover up the puppies with, so they wouldn't be exposed to the sun. So why did you cover them like that with only a bamboo strainer?"

Embarrassed, Mrs. Dau could only answer with these words: "I beg you, Madame."

Asking the cook to tie the mother dog by her leash to the

house post, Mrs. Dau took the basket of puppies and slowly placed it on the threshold.

Madame Representative glanced over at Ty, the daughter, then chided Mrs. Dau in a shrill voice, "How dare the two of you—you and your husband—tell me that your daughter is seven years old already? How come seven and still so puny? I should have known! How can one ever expect to get one word of truth out of your kind!"

"Venerable madame, we do not dare to lie. She is indeed seven. Her brother is five, and there is another daughter who is two. I have three children in all."

Representative Que came in from the yard just then and shook a finger in Mrs. Dau's face, showing that his temper had been ruffled. "Shut your mouth! Don't start in on any of your impertinences around here! However many children you have, that's your business! The more you give birth to, the more you've got to dispose of. So what? Open that basket, let me see the puppies!"

Madame Representative seconded her husband's words. "You see! How can one listen to nonsense like that!"

Then, looking around at Mrs. Dau, she said, "Mind yourself now, hear! Otherwise I'm going to kick you all out and won't bother with any more business. Do you think maybe I'm on the same level with you, eh? Even before I began to speak, you started to talk back! Vulgar woman! The little girl there is no bigger than that, and you dare insist that she is seven. Do you think you're talking to the dogs or something?"

The little girl, Ty, had shrunk back behind the house post, with a listless expression. It was as if she were worrying that maybe at some point she had lost a year of her life. Mrs. Dau continued to sit in the same spot, numb and motionless. Her eyelashes glinted with teardrops.

Purplish veins appeared on both sides of Representative Que's forehead, a foreshadowing of angry words. "So she still won't open her basket to let the puppies out, huh? If she's so reluctant about it, then she can just take them back and raise them herself."

Her tears falling slowly one by one on the brick threshold, Mrs. Dau painstakingly undid the knots at the basket rim and removed the bamboo sieve. Representative Que quickly seated himself next to the basket. The four pups, one by one, were taken up by the nape of the neck, and the ears, eyes, tongues, paws, stomachs, tails, and chests were carefully inspected, each young hair getting its due attention. The Representative next admired the mother dog. A moment later, with a somewhat softer appearance, he came inside the room and settled himself on the plank bed, crossing his legs in the shape of the Chinese character for the number five.*

Looking down on Mrs. Dau he said, "Where is the contract? Hand it here."

Mrs. Dau fumbled for the document, which had been tied to her bodice strap. Cringing, she placed it on the plank bed.

Holding the contract, Representative Que repeatedly examined the place that bore the stamp of the village chief administrator. After a long pause, he turned and ordered a boy attendant, "Go and bring several bowls of rice leftovers. Bring enough for me to feed the pups, and we'll see if they eat it."

The boy responded instantly and "on three feet and four legs" was off to the servants' quarters.

Mrs. Dau and her daughter were crouched next to the house post, each peering into the tearful face of the other.

The four puppies swarmed over to the edge of the threshold, each assuming its place at the mother dog's breasts.

Representative Que good-naturedly commanded his spouse,

---

* 五 That is, with one foot resting on the other knee.

"Check to see that they are all indeed without spots on their tails."

"I too am looking. It seems none of them has."

Chapter 13

The boy returned with a small basket full of leftover rice. Representative Que ordered Mrs. Dau and her daughter to move the pups over to the other side of the threshold. Hastily, he himself ran out, took the basket, and scooped out a bowlful of rice for each puppy. As Mrs. Dau had truthfully informed him, all four pups already knew how to eat. The mother dog, on the other hand, seemed tired and anxious and only nibbled a few bites, then stopped.

Appearing calm and easy, Representative Que looked at Mrs. Dau, "Where did you buy the female dog?"

"My mother bought it, sir, in Lau Cai, and gave it to me."

"Hm, how about that! It may very well be of Mongolian descent then. You can't get dogs like that in the countryside!"

Madame Representative was quick to direct praise to herself. "Since I'd heard from several different people that she had this very intelligent bitch, I spared no effort in trying to get it. And finally this morning I was successful. Ordinarily, though, who would be so stupid as to buy up a whole litter of puppies that had just barely opened their eyes? And so, what do you think of the four of them?"

Representative Que nodded and mumbled, "Beautiful, all of them. Each with its own special characteristic—one with an extra toe, one with a tiger skin, an all-black one, and one with all four cherry-blossom paws. All with floppy ears and short faces, spotted tongues, and eyes in the shape of banyan leaves. Really handsome."

While still talking, he strutted back to the plank bed. Then once again he settled himself with his legs crossed in the form of the Chinese character for the number five, then briskly pulled over a water pipe, and began smoking, slapping his thighs in self-congratulation.

"The more one knows, the harder one has to work! Province Chief Dang, Representative Bui, Judge Tien, and District Chief Xung at the province capital all know how skilled I am at choosing dogs, and that's why they all insist on having me buy dogs for them. I have decided that when these four are fairly well grown, I'll give one to each of them. But I'd be hesitant to give away the all-black one and would rather keep it myself, since it's supposed to be the kind that will bring profit to its owner. With such a dog in the house one is sure to be prosperous."

Madame Representative interrupted in a half-serious, half-playful voice: "Nobody gives things away free. Whoever wants a good breed will have to hand me the money. Otherwise I'll just keep the whole bunch of them myself."

"In all, we have fourteen dogs as it is. Why should you want to keep all of these, too, and have to feed them all?"

"I'd like to keep them as watchodgs. It's better to raise dogs than to raise servants. This house is so large; ten or more watchdogs wouldn't be too many, would they?"

Then laughing heartily and shaking her finger at Mrs. Dau; she said, "The dog food in my home is worth much more than your kind of 'human food.' "

Mrs. Dau, visibly hurt, lowered her head and silently wiped her tears, not knowing what to say.

The pups had stopped eating, and one by one they went back to their mother, leaving several heaps of unfinished rice. Representative Que ordered the boy attendant to gather it all into a basket and give it to Ty. In a mock-humane voice, that representative of the people addressed the miserable little girl: "You, little girl! Take that basket of rice and eat it. Don't waste heaven's resources. You can eat it with your fingers; you don't have to have a bowl and chopsticks."

With tears rolling like drops of rain, Ty squeamishly eyed the basket of leftover rice but felt no desire to stretch out her hands to receive it.

The representative of the people was furious. "Are you not going to eat up that leftover dog food?"

Madame Representative completely blew her top. "Did your mother teach you that, you little devil? You keep up that kind of haughty attitude around here, and I'll have every last one of your bones splintered. Here now, let me just tell you this: you don't *deserve* my family's dog food. My dogs cost several dozen piasters each, but your kind of people—as you can see, I was able to buy one of you for a single piaster. Don't you be haughty to me, now!"

Representative Que told Mrs. Dau, cruelly, "You disgusting woman! Are you just going to sit there and stare? Don't you know how to make your daughter behave? Are you perhaps afraid that if she should eat dog food you'll be shamed?"

Apparently because she could not bear to see her mother scolded this way, Ty quickly took the rice. Timidly, she took up a handful and stuffed it into her mouth, then languidly chewed on it like an ox chewing rice chaff.

Madame Representative gritted her teeth and shook her finger in the little girl's face; "I'm telling you once and for all—you've got to finish that basket of rice before tomorrow, and only then will you get anything else to eat!"

Mrs. Dau leaned her head against the house post and sobbed silently. Representative Que shouted out; "Hey you, are you going to take your money or aren't you? Or maybe you're still wanting to hold on to your child and the dogs?"

Mrs. Dau quickly wiped away the tears and stood up. "Venerable sir . . ."

Not letting her finish the sentence, Representative Que turned to prod his wife. "Pay her and make her go home. Letting her sit here forever like this, I just can't put up with it any longer."

Madame Representative went to open the trunk to get the money. The bells fastened to the lid [as a sort of burglar alarm] clinked and clanked a few times, and then Madame Representative threw two strings of coins out onto the threshold. "There! There's the money!"

Mrs. Dau cautiously picked up the coins and was about to untie the strings to recount them. Madame's voice was high and rasping. "Nobody would think of shortchanging you! There is no need to count them!"

Mrs. Dau tucked the coins down behind her back, then, sobbing, she said to Ty, "Child, stay here and attend the venerable sir and madame. Mother has to go."

Ty embraced her mother and cried like the wind and the rain. "Mama, don't go too quickly! Please stay here with me a little while longer."

Representative Que arose abruptly, extended his giant hand, and slapped the girl on the face. He then roared out like a stage general, "You, boy, haul her out to the kitchen."

At once, Ty was separated from her mother and was made to follow the Representative's attendant out the doorway. She turned back to look at her mother. Her lips were trembling, and she was sobbing.

"Mama, please bring brother Dan over tomorrow to play with me, because I miss him very much."

Mrs. Dau's breasts were round with milk, and it had begun to drip out, getting her bodice wet. Mrs. Dau was uneasy about it and worried about the baby girl at home since, according to the experience of mothers with babies, should they be away from their children and should their milk begin to drip out in such a way, it was a sign that the babies were hungry and crying for milk. She did not dare to think any more about her daughter Ty but gathered up the basket, the bamboo sieve, and also the tattered conical hat and hurried out through the gate of Doai hamlet.

The sun had already sunk below the horizon. Flocks of crows flew down onto the graveyards. The buffalo boys, hastening the cattle back to their resting places, were sounding their coconut-leaf horns. By the time she reached Dong Xa village, night had fallen.

The communal house was empty. Inside, a band of mosquito bats whirred. A lamp flickering on the altar strained to spit out its weak yellow rays, to give light to a few tablets of black incense smoldering below the altar door.

In the various rooms of the communal house there remained only darkness to emphasize the eerie atmosphere of the place. Some time ago, the people had removed their noise and activity to the house of the village chief administrator.

As if she had guessed that this was the case, Mrs. Dau started off alone for the place where the noise of the prisoners could be heard. Finally she went inside.

Under the brightness of the two-wick lamps, the scene within the chief administrator's house was at that time just like the earlier scene in the communal house. Mr. Dau and the other men who had not paid the required amount of tax sat with their elbows roped to the supporting room pillars. Men and women waiting to pay their taxes were still crowded at one of the door-ways.

As before, guards and their deputies reclined on the floor near the opium pipe, in attendance on the canton chief. The treasurer, the council chairman, the vice-chairman, and other village notables sat and sprawled beside a clutter of books and notebooks.

When Mrs. Dau's sweaty, tearful countenance appeared at the doorway, she was at once met with a chorus of yells from these notables.

"So you managed to sell your child, did you. Bring the money on up now, quickly!"

"Yes."

Saying this, she pulled out the two strings of one-cent coins that had been tucked under her waist strap and also the eight dimes—the money for which she had sold her potatoes—that had been securely fastened at the bodice strap. She put back one dime out of it, then tiptoed up to lay the two piasters and seven dimes before the village chief administrator.

"Please, sir, I did not have the time to change it to paper money, so please accept it from me!"

"Then for each piaster you must pay a three-cent surcharge. Hand it here and I will accept it. But why only two piasters and seven dimes?"

Uncomprehending, Mrs. Dau gave over the remaining dime to pay for the currency exchange and answered in a trembling voice; "Sir, I thought that each body tax for this year was only that much."

"That's correct. The amount of each body tax is only two piasters and seven dimes this year. But your family must pay two accounts, don't you see? One is for your husband and one is for Hoi."

"Sir, but my brother-in-law has been dead since January! Is it possible that my husband has not registered his death?"

The village chief administrator became annoyed. "Even if his death has been registered, he still has to pay his body tax. Why didn't he die in October of last year?"

She was more confused than ever, and sensed that they were deliberately doing all they could to bully her. "But, sir, he has been dead for nearly five months. Why must he still pay body tax?"

The village chief administrator shouted; "Go and ask Mr. Frenchman, I don't know."

The secretary solemnly explained, "Even in death one cannot always avoid paying taxes to the government! It is because, even though your brother-in-law died in the Annamese month of January, the 'death registration' record of the village was compiled at the beginning of the Western year, that is, the Annamese eleventh month of last year. Hoi's name appeared in that record since he was still living at that time. When the list is sent to the province capital, the administration there, in order to form the list for the Treasury, goes only according to the number of men given therein. When it is tax-collecting time, the Treasury goes by the amount of taxes given on this list and must collect it. Your brother died in January, but even if he had died in December, it would still have been the same story. After the record is once completed, it can never be altered. Whether the dead are registered or not makes no difference! Therefore, this year our village cannot deduct the body tax for your Hoi. As he is dead, without wife or children, the village chief administrator has to collect it from his relatives. If your husband does not pay for him, who will?"

Half-speaking, half-whining, Mrs. Dau replied, "I am a woman, and don't know about this sort of official business. . . . How unlucky that my brother-in-law should pass away, for it's just like losing the right hand of our family! With him alive, surely we would not be so miserable. But unfortunately he died, and now of course his body tax has to be paid by my husband. But I beg you to let it be delayed until tomorrow. Today I will pay for one account, but first, please free my husband, since he's already weak from illness and has been tied up all day. Otherwise he may die too."

The village chief administrator, his eyes distended, snarled, "If he dies, I will bury him myself! You think *I'd* be scared if your husband died? If you don't want your husband tied up, then bring two more piasters and seven dimes. Otherwise I will keep him tied up, tied up until all the tax money is paid."

Mrs. Dau, as though at her wit's end, squatted down at her husband's side and wailed, "Heaven, oh heaven! I have sold my daughter together with my dogs and four baskets of potatoes in order to raise two piasters and seven dimes, thinking I had enough to pay my husband's body tax so that he would not be beaten tonight. But whoever thought of having to pay a body tax for the dead? What an awful thing to happen to me! Oh heaven, my brother-in-law is dead, and still he has to pay his tax— heaven, is such a thing possible? What can I smash my head against to raise two piasters and seven dimes now?"

The guard foreman sat up quickly, the veins showing on his neck, and shouted, "Is this the place for you to cry, eh, woman? If you want to live, shut up—or else I am going to give you another beating!"*

Trembling, Mr. Dau advised his wife; "Please go back home to the children. They will be out of breath from crying. Just leave me here; I won't die from having to be tied up for another night! Don't say anything more, or they will beat you, and you will only suffer the more for it!"

Still Mrs. Dau could not calm herself.

The treasurer, who had just finished recounting the two strings of coins, called to Mrs. Dau, saying, "Hey woman, stop

* She had been beaten at the communal house that morning.

your crying, and come over here and take a look: for each piaster, four cents are missing! From the dime that you paid for exchange fees, eight cents must be deducted for this, so that means you still owe us four more cents."

Mrs. Dau again wailed, "What a terrible fate! I had thought all the time that there would be a dime left to buy rice for my children. Now everything is gone, and still there is not enough! That Madame Representative is so rich—heaven only knows—and still she cheats!" Dejectedly, she sat down and cried.

Mr. Dau insisted, "Please listen to me, dear! If you love me, then please go home to the children. Don't sit here crying, it just makes me get all churned up inside!"

Friends, who were tied up alongside Mr. Dau, asked, trying to express their compassion, "If you have sold your eldest daughter, then who are the two younger children at home staying with?"

Sobbing, she replied, "They are staying at home all alone. Who else is there, gentlemen?"

The men looked uneasy. "What a pity! A five-year-old boy having to take care of a two-year-old girl! What a pity!"

"According to what those officials just said, even the dead have to pay taxes. That means your family still owes them another payment. If you do not have the money to give them, then even if you stayed here until tomorrow morning, you still wouldn't be able to plead for his release. The more you say, the more worn out you will be, and none of them will take pity on you. It's better that you go home so the children won't have to suffer."

"Right, he's right! Please take heart and leave your husband here, and go back to your children to rest. It will just be all the more painful for you to stay around here, so what's the use of it? And if you are not able to control yourself, your mouth may itch to say a few things that could only end in getting your husband beaten."

Those speeches, though full of kindness, could not really help Mrs. Dau, and in any case she already thought as they did. Sadly she murmured in her husband's ear, "Ty saved a dish of potatoes for you. I will bring it over for you; is that all right?"

Mr. Dau shook his head, "My mouth is very bitter. I don't feel like eating anything just now. You just go on home to the children. Don't worry about my eating."

Saying good-bye to her husband with tears streaming from her eyes, Mrs. Dau stumbled out with the basket, the bamboo sieve, and the torn hat.

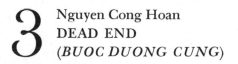

3 Nguyen Cong Hoan
DEAD END
(*BUOC DUONG CUNG*)

Dead End, first published in September 1938, again describes the problems piled upon the peasants during the French colonization of Vietnam. These problems—the French and Vietnamese officialdom, the landlords, the high taxes, and so on —were such that for the peasant there seemed to be no way of escape. The author, Nguyen Cong Hoan, is one of the best "literary realists" (*van chuong ta chan*) of his time. All of his works—and there are a great number of them—deal with the real-life circumstances and the social customs of the middle-class and poor Vietnamese. He lives presently in North Vietnam.

Following is a translation of three short chapters of the aforementioned book. Chapter 4 describes the hardships brought upon the peasants by the French monopoly on distilling alcohol and the collusion of French and Vietnamese officialdom against the powerless villagers. Chapters 18 and 19 speak of the tax burdens borne by the peasants as local officials and landlords refused to pay their own taxes and instead cooperated with the district and provincial officials in their exploitation of the poor.

Chapter 4

Representative Lai's villa is located in the very center of the village of An Dao. But his villa and the village of An Dao are two completely separate worlds.

The villa covers a spacious area of some two *mau*, completely surrounded by four walls about three meters high, which hide everything from view except for the house belonging to Anh, placed clumsily in one corner. The glittering glass bottle fragments that jut from the tops of the walls are like the bayonets of guards posed in straight rows.

In the middle of one of the walls, at the end of a road, there is an immense gate with a guard tower, but it is rarely opened. Ordinarily, people come and go through the adjacent "bee-hole gate," which is a mere fifty centimeters wide [for purposes of easier surveillance]. It was also kept tightly shut all day when not in use.

Representative Lai is frightfully rich. Other people's money, rice, paddies, and dwellings can slip into his possession with a wave of his hand.

Education does not appeal to him at all. When he was young, he considered books his number-one enemy. Even now he still brags about an escapade when he was fifteen years old. At that time he was in the "fourth grade."* One day when he had not memorized his lesson, he was reprimanded by his teacher. He jumped up and, carrying his books with him, strode out of the schoolhouse. From that time on, regardless of how his parents might coax or reprimand him, he would never again return to the prison that had robbed him of the freedom of his otherwise happy boyhood.

Then in the next year, as he became wiser, he realized that he

---

* This would be second grade, if compared to the American system, since the grades of the five-year Vietnamese primary school are counted in reverse order.

had been kept from childhood in a prison harsher than school: his family. There the jailers were many times more severe than his teachers had ever been. So he looked for an escape. One night he stole five hundred piasters and, with an older friend, went up to Hanoi to experience some of the "social life."

Getting his start in social life at that early age, he was able to master all the tricks and became cunningly clever at them all. He became very proud of the fact that at the age of sixteen he was already accomplished at *trong co dau*,* that at the age of seventeen he could take twenty shots of opium in series, and that at the age of eighteen he already had numerous mistresses in Hanoi.

He had only twice shouted insults at his parents, but while still at home he had seldom attended to them in the proper ways. Had he not, at the age of nineteen, become totally addicted to opium and thus gotten himself into a situation without enough food to eat or money to spend, he would doubtless never have returned home at all and would indeed have carried out his earlier pledge never again to accept village council chairman Hoe and his wife as his parents. Only after a night of careful pondering, deprived of opium to smoke, had he finally come to his senses and realized that he had been stupid not to take full advantage of his rights as a child, especially a son, of a family whose riches were counted in the tens of thousands of piasters.

Mr. and Mrs. Village Council Chairman were happy to see their son come home, thinking that he had repented. They coaxed him into paying more attention to his own welfare, and found him a wife. A beautiful wife and the "goddess of opium" —these were the two firm ropes that tied him to his native place. The parents then began instructing him in the ways of getting rich. As he became a master of this worthy art, he soon came to

* A kind of drummed accompaniment for the playgirls to dance to.

admire himself for having been many times more successful than his parents had been before him.

When Mr. and Mrs. Village Council Chairman died, the villa covered only about eight *sao*,* and the paddies and dry fields covered about a hundred *mau*. But in the space of ten years, the walls were built up to enclose the villa, and paddies gave birth to more paddies, so that at the present time Representative Lai has precisely 400 *mau*.

Now he only lies and smokes, so as to savor his fifty years of age. However, from time to time, if a chance should present itself, he will make some effort to enlarge his fortune still further. On the whole, though, he is quite self-satisfied. . . .

The village officials led the customs officer up to the large gate at Representative Lai's villa. When the village chief administrator reached up to ring the bell, a horde of dogs began to bark noisily. A moment later, a man peered down from the watchtower. "Who is it?"

"Go and report to the Representative that the honorable Customs Officer has come."

Five minutes later, from inside the gate came the sound of a latch being removed and of a lock opening. The two wings of the gate rolled apart noisily on two wooden wheels out onto the brick pavement, exposing a half-naked field laborer who, legs apart, was exerting all his strength to open the thick ironwood gates as far as he could move them.

The French customs officer, already accustomed to the layout inside, continued straight into the yard, paying no heed to the swarming, barking dogs. In order to get into the shade, he passed along next to the buffalo and cow compounds and the rice storage bins, then stepped up and across the threshold into the guest room.

*One *sao* is equivalent to 360 square meters, one tenth of a *mau*.

One might say that the guest room was rather on the voluptuous side. At one place there was a Chinese girl, pinkishly fair like a peeled egg, smiling and lying with her inner thighs exposed. In one corner was another girl, without a single stitch of clothing to cover her whitish and chubby figure, who pretended to be embarrassed; one hand covered a place that really need not have been covered, with the other hand raised skyward, holding . . . what turned out to be a blunt-ended light bulb.

These things, appealing though they might have been, all turned out to be color paintings and white statuettes full of dust. If the sensual guests did not become ecstatic over them, it was no wonder, since there were so many distracting forces inside the room to dampen their ardor.

First of all, there was the putrid smell coming from beneath the divan. It was the brass smell of the urns, lamps, trays, and pots that had been piled there in storage. It was troublesome to remove them since the divan [of an inverted box-shaped construction, made of hardwood, and open around the bottom] was so heavy it would take several people just to lift it, and the utensils could not be removed from the outside since the sides of the divan reached almost to the floor. Then there were the other furnishings, the portraits, and the hundreds of wall decorations, all in grievous disorder. Some were genuinely beautiful; some were extremely ugly; some were brand-new; others were very old. It indicated that the owner must have collected these things bit by bit from the houses of others. The room display showed the present owner to be a person oblivious to all artistic consideration, yet one who knew how to take pains in preserving "heaven's resources."

But the most distracting object of all was the portrait of Representative Lai. We must remember that Representative Lai had become a representative only recently. Since the villagers must obey him and call him a "mandarin," he has no need to respect anyone else's sensibilities. Thus, immediately after his election, he had his photograph taken in ceremonial court dress and then had this photograph used as the model for the painting. The painter, moreover, is a personal friend of his—all the more reason for the painter, too, to ignore all obligation to respect other people's sensibilities. He painted the dragon dress purple, then added two intertwining dragons on the cap, together with a gold tassel. But—heaven forbid—this complete, majestic court gown was used to decorate a body with a face that strikes terror into those who look on it—wrinkled and emaciated, with two deep and serpentine creases on the cheeks, making the already slanted eyes look all the more slanted!

The painter, however, wanting to flatter this wealthy person, had carefully mixed up a pink color for the face, which made it as rosy as that of a healthy American. Still, the truth is that Representative Lai comes from the tribe of people that constitutes the world's sixth race. For if he were white, he would have been a European; if yellow, he would have been an Asian; if red, an American Indian; if brown, an Australian; and if black, an African. But he is a shade of green, which is undisputably the complexion of the race of drug addicts.

By the time the customs officer arrived, Representative Lai was decently dressed. He pretended to be in a hurry. Nevertheless, his eyelids were still half-closed, and the smell of opium was still strong so that anyone could easily guess that he had just been through a "dream session." Perhaps the reason he had felt the need to pump himself full of opium (at least ten shots) was that he imagined it might somehow reduce his bulk, enabling him to move about with greater alacrity.

He cackled and strode effusively over to the customs officer, as if he were about to embrace an old friend. He bowed low and grasped the hand of the Frenchman with both his hands and stammered, "Greetings to your honor. Why has your honor not come here for such a long time?"

The French customs officer shrugged his shoulders. "I came here on important business."

Representative Lai was taken by surprise and simply stood there gazing at his guest. "What's the matter?"

"There is illegal alcohol [moonshine] in one of your paddies."

"Illegal alcohol?"

"That's right. Mr. Village Chief Administrator, will you please tell the representative clearly in which paddy it is?"

The village chief administrator explained:

"Your honor, sir, it is the seven-meter-long paddy next to the Ma Gioi paddy*—the one that Sinh ceded to you last month and that you leased to Lanh for sharecropping."

Representative Lai frowned and tapped the table with his fingers. "Do you mean the paddy next to the one owned by Pha?"

"Yes."

Speechless for a moment, Representative Lai then laughed. "It's strange, your honor. Please consider the fact that with a property like this, what reason should I have to distill alcohol?"

"That's very true, but you are the owner of the land, and according to the law you're found guilty. The evidence is still there, so you had better go out to the paddy with me to take a look and sign the report."

"Phat!"† This angry call startled everybody.

"Yes."

"You report to Madame Five‡ and ask her to go with the chief

* Here, simply a name that came to be attached to a particular paddy.
† Name of a particular servant.
‡ The fifth wife.

administrator to find out whether it's true that someone put alcohol in our family paddy."

Then he said to the customs officer, "Now, there's really no need for the two of us to go out. Please, your honor, stay here inside. It's very sunny out."

Then, turning, he called back toward the inside of the house, "Hurry up, what's taking you so long?"

"Yes."

Soon a servant appeared, carrying a tray of liquor. Two bright, clear champagne glasses clicked against each other, and the champagne fizzed. Representative Lai put out his hand in invitation: "Your honour . . ."

The guest lifted his glass, stretched his neck, and gulped it down. Representative Lai poured some more, saying, "This glass is too shallow. If your honor will allow me, I'll get a couple of wine goblets, since they will hold more. Your honor surely must be very thirsty."

The French customs officer smiled. "It's up to you."

"This champagne is quite good quality. While my father was still living, he never got around to using it and left about thirty bottles in a corner of the rice bins. I only recently found out about it. Otherwise it would have been wasted."

He laughed aloud in order to cover up his anxiety.

After finishing about half the bottle, the French customs officer was a bit flushed, so he stopped for a moment and commented, "About this alcohol business, I suppose you will be severely penalized."

"I don't know why the law is so unjust. I am a representative who is very faithful to both governments,* and I wouldn't think of doing anything illegal."

* Both the direct French administration and the vestiges of the traditional Vietnamese system.

"True, I know this and would never suspect you of such a thing. However, the law is the law."

"I have a great many paddies, not only in this province but also in other provinces. Do I have to send people to keep constant guard over each of them? If the customs regulations are going to be this strict, then those who bear grudges against me can easily cause me to lose all my properties in a single day."

The guest did not reply, only smiled. Representative Lai continued, "In my village there is one fellow in particular who has for a long time made a profession of distilling alcohol. He is Patrolman Thi. It may be that he's the one who put illegal alcohol in my paddy."

The village council chairman informed him, "Sir, if it were in fact Thi, then he probably meant to put it in the paddy that belongs to Pha, because of the long-standing feud between the two of them."

The customs officer replied, "Maybe so. After all, it was this Thi himself who reported the matter to me."

"There, the whole thing is as clear as that, and if your honor should penalize me, it would be very unjust to me."

The Frenchman shrugged, "But what can I do? You and I have been dear friends. . . ."

At that moment, Madame Five returned and certified that the paddy in question was indeed theirs. Representative Lai thought hard. Then, suddenly, as if recollecting something, he reprimanded the servants. "Look, aren't you people going to take these gentlemen next door to have a drink?"*

After waiting until all the others, except for the customs

---

* These are the village officials who had, presumably, come in with the French customs officer. Representative Lai is trying to get rid of them so that he can talk business with the Frenchman. In Vietnamese writings insignificant people usually pop up suddenly.

officer, had left the room, Mr. Representative smiled cordially. "Naturally, I will have to accept responsibility for this grave matter, but between your honor and me, can't you somehow help me out? I am not as literary and polite as other people, and that's why I ask your honor so bluntly."

The French customs officer shook his head. "I can't. I was sent down here to inspect illegal alcohol. People know about it at the office, and so does everyone in this village."

"So what can *they* do? The village officials are all servants of mine, you see. Whatever I tell them to do, they will do. Your honor, please tear up that report, and I will certainly not forget the favor."

"I cannot, sir."

"I am a representative who is very faithful to both governments. Therefore I do not want to have any bad marks in my record. That is the only thing I am concerned about. What do I care about the fine? With a villa like this, what do I lack in the way of money? Your honor is probably aware of the fact that in serving you officials I sometimes spend several thousand piasters without regret. Look, as you know, I often come up during the holidays to try to be of some service to you."

The customs officer nodded and replied, "But I do not want to do things illegally."

"Yes, I understand, but it would only be in keeping with our friendship. I would never forget your doing me this favor. Before, even though I never looked to your honor for anything in return, I always treated your honor generously. If only you'll do me this favor now, I'll continue to do so in the future—even more."

The Frenchman thought for a little while, and then asked quietly, "Whom do you lease that paddy to?"

"Nguyen van Lanh."

"Where does he live?"

"He lives in Ha Trang canton, about ten kilometers from here."

The French officer thought for a moment and then nodded. Representative Lai eagerly pressed ahead, "Although he lives far from here, he is the one who should be responsible for this illegal alcohol business, since I have leased the paddy to him. Your honor will, I hope, arrest him and penalize him. It's more just than arresting me."

The French customs officer got to his feet, smiling. He shook hands with Mr. Representative and sighed, "I am taking on this difficulty just to help you out, you know!"

Mr. Representative replied obsequiously, "How do I dare express my gratitude?"

Then he walked his guest out the gate, gazing after his benefactor with a smile.

Chapter 18

The sound of the dog barking outside at the gate made Pha nervous as he craned his neck to look. At first he thought it might be someone through whom Quay and Hoa had sent their tax payments. But it was not. It was the patrilineage representative,* who had come to urge him to go and make sure his own taxes were paid on time.

Pha replied, "Yes, as for myself, I've got the money. But I am waiting for the money from my brothers so I can go and pay it all at the same time."

"So have you asked someone to go to Thai† to tell them?"

---

* One who represents the clan in dealing with officialdom, other clans, etc.
† This is probably short for the city of Thai Binh, the capital of Thai Binh province, Tonkin.

"I have, but I could only get word through to my brother Quay. As for my brother Hoa, there is no way of knowing his whereabouts."

After smoking his cigarette, the patrilineage representative said, "The tax will all have to be in by the day after tomorrow, and I don't know how the village officials will manage to avoid a big deficit."

"It's because they're collecting the tax earlier than usual this year, and those who go far away to work have no way of knowing about it so they can get their money sent back in time."

"No, it's not that. It's just that the officials are lazy. The only things they can do well are drinking and smoking and pushing their business off on someone else. From the day they started collecting taxes, they've just let the militia and the soldiers* sponge on them [at the expense of the village treasury]. These people are down here doing nothing at all that's worthwhile but only lounge about at the village council chairman's house, clamoring for food, opium, and money for gambling. And, to top it all off, they chase after the girls all night."

Mrs. Pha joked, "The village officials are sure to lose money on that."

"No, but they aren't going to profit much."

As he finished saying this, there was a sudden commotion at the outside gate. The patrilineage representative quickly withdrew from sight, visibly frightened. A soldier with an angry

* The Vietnamese words are *pho doi* or *cai* (corporal) and *linh* (soldier or private). They were ordinarily stationed only in the principal towns of each district or province. As members of the French colonial army, they belonged either to the *linh kho xanh* (green-sash militia), which could be called for special duties by both the French and the local Vietnamese officials, or to the *linh kho do* (red-sash militia or *tirailleurs annamites*), who were under the sole control of the French.

appearance, together with the head of the village patrolmen, strode up and entered Pha's house, followed by Binh, his arms tied tight behind him at the elbows.

"Is there a guy named Pha here? . . . Are you trying to evade your taxes? . . . Why aren't you down at the communal house to pay them then? Want to be put in jail, eh?"

The soldier waved his finger angrily in Pha's face. Pha was frightened as he replied, "Your honor, sir.* I am waiting for my brothers to go and pay with me at the same time."

"Wait a minute now! This isn't something like eating, where you've got to wait for each other first. In two days all the taxes have got to be in. If the magistrate should come down here, you'll 'lose your mother quick' [swearwords]. Patrol chief, tie him up and lead him to the communal house."

Obeying the order, the patrol chief approached Pha. The latter quickly countered, "I beg you, your honor, to release me. I have the money ready here."

Mrs. Pha was distraught. She went into another room and came out with a few piaster bills spread in her fingers.

"My husband is telling the truth. Please don't arrest him."

The soldier shouted, "All right, let him off."

Then angrily he strode out.

Pha had successfully dodged the disaster and felt so relieved that he quickly got dressed and went for a walk down to the communal house. When he passed near Representative Lai's gate, he saw a crowd of people there.

It was a tumultuous scene in front of the bee-hole gate of the "rich-by-the-tens-of-thousands pawnshop." Every person there wore a look of sadness stemming from hunger and anxiety. Each tried to squeeze his way a little closer to the gate, which was

* Thay quyen.

tightly shut. From the tower above the big gate, Phat was giving one order after another. "That woman holding a pair of lamps there, stand aside and let Mrs. Rot come in first." Or: "That person holding the quilted dress there, take it home. We don't take dresses around here."

When the gate opened to let one person out, dozens of people tried to squeeze their way in. A rattan rod beat upon their heads from above like rain, and Phat shouted himself hoarse. The gate slammed shut again, after having swallowed only one person. Mrs. Thu elbowed her way out into an open space. Her head-turban was loose, and her face all scarlet. Yet she was satisfied as she laughed and boasted, "Mr. Representative refused to take the earrings, because he said they were imitation gold, but Madame lent me two piasters."

Everyone cast a covetous glance at Mrs. Thu, hoping that he could be as lucky as she. Pha asked, "How much was the interest?"

"Five cents a day on each piaster."

Seeing the satisfied face of this woman who had been able to obtain the money for her taxes, Pha sighed and went straight to the communal house without so much as one backward glance.

Moi's son, Chich, his arms outstretched, was beating the surface of the drum with all his might and at the same time amusing himself by repeating in groups of three the words:

"Tax, tax, tax! Tax, tax, tax!"

As he stepped through the doorway, Pha heard the voice of the village chief administrator shouting loudly, "Who cares? Clamp his hands whether he's sick or not. You musn't let personal considerations get in the way of official business."

Pha looked in and saw that in the corner of the communal house, Co, a former farm hand of the Representative, was hunched up on the floor, as he contorted his face to say, "I beg you, venerable sir, please let me off until tomorrow. My wife is taking our daughter to sell, and she ought to be back home any time now."

"Only dogs would buy that dirty girl!"

Then the chief administrator glared and stamped his feet. "Come on, you guys, why don't you bring out the hand clamps, as I told you?"

In unison, the two patrolmen complied and hustled in with two bars of bamboo. They forced Co to extend his hands, then fitted the two bars on both sides of the fingers and twisted the strings tight.

Co winced, and his mouth gaped open as he moaned, "I beg you, venerable sir! I beg you, sir!"

"Tight! Tighter!"

As the chief administrator removed one of his worn-out wooden clogs and beat repeatedly on the head of one of the patrolmen, he shouted, "Parents of yours,* are you not going to make them any tighter?"

The victim's cries, calling upon heaven and earth, made everyone turn around and stand in silence, their faces pale with fear.

The chief administrator gnashed his teeth and shook his finger in Co's face. "If you want to evade your taxes, just go ahead and try, and see how you make out."

Then, exhausted, he breathed heavily and looked over at the other tied-up people who were sitting in a line out on the veranda. At the same time, all those eyes looked downward in fear.

The chief administrator shook his finger at those poor people and threatened, "In a little while, when your grandfather† is less tired, he'll get around to you."

* Swearwords.
† Swearwords, here serving as a substitute for the first person pronoun.

Pha went up onto the raised floor of the communal house and stood by the mat where the taxes were being collected. Threads of smoke arose from where the canton chief lay alongside the corporal. This smoke produced a strong odor, together with the "factory alcohol" on the trays set before the village council vice-chairman, the soldiers from the district headquarters, the former village chief administrator, and the treasurer. Pha became frightened and had a choking feeling in his throat. He remembered the time he had gotten drunk at Mr. San's house.

Suddenly the collector announced, "Pha, come pay your tax."

Pha squatted by the mat, holding a wad of money. "Please see how much I have to pay."

The collector began making a computation and grumbled, "Why didn't you do it yourself beforehand at home?"

After a while, he looked up. "Thirteen piasters, seven dimes, and one cent."

Pha was taken aback as he asked, "Why so much, sir?"

"It's not so much. The land tax for each *mau* is three piasters, seven dimes, and two cents; and the body tax is three piasters, three dimes, and three cents for each account. Your family had to pay three accounts."

Pha was all the more bewildered. "Look, I have only eight *sao* of land."

"Then it's thirteen piasters and fifty cents."

"But my brothers' body taxes are to be paid by them."

"I don't know; it's the magistrate's orders."

The village chief administrator glared and snarled from a distance, "If he's not going to pay, put him in the pillory. How long do you think it'd take you to get through to him by reason? You people are just too slow. If by tomorrow we haven't raised enough money and if I am reprimanded by the magistrate, I will report on everything, and the whole group will be put in prison, not just myself alone. So why should I fear?"

The collector was embarrassed and began to lose his temper. "Thirteen piasters and fifty cents, quick!"

Pha said politely, "Then I will please be allowed to pay for my body tax and the tax on the eight *sao* only."

The collector grumbled, "Monkey!"

Quickly he computed: "Seven piasters and five cents!"

Pha thought out loud, "But that means you are still making me pay for a whole *mau*."

Affecting an innocent appearance, the collector said, "Oh, er . . . I mean, then, seven piasters."

"Then you're only deducting five cents for two *sao*. Also, Mr. Viet, the patrol chief, only had to pay three piasters for his body tax."

The collector scowled and became sullen. "But you're not him. Now don't try to be a smart aleck! I'll put you in the pillory. Understand?"

The corporal finished a smoke, sucked from the spout of the bottle, and then sat up, saying, "Who's the smart aleck? Drag him over here. Look, my hands are getting itchy."

Pha trembled, looked down quickly, avoiding the corporal, and counted out exactly seven piasters to pay the tax.

The collector wrote something down on a piece of paper. "Here, I'm giving you a receipt for the eight *sao* and the body tax for Hoa. As for Quay's and your own account, we'll let you pay when you get the money."

Pha was taken by surprise, but he did not dare to speak loudly. "My brother doesn't have anything—please let him pay in the one-piaster category."

The collector grumbled, "One piaster? Only the propertyless can pay one piaster."

Pha glanced quickly at the corporal. The village chief administrator charged over to him. "Isn't he going to pay? He just recently got hold of thirty piasters.* What's all this about being propertyless?"

The corporal turned around, saying, "Then tie him by the neck and give him a good thrashing. Their kind is like that. Unless you beat them, they'll never hand over the money."

Pha quickly took the receipt and went straight outside without looking back.

When he passed by Du's house he stopped for a visit and to air his grievances. Du held up the receipt and glared at it, saying, "They only wrote down three piasters and three cents for the body tax, and two piasters and nine dimes, and eight cents for the eight *sao* of paddy land."

Remaining thoughtful for a while, Du nodded his head and said grudgingly, "During this taxing time, those termites must have stripped the villagers of up to several hundred piasters."

Chapter 19

When informed that the magistrate himself was coming to push the tax collection to a successful conclusion, the village officials came down with a case of the jitters. They hurriedly commanded the patrolmen to search out and arrest the relatives of all those absentee residents who had not yet paid their taxes.

Thus, in addition to those who had already been detained and tortured at the communal house, nine other people, Pha among them, were tied up and hauled over to the tax-collecting place.

Early that morning, Moi was forced to make a clean sweep of everything. Opium pipes, cards, and all the half-eaten food had to be hidden away in the back of the communal house.

At the village entrance, several fishtail banners [*co duoi ca*]

* As related in earlier chapters of the book, Pha was forced to borrow thirty piasters from Representative Lai.

drooped along the roadway. The village officials had all gathered under the banyan tree to wait. When it was time, an automobile sped in, blaring its horn. Two yellow parasols were immediately opened up. The automobile stopped. The magistrate descended. Among his retainers, in addition to the familiar personages of the record clerk, the sergeant, the personal guard, and the soldiers from the district headquarters, a stranger was seen walking along at the very end.

As soon as he got out of the automobile, the magistrate scowled and demanded of the village chief administrator, "How much is lacking?"

"High Magistrate, sir, ninety-seven piasters."

The magistrate snarled, "You people are stalling. Watch out or I'll throw you all out of your jobs. Order the patrolmen into every house, and have them herd all the buffaloes and cows out here for me."

The village officials themselves all owned buffaloes, and in the way they nervously glanced over at the chief administrator you could see that they were getting scared. The chief administrator rubbed his hands, and said, "Sir, none of the buffaloes are home, as they have all been in the paddies working since early morning."

The village council chairman added obsequiously, "High Magistrate, sir, let me order the crier to beat the gong and call them back."

The magistrate nodded, saying, "Order both gongs to be sounded and the patrolmen to be sent out into the paddies to bring in every last one of the buffaloes. Only that will do."

The magistrate climbed up to the main room of the communal house, sat down on a chair, and leaned his elbows on the table, where a white tablecloth had been spread. One of the patrolmen waved a feather fan. The village officials submitted the records, and while the record clerk read out the names of those who had not paid their taxes, the village chief administrator led a long string of men and women, their arms tied behind them at the elbows, in front of the magistrate.

The latter snarled, "How do you people dare try to evade government taxes?"

Each person in the crowd replied noisily in his own way. The record clerk extended his hand to stop them. "Silence! Pham Lieu, where are you? State your case."

"High Magistrate, sir, I do not own one single *sao* of paddy or other land. I am a hired laborer and rent out my services to the representative, so I thought that I could pay the "propertyless tax" of one piaster. But the village chief administrator did not agree and tried to force me to pay three piasters and three cents. I pray that you, High Magistrate, who are the light of heaven, will shine [your grace] upon me."

The village chief administrator twitched his ear and swiftly reported, "High Magistrate, sir, though this fellow has no land, at the beginning of this year he was absent from the village for more than three months."

"High Magistrate . . ."

The magistrate glared and snarled, "Silence. Slap him in the mouth."

At once the village chief administrator's five fingers slammed into Lieu's cheek, and his whole head could have been knocked away.

The record clerk summoned, "Nguyen Thang."

Before Thang could speak, the chief administrator broke in, "High Magistrate, sir, this fellow is determined to pay only the basic tax of two piasters and fifty cents, while the side taxes and mutual benefit money he refuses to submit. Also he has claimed that we are harsh and corrupt."

Thang opened his eyes wide and argued back, "Sir, the village chief is giving a false report. . . ."

The record clerk shook his finger and admonished, "Silence."

"Vu huu Chu."

The village chief administrator said, "Sir, Chu's mother is present."

An old woman, whose head was completely bald, whose facial skin was nothing but wrinkles, and whose limbs were somehow stunted, twisted up her face and regarded the magistrate with beseeching eyes. Since her arms were tied, she could only bow her head for a kowtow, her voice barely audible. "High Magistrate, sir, please pity this old woman who is already eighty-two years old. My son has been dead since the twelfth month and has been reported dead accordingly, but now the chief administrator is trying to make me pay the body tax for him."

After saying this, she wept. A double line of tears streamed down her cheeks and across the twisted lips.

The record clerk was moved, but he explained, "That's right, your son died in the twelfth month. But by the end of the eleventh month, which means the beginning of the Western year, the village had already sent in to the provincial capital the death record and the record of those who have to pay taxes. The provincial administrator, in accordance with the record of man labor, makes out a report to the Treasury that, when tax time comes, must be collected in the amount stated in that report."

When he saw that the magistrate had gone over to one side of the communal house to spit, the village chief administrator fixed his eyes on the old woman, shook his hand at her, and cursed in a low voice, "Parents of yours,* you female raven, come on, argue some more. Why didn't your son play it smart and die at the beginning of the eleventh month of last year?"

The old woman, unable to endure this abuse, moaned aloud, "Oh, my son. Oh, oh, father of Voi, oh. How shameful this is for

* A curse.

your mother! To think that you cannot escape this, even in death!"

All were moved but watched the tragic scene in silence.

The magistrate ran up to her and snapped, "Silence!"

The village chief administrator glared angrily, quickly raised his hand. and was about to slap her. But the magistrate stopped him, saying, "Never mind. As for the rest of them, though, if they do not have the money to pay their tax, then lock them all up."

For some time Pha had been eyeing the magistrate nervously. He was not afraid but rather hoped that his turn to answer would come soon, so that he could have a chance to denounce the village chief administrator for having overcharged and arrested people unreasonably. He had felt sure that the magistrate would be on his side, since he recalled what he had been told the other day by Representative Lai, that although he [Pha] had in effect lost twenty-five piasters to the magistrate,* that money could not all be wasted [and he could surely expect to rely on the magistrate for special consideration, if need be, in the future]. So he had felt that the magistrate would surely remember and would thus be willing to defend him against the chief administrator. But now that the magistrate said they were all to be locked up, Pha was very much disheartened. He called out in the hope that the magistrate would recognize him, "High Magistrate, sir!"

The magistrate looked at him as if vaguely recollecting. Pha's heart beat with joy. When the magistrate remembered who he was, he then pointed at Pha and instructed the village chief administrator, "That fellow is fairly well-off and still he isn't paying his tax. Why don't you give him a beating till he throws up?"

* As a result of an episode related elsewhere in the book.

As he was saying this, he glanced out into the yard and noticed that one of the patrolmen, his face all bloody, was leading in a buffalo. All the village officials in turn looked at the animal and at the injured man, and none of them seemed in the least surprised.

The patrolman came up to the communal house floor and angrily complained, "High Magistrate, sir, to carry out your order, we went out to the paddies to bring in the buffaloes, but they all ran away. This is the only one I could catch, but the buffalo herdsman beat me up. I pray that you, High Magistrate, the light of heaven, will shine upon this. . . ."

The village chief administrator reported, "Sir, this buffalo belongs to Representative Lai."

The magistrate was annoyed and berated the patrolman, "Didn't you know that this was Representative Lai's buffalo? Why are you so stupid? No wonder they beat you up, when there are so many other buffaloes in the paddies."

Another patrolman led a second buffalo in but remained in the communal house courtyard. After learning that it did not belong to Representative Lai, the stranger who had accompanied the magistrate quickly stepped out to inspect it. After a while he came back, saying, "High Magistrate, sir, I will pay fifteen piasters for it."

Just as he was thrusting three five-piaster bills before the magistrate, a despairing woman came running into the courtyard, breathing hard. "High Magistrate, sir, this buffalo is mine. I am not guilty of anything. I have paid my land tax. Please release my buffalo. It cost me seventy to eighty piasters."

The magistrate coolly pointed to the people who were tied up, "You'll get it back from these people."

Then he lifted up his chin as a sign to the soldiers, and they dragged the struggling woman away. One continued to hear the echoes of her wailing and of the cracks of the rod they were beating her with.

After waiting a long while, the magistrate inquired of the village chief administrator; "How many buffaloes are there in this village, and why could they bring only two of them in?"

The chief administrator began to stammer. The magistrate glanced at the buffalo buyer, smiled, murmured something or other, and then stood up, "Village Chief Administrator, lead me into the village—to the wealthy families."

"High Magistrate, sir, we'll invite you to Representative Lai's house."

The magistrate scowled and snarled, "Besides the Representative, aren't there any other families that have enough bowls to eat with?"

The village council vice-chairman prompted them, "Ah, the handicraft man, Nang."

The village chief administrator, who suddenly recollected that Nang had agreed to pay only three piasters and three cents, then led the magistrate to this man's house.

As Nang greeted him, the magistrate said, "You're wealthy, and you ought to lend money to the poor to pay their taxes."

Nang, the handicraft man, firmly disagreed. "High Magistrate, sir, the village chief adminsitrator is giving you false information."

The magistrate did not reply but instead raised his jaw as a sign of command. At once, two soldiers from the district headquarters held Nang and his wife in place while the sergeant and everyone else went searching for money in the bedroom.

Nang continued his plea, with all the words he knew.

Unmoved, the magistrate asked him, "Where is your tax receipt?"

Nang did not know what the magistrate wanted it for, so he

took it out of his shirt pocket and gave it to him saying, "High Magistrate, sir, I have already submitted all of my tax."

Without replying even half a word, the magistrate handed the receipt to the clerk, "If he is unwilling to lend his money to the inhabitants, destroy this receipt and transfer the amount of money that he has submitted to someone else's name. If in the end he does not pay for himself, then report it to me, and I will confiscate his house."

Nang trembled in anger. The sergeant came out of the bedroom with four strings of coin and a few paper bills.

The magistrate was overjoyed. Nang's wife screamed in grief over the loss of the money. However, the rest quietly went on with their business. The magistrate ordered: "Count and see how much it is."

Nang contorted his face as he said, "High Magistrate, sir, this is too much for us to lose."

"You won't lose anything. It's only because the official business is so urgent that I have to do it this way. You can make those who haven't paid their taxes write out IOU's to you in turn."

The sergeant finished counting and reported, "High Magistrate, sir, forty-eight piasters and five dimes."

The magistrate mumbled; "With the fifteen piasters, that means sixty-three piasters and fifty cents."

The village chief administrator said, "Sir, we're still thirty piasters and five dimes short."

The magistrate stood up, and everybody followed the village chief to Mrs. Them's yard. She was a widow. She had been informed that the magistrate had come to search for money at Nang's house, and now that she saw them beating a noisy path to her own house, she quickly shut the gate and rushed into the yard, stamping her feet on the ground and shrieking out, "Oh village and country, oh! Bandits! Bandits at Mrs. Them's!"

She had thought that if she shouted in this way the villagers would come to her aid, but it was in vain. The patrolmen pounded on the gate. When the gate was opened, she sank to the ground like one who had been knocked down by an evil wind and moaned incoherently. People carried her into the house, laid her down, searched for the keys that were in her pocket, and opened up all the trunks and drawers. After this search, they came up with forty piasters more.

After Mrs. Them came to her senses again, she wailed horribly. The magistrate, having become a bit uneasy, tried to explain to her the humanistic implications of her "lending." But the widow chose not to understand the noble purpose of the deed that she was being forced to perform. She moaned for her husband and cried tragically for her children. Unable to endure the wails of this stubborn woman, the magistrate ordered one of his personal guards, "Do as you did yesterday."

At once the two guards went to the surrounding houses, and, whether anyone was at home or not, they went straight in and then carried out candle stands, brass pots, and even pigs—that is to say, anything having a value of about a dime up—and threw it all into Mrs. Them's yard. Now the sounds of wailing came from everywhere.

The magistrate, pointing out these articles, said to the village chief administrator, "Straighten this thing out among the villagers themselves. These articles here are to be used as compensation for this woman. Make an assessment of the value of each article and deduct it from the amount of money taken from her. Then make those who haven't paid their taxes reimburse her for the rest."

Then, ignoring the wailing people, the officials and soldiers calmly walked back to the communal house.

The magistrate sat down to rest on a chair and exclaimed joyfully, "If you don't do it that way, you'll never get it done at all."

The village chief administrator obsequiously put five piasters on a dish, scratched his ear, and said, "High Magistrate, sir, you've truly shown great affection toward us, for otherwise we would not have known what to do. This is our insignificant but honest thanks to you."

The district magistrate grasped the money, put it in his pocket, and stood up to leave. From the record clerk down, the village chief administrator saw each of them off with some money, according to their rank, even though they all sat in the same car with the magistrate.

4 Hoang Dao
MUD AND STAGNANT WATER
(*BUN LAY NUOC DONG*)

Mud and Stagnant Water, which was first published in Hanoi and immediately banned in September 1938, describes administrative, political, economic, and spiritual aspects of what the Vietnamese peasants faced during the French colonization of their country. The author, Hoang Dao, whose real name is Nguyen Tuong Long, had formerly been a judge in a French colonial court (Tay An), and later turned writer and propagandist along with his two famous writer brothers, Nguyen Tuong Tam (Nhat Linh) and Nguyen Tuong Lan (Thach Lam). Hoang Dao attained fame through his editorship of the newspapers *Phong Hoa* [Winds of Change], 1933–1937, and *Ngay Nay* [Today], 1937–1940, and also through his participation in the Vietnamese Nationalist Party. He died in 1948. The following is the translation of three short chapters of Part Two, "The Economic Aspects."

Although this account contains much of the same sort of material as the previous readings, the French administration felt obliged to ban its distribution because of its first-person, essay-type format. Students of Vietnamese society during the French period found it more expedient to write in the so-called "documentary fiction" style, such as the short story or the novel. Present-day researchers on Vietnam should thus take the content of the Vietnamese novel and short story seriously, since the novel and short story were more often than not the only written forms permitted for the discussion of serious matters.

Chapter 2 The yearly apprehension

I will always remember a certain afternoon in the innocent days of my boyhood, a dreary afternoon that brought me for the first time into the heartbreaking environment of the peasants. At that time I was studying in a district school, and every day I had to pass by a small marketplace where the stores were low and dilapidated.

That afternoon I started home early, stopping by the market-place on my way to look for birds' nests. The market session was over, and all that was left beneath the shoddily constructed stalls was rubbish and some sugarcane bagasse. A few women were hurrying to pack up their things. A sensation of melancholy stirred in my heart, the sensation of standing before an abandoned place.

Suddenly I noticed a man standing at the corner of the market. Now the only thing I can remember is that when I first noticed him he had a preoccupied look. He was leaning on his carrying poles and was standing next to a couple of baskets, one of which, to my surprise, contained a small boy. When he saw me approaching, the man seemed to want to say something to me but then hesitated and did not. I looked at the boy, and the boy returned my look, smiling.

Curious, I asked, "Uncle, why are you making him sit in the basket?"

I imagined that to be able to sit in a basket and to be carried on the man's shoulder pole would certainly be as comfortable as sitting in a vehicle. But I was very surprised to hear the man's answer: "I am selling him, young sir."

"Selling him? What for?"

"To pay my taxes."

Then the man smiled bitterly. "All day long nobody has inquired. It has really been miserable. Here, if you want to buy him, I'll let you have him cheap."

Although he was surely only jesting, his face at the same time showed a certain hope, like that of a drowning man trying to cling to a thin piece of wood in the hope of escaping death. . . .

From that time on, slowly, the things I heard and witnessed brought me to a general realization: the peasants, who never have enough food to eat or enough clothes to wear but who must always pay the full amount of taxes, will sacrifice everything in order not to be marked as tax evaders.

One could try no harder than they to meet their responsibilities. But human energy is limited. Ideally the responsibility of the government should be to collect taxes only in accordance with the ability of the individual to pay, especially in the case of taxes paid to the village chief administrators. As everybody knows, the principle of taxation should be that a tax is levied in proportion to the income or the productivity of the population. To go against this principle is no different from "cutting up the chicken in the hope of obtaining gold,"* and the result will be extreme poverty and misery for the whole nation.

A second principle in taxation is that the collection should be so organized that the amount paid by the population should not be at odds with the amount actually remitted to the national treasury.

Whether or not these principles are applied in the countryside is a matter that should be investigated if we are truly concerned about letting the peasants have a brighter life.

Before discussing the question of whether or not the taxes that the peasants have to pay are proportionate to the crop yields, I would like to describe the tax collection techniques, especially the ways in which the body tax and the land tax are collected.

* This refers to an old Vietnamese tale, very similar to the story of "killing the goose that laid the golden eggs."

The body tax and the land tax are the two forms of direct taxes that the peasants must worry about before all else. Every year when the fields turn golden yellow, the peasants hear the earnest appeals about their responsibility to the Treasury. First of all, the village chief administrators receive a summons ordering them to call together committee meetings to decide on how much each peasant must pay.* This committee decision is usually full of injustices. The members of the committee are for the most part people of senior status, that is to say, rich people in the village. For this reason, they agree among themselves to keep all the advantages to themselves and to heap all the losses on the heads of the poor people, who do not have anybody to protect their rights.

Even when these injustices are carried out, we can discover still other attendant evils. I assume that everybody must by now be aware that tax collection time is a time when greedy and influential officials can do whatever they wish. At that time they can give free rein to arrogance. Confiscation of household goods (sometimes even articles of worship), beatings, arrests, imprisonment, and other illegal activities all of a sudden become daily happenings that are openly perpetrated. At that time, the officials will point out to the peasants that they are not working for anybody free of charge, and so besides the tax money they need to collect some "side money" as well. The amount of this "side money" depends on the influence of these rich people and on the naïveté of the peasants.

At tax-collecting time, only those who go into the countryside can understand the peasants' plight. In an atmosphere of fear, there is the heavy beat of the drums urging the people to pay their taxes; the frightfully arrogant yells and threats of the administrative chiefs; and, mixed in with all this, the pleas of

* This was not the case in pre-French times.

the hungry peasants who do not have the money to pay. In the marketplaces people bring out their trays and pots, dishes, pigs, dogs, and chickens to sell at very low prices; inside the houses of the rich, poor people gather to borrow money. Some bring along antique vases handed down from their ancestors; others bring their paddy ownership certificates in the hope of borrowing a bigger amount, and the interest will be three times the amount of the loans.

But the most pathetic case of all is that of the man who carries with him to the market his own son to sell, such as I first encountered when I was young.

If the peasants are apprehensive about paying their taxes in this manner, it is certainly not because they do not do their utmost to fulfill their obligation to the Treasury. It is only because the taxes are too high and are not in proportion to the peasants' income.

Therefore, reform of the various taxes, as well as of the techniques of collecting them, must be carried out immediately if we are sincere in our hope that those pathetic situations will be things of the past.*

Chapter 3 The land tax

It is as clear as day that the peasants always try their best to pay their taxes. But their zeal is not directed toward the nuts and bolts (such as they exist) of taxation procedures. No matter how hard a person tries, if he is unable to meet the demands, then the result is more suffering, and that is all. The crux of the matter is that the taxation system should be structured in such a way that it benefits the whole population, so that the whole nation may be enriched by it.

It is necessary to have taxation. Nobody would argue against

* This is a rather weak conclusion by 1938 standards.

that. The people are protected by the government, and therefore they must pay a tax so that the government can employ the tax monies in useful projects, as a matter of course.* But *how* should they pay taxes? How much? These are the questions that should be answered and that other countries have solved. Since very early times, economists have agreed, on the basis of experience, that taxes should be reasonable, that tax records should be clear, and that tax collection and its subsequent allocation should be done in a just manner.

Those countries that have the kind of tax system just described are indeed fortunate. On the other hand, those countries that collect excessive taxes only bring great suffering upon themselves. This is because excessive taxes deprive people of the incentive to work, besides causing them to be discouraged and to lose hope. Experience teaches us that, in those places where taxes are so high that the inhabitants, no matter how much they try, cannot find enough money to make up for the earnings being taken away by taxes, production will be stagnant and the people hard-pressed. Excessive taxation produces another problem, that of pushing people into the path of "tax evasion." Economists have computed that, on an average, if in a given country each citizen is taxed only some 5 or 6 percent of his income, then the tax system is reasonable; if the amount of tax goes up to 11 or 12 percent, the population can still manage; but if it is above 13 percent, it becomes a restraint on the whole country and on the mutual welfare of the citizens.†

According to this sort of computation of percentages, are the taxes imposed upon our peasants reasonable? Do the taxes that they have to pay provide them with any enthusiasm or initiative

* This is very moderate for 1938.
† The author overgeneralizes here. These rates, of course, depend on size of income.

to work? At a glance, anybody can see that the peasants, in fact, have to pay excessively high taxes and that the number of tax evaders is not small, regardless of the fact that they remain excessively poor; as for handicrafts, they are so few and so unremunerative that there is really nothing worth mentioning.

However, people may reply that "one should not judge the figure by the face." They can rely on the old rumor that "Indochina is rich"—the Indochina that people not so long ago believed to be a place from which, after a few years' work, one could return with hundreds of thousands or millions of piasters.

Therefore, in order to reveal the truth, we must examine the facts. We need to know the size of the peasants' annual income and whether or not the amount of money they pay in taxes, compared to their income, is unreasonable.

To do this, we must look at the body tax and the land tax.

The body tax is, theoretically, two and a half piasters annually for every man in Bac Ky [Tonkin]. But in reality the peasants have to pay a larger amount, the additional sum depending on the locality. This sum of money is to the poor peasants—that is, to the great majority of the agricultural population—a yearly source of anxiety. It is already very difficult for them to find enough to eat from day to day, so where can they get the money to pay taxes? The result is this: only those who can manage to pay their taxes are still free individuals. The rest of them become slaves to rich families who pay their taxes for them.

We must realize that things were much better for the peasants formerly. That is because formerly [during the early years of the French occupation] the villagers were divided into two groups: *noi tich** and *ngoai tich*.† The *noi tich* had to pay two and a half piasters, while the *ngoai tich*, who were mostly very poor or

* Literally, "inside the register," meaning taxable people.
† Literally, "outside the register," meaning people exempted from taxes.

propertyless people, had to pay only half a piaster. But people have abandoned this differentiation. The village councils agree to this because it is advantageous to the senior-status inhabitants, and the government claims that, with respect to taxation, it is introducing the idea of equality among the people. This kind of "equality," however, is unjust and disastrous in the extreme, because the peasants are equal only with respect to taxes, but not with respect to income.* For most of them, a three-piaster body tax is a very large sum of money, larger than their annual profit. A revision in the body tax is necessary so they will not become slaves. So they will not retain their resentment, there is no better course of action than either of the two following solutions: (1) to abolish the body tax and replace it with a [progressive] income tax; (2) to reclassify the body tax into different categories, with the poorer peasants exempted.

The land tax is not so unjust as the body tax, and therefore the peasants do not resent it to the same degree that they resent the body tax. On the average, for every *mau* of paddy land they should [theoretically] pay from 1.40 to 1.50 piasters, but usually the peasants have to pay about two piasters per *mau*, since, in taxing a certain village, the government puts a tax on every-thing, from fields to houses, wells, ponds, and roads. That is not to mention the extra money one must pay to village chief admin-istrators and numberless other payments.

Meanwhile, even in good harvest years, the average single crop yield per *mau* is only five or six *ta* [a *ta* is a hundred kilograms] of paddy rice, which means about twenty piasters' worth. Of this twenty piasters, about half has already been consumed during the plowing, harrowing, planting, and harvesting, while only about half is left as income for the peasant landowner. For every ten piasters, on the average one has to pay two to two and a half

* That is, "regressive" taxes.

piasters in tax; therefore, the land tax will be as high as 20 percent of the peasants' incomes.

A land tax that is as high as 20 percent of the peasants' crops cannot be considered light. Because of this, in bad harvest years, small landowners—who compose the majority of the peasant population—are forced to sell their land at very low prices. The result is that rich people, who lend money at high interest, are gradually taking over all the land in a village, forcing most of the peasants to become their servants or, in effect, their slaves.

Thus in order to bring a stop to this extremely demoralizing situation, the present authorities must turn their attention to and protect the small landowners, decrease their taxes in bad harvest years, allow them to form their own cooperatives in order to help one another out, and, most importantly, reorganize the tax-collecting system and make it more viable.*

Chapter 4 The freedom to drink
The alcohol problem has been much discussed. It is a subject that, for the peasant, looms very large. It is so complex that it can even give rise to "pen fights," with the ink never ceasing to flow.

People can take a moral stand and cast an easy verdict on the whole problem of drinking, hoping that in the future nobody will get drunk any more. Naturally, then the government would in that eventuality no longer have any prospect at all of collecting the alcohol taxes.

But while waiting for that ideal day, we must look more closely at the present reality. It is not that the peasants have only now taken to drinking. The enjoyment of song and wine has existed since mythical times. Alcohol, like many other poisons, can excite people's spirits or else make them depressed.

* Again, this is a very moderate point of view for 1938.

When the French arrived in Indochina, in the provinces of Bac Ky [Tonkin] there were over four hundred recognized distilleries, which together paid about 14,000 to 15,000 *quan** in taxes annually. Besides, there were innumerable people engaged in the distillation of alcohol who escaped tax payments altogether. The reason for this was that the peasants had rice and could easily distill their own alcohol. Since alcohol is an element used in religious rites, the courts at the time levied taxes—and it was a very light tax burden at that—only on the larger distilleries. As for the poor people who distilled their own alcohol for use in the villages, the courts always gave them complete freedom.

Faced with this situation, the French government naturally found ways to increase the tax so as to profit their Treasury. Paul Bert, the famous colonizer who became the first governor-general of Indochina, was among the first to consider the possibility of an alcohol monopoly. But he was careful and hesitant, since he wanted to think of a way to establish this monopoly without making the population overly resentful. In a communication sent to the Residents-General in 1886, he said that since alcohol was a product used by the Annamites in rites of worship, to impose a tax on it would, in the eyes of the poor, constitute a serious move. Especially since the peasants were already paying a land tax, which meant a tax on rice, if they then had to pay an additional tax on alcohol, which was a product of rice, they would naturally consider that on rice alone they had been forced to pay two kinds of taxes.

Because of this caution, it was seven years before the government issued a decree clearly defining its policy on the subject of alcohol. According to that decree, any individual, village, or

* 140 to 150 taels, or *lang*. These taxes were paid to the court government at Hue.

organization that wanted to distill alcohol had only to report to the province chief. Because this was a policy of freedom to distill alcohol, there were few who resented it. However, that policy was gradually abandoned, and we came to see the Fontaine distilleries* become bigger and bigger. It was thus that the monopoly on alcohol distillation came to exist in our country.

The results of this monopoly were clear to everybody. The profits of the Fontaine company became larger and larger every day; the number of individual distillers who were arrested and imprisoned increased daily; and the resentment of the population became more and more obvious.

The alcohol produced by the Fontaine company, which the peasants call "factory alcohol" [ruou ty], cannot be used by them in worship, since, according to them, it is produced by "chemical methods" and thus is not as "pure" as the old-fashioned alcohol distilled at home. Moreover, they do not think that it tastes as good. For these reasons, the illegal distillation of alcohol prospered and at the same time demonstrated the injustices of the monopoly. The peasants could not understand why they were being forced to drink bad alcohol while being forbidden to drink good alcohol. As the profession of illegal distillation became more prosperous, naturally the rampage of searches and arrests began its course. Cases of injustice became abundant. Customs officers who could find no way of arresting the actual distillers usually turned around and arrested the landowners. In this regard, people saw many ironic cases, too. They were ironic because they were unreasonable. There were people who left, never to come back to the countryside, who were nonetheless fined because, in some abandoned field they happened to own, the customs officers came upon a basket of distillation residue.

* The Fontaine distilleries, owned by Frenchmen, were given complete monopoly in Annam and Tonkin.

Moreover, people who lacked a conscience might, owing to small grudges or a search for profit, deliberately leave alcohol residue in someone else's house and then report it to customs. Thus, many good and honest people in the countryside are being terrorized and are worried about the possibility of being found guilty at any time. The uniform of the customs officer has thus become a symbol of terror in the countryside.

The popular resentment against the alcohol policy has made the government officially abandon its protection of the French monopoly during the last few years. But since the requirements for establishing a distillery are so strict, only a few companies dare to come out on their own and try to compete with the Fontaine company. Although legally the monopoly has [theoretically] been abolished, in every other way it is more monopolistic than ever.

This kind of fake change is not at all advantageous to the peasants. We know that the government is aware of this and is trying to find a way to reform the present system. We think that the simplest way is to let the population once again have the freedom to distill their own alcohol, as prescribed in the decree of 1893.

Moreover, other things that clamor for immediate changes are the harsh statutes like statute #94 of the 1921 decree on alcohol, which orders the arrest of those whose houses or fields contain distillation residues. The tactics used by law enforcement officers in increasing the amounts of alcohol sold in their areas must also be changed. There is nobody who does not know that the alcohol tax has become a kind of direct tax comparable to the body tax —with each person being forced to buy a large bottle* of alcohol a month, whether he wants to get drunk or not. This is something that ought not to happen in a civilized country. It is

* *Chai bo*: one liter or more.

a matter that makes people resentful and something that the government must recognize and do away with. Alcohol is a kind of poison; he who wants to use it must be ready to accept its consequences and should rightfully pay tax on it, but he who does not want to drink, a citizen who values his health and who should be an example for others, should not be forced to drink, as at present.

A most important issue nowadays, therefore, is the "freedom to drink alcohol," or, to be more exact, "the freedom not to drink."

5 Tran Van Mai
WHO COMMITTED THIS CRIME?
(*AI GAY NEN TOI?*)

During the height of the starvation caused by the French and the Japanese in 1944–1945, Tran Van Mai managed to put down in writing some of the things he witnessed. The author, who is very well educated and who has written many books on a variety of subjects, was a very well-to-do person at the time of the starvation. This book was first published in Saigon in 1956. With the personal permission of the author, the book is here translated in its entirety with the exception of one short chapter of two pages.

Foreword

This book is not a piece of fiction. These are things that I myself witnessed and was able to put down in writing at the time they happened.

Nearly two million people died in the starvation of the years *than-dau* [1944–1945].

Who committed this crime?

The reasons are very deep and complicated. Consequently I here limit myself to presenting in an objective manner various examples of things that happened within the confines of a particular village and a particular province. However, I think these things will suffice for the reader to judge for himself the total situation.

I do not wish to stir up enmity among any social classes whatever. In coming back to this old story, I want only to remind people of the heartfelt yearning of the tens of thousands of victims.

Our society must change for the better!
Human lives and human rights must be respected above all else!

Saigon, September 12, 1956

Chapter 1 The rice-robbing policy of the colonizers

From the beginning of the Second World War the French colonizers realized that their position in Indochina was threatened both by the spreading national liberation movements and by the increasing pressure of imperialist Japan. To make sure the people would not be able to revolt, the colonizers used extremely "scientific" methods to create a severe and long-lasting famine.*

* This is what most Vietnamese believed at the time and still believe. However, as history shows, at best one might discover that the French were very uncertain about their own future and were hoarding rice and taking other "precautionary" measures, which led, along with other factors, to famine.

The area affected the worst was Bac Viet [the northern part of Vietnam], from which our people came originally.

The colonizers began collecting rice from the time of the October harvest of 1943 up through the seasonal harvest of 1944 —three harvests in all. The colonial government ordered that:

1. People who had five *mau** or less of paddy fields had to sell 50 kilograms of paddy rice per *mau* to the government.

2. Those owning from five to twenty *mau* had to sell 120 kilograms per *mau*.

3. Those owning from twenty *mau* up had to sell 200 kilograms per *mau*.

4. Graveyards, dry fields, and gardens were all counted as paddy fields. One had to turn in the rice even if the crops failed.

The colonizers fully realized that when the harvest was good the amount of rice produced in Bac Viet was just barely enough to feed the population. The small amount of rice that Bac Viet sold to the northern part of Trung Viet [central Vietnam] had forced the laboring population into a situation of constant hunger. On this even the colonialist researchers themselves agreed.

The rice-collecting decree thus could not help but carry with it the intent of murder!

But that is not all. The activities involved in this rice-collecting business were those of "robbery in broad daylight." In 1943 the government paid the people 1.40 piasters for a ten-kilogram container† of rice, while the going market prices were from 2.50 to 3.00 piasters. During the *chiem* harvest‡ of 1944 the government still paid the producers 1.40 piasters per can of rice, while market prices were from 6.00 to 7.00 piasters. During the sea-

---

* A *mau* in northern Vietnam produced on the average about 500 kilograms,
† The Vietnamese word is *thung*, which originally had the literal meaning of "can," but which came to designate a standard ten-kilogram unit of rice, whether in metal cans or in boxes, baskets, or other containers.
‡ A second yearly harvest that falls around June in most regions of Bac Viet.

sonal harvest of 1944 [that is, the autumn harvest] the market price for a can of rice shot up to 20 to 30 piasters per can, and then again up to 60 to 70 piasters. But the government continued to collect the rice at a price of only 1.40 piasters per can.

All those who owned any land were called to the district or provincial capitals to sign papers for the sale of their rice. The amount of land owned by each person had been clearly recorded in books that were filed by the registrars of each village, so that nobody could quarrel with or defraud the government.

A few days before they were forced to send their rice to the government, the producers had to go to the houses of the village chief administrators to get the sacks to package the rice for shipping. The village chief administrator* allowed the rich and the influential in the village to choose the good sacks, while the poor and the underlings had to accept bad sacks that were ragged and full of holes and that required a great deal of work to mend them.

The majority of those who had to sell their rice had to transport it by boat. Those who had little to sell either transported their rice by oxcart or else joined together with neighbors in the hiring of a boat. They often had to go from fifteen to twenty

* The Vietnamese word is *ly truong*, derived from the Chinese. A literal translation would be something like "village headman" or "village chief" (as it is usually translated into English). However, the *ly truong* had relatively little decision-making power and merely carried out the decisions of the village council. The village council, called *hoi dong ky muc* in Vietnamese, might also be translated as "council of elders" or "council of notables." The village council, which appointed the *ly truong* as an executive administrator, was headed by a council chairman (*chanh hoi*), whose opinions carried the most weight in the formulation of local decisions. Traditionally, the village councils were more or less democratically chosen by all the village inhabitants, but after the French take-over the council positions tended to be usurped by collaborationists and by those who, if not themselves concerned primarily with their own selfish interests, were used to protect the selfish economic and power interests of others.

kilometers in order to get to the river depot where rice was being collected. On the river banks the rice sacks were piled up in lines that resembled unending colosal dikes. Boats, heavy with rice, anchored in the rivers next to each other like bamboo leaves. The landowners usually had to wait from five days to a week before they could get their rice up to the bank to deliver it to the contractors. Even then, the contractors might give them trouble over whether the rice grains were fully grown or not or whether the sacks of rice were the right weight. The peasants would plead with them patiently, enduring all things to get the whole thing over with. Finally, to receive a receipt, the peasants had to let the contractors trim the figures. As long as they got a receipt saying that they had sold the full amount of rice to the government, they would not have to go to jail.

Chapter 2 A bank that engaged in robbery

Learning from their experience of being forced to sell rice in 1943, landowners* seeking to decrease the amount of rice they would have to sell to the government tried to find ways to conceal the amounts of land they really had. They signed official papers parceling out land to their children and their relatives in amounts below five *mau* each, since for areas less than five *mau* one was required to sell only eighty kilograms per *mau*. But in order to safeguard their original properties and to prevent possible "swindling" in the future by consignees who might take the legal papers too literally, as soon as they officially signed their land away to someone, the owners would then have the consignee make out a separate certificate saying that this land had been sold back to the original owner and that full payment had already been received for it. The landowners kept these

* This use of the term "landowners" includes independent owner-cultivators and even part-time tenants, as well as the relatively small class of noncultivating landlords.

papers only for proof [to cover future contingencies] and did not enter them in the official registration. The business of transferring names and changing fields confused all the land records of the villages. Village chief administrators and registrars sided with the landowners since they too were against this [government] policy of stealing rice. But the result was nil, since the colonial government was smart enough to see through this strategy and ordered the authorities to collect rice according to the old records.

There were many landowners who did not have enough rice to deliver because of crop failures. They saw clearly that there was no escaping from jail. They were frightened and resentful. There were many who were so discouraged that they might easily have welcomed a big bomb falling on their village and killing them all outright, so bringing an end to the whole story.

The unavoidable happened. Landowners who could not deliver enough rice were arrested, jailed, or sent away for hard labor. In order to get all the rice the population had, the government forbade landowners to store more than twenty *ta* [2,000 kilograms] of rice. Authorities came from everywhere to inspect. The farming population ran off with their rice as if running away from bandits. Those who had a lot of rice took theirs to those who had but little in order to store it. But the government went on to prohibit those who owned five *mau* or less from storing more than ten *ta* of rice on their premises. Those who owned one *mau* or less were not allowed to store more than five *ta*. Thus nobody could store enough rice to eat or to use for the next planting. The future was very black.

After a succession of strict inspections and arrests, the government, realizing that it had already collected most of the rice, went on to establish a so-called *can* policy.* "Paying in money"

* Collecting in cash what they were unable to get in rice.

(*can tien*), as suggested by the term itself, was the most clever and demonic way of robbing.

The government sent out its contractors to represent it in collecting the rice or, to be more exact, in callously robbing the people of their money. People were forced to sell their rice to the government at the price of 1.40 piasters per ten-kilogram container. The market price during the *chiem* harvest ["second crop," usually in May or June] was 7.00 piasters. But those who did not have enough rice to sell to the government, in order to escape jail, now had the "fortunate" option of asking the government to allow them to *can*. That is to say, they had to go up to the district or province level and ask the contractors to accept payment in money for the amount of rice they were unable to deliver. For each ten-kilogram unit that they could not deliver they had to pay the difference between 7.00 and 1.40 piasters, or 5.60 piasters. For example, a landowner who was supposed to sell the government one hundred units of rice at the price of 1.40 piasters per unit had to pay the contractors 560 piasters just in order *not* to have to sell this amount of rice.

Those who did not have rice asked to pay in money and even those who had enough rice to meet their payments also asked to pay in this way since they could sell their rice to local villagers right where they were for as much as 7.00 piasters, without having to contend with the expenses involved in transportation, the waiting, and the numerous other inconveniences of selling to the government.

For this reason, in the districts and provinces, banks were suddenly established that, in effect, engaged in robbery. They were continuously flooded with people who were making money for the colonizers.

There is no knowing who got all of the money that had been stolen from the people. As for the rice that they had collected, the colonizers stored it in vast warehouses. While starvation was rampant among the population, the colonizers were determined not to release this rice either for relief or for sale. As Resident *Va-Re* [Pierre Varet] declared, "The more of them that die, the better!"

Chapter 3 Holding on to one another, crying, waiting for death
The Vietnamese people are accustomed to leading a hard working, frugal, and patient life. They believe that if they eat less, save some money, and work hard, then no matter how difficult life is for them, they can still "patch things up" and somehow manage to have at least one meal of greens and one meal of rice gruel each day. The changes in the economy of Vietnam between 1940 and 1945, however, greatly disrupted the people's livelihood, worst of all in the countryside.

In 1943 a ten-kilogram can of rice sold for only 1.00 piaster. A dozen eggs sold for only eight cents. In 1944 one had to pay 2.00 piasters a dozen.

The speculators hoarded, took advantage of their situation and their powerful influence, and very rapidly became rich. Prices of goods soared upward. Wages for labor, however, were raised very little and very slowly.

During the seasonal harvest of 1944 the wage for a harvester or a rice grinder was two meals of rice and salted cucumbers, an extra bowl of rice, and one piaster per day. A very strong laborer could earn only enough to feed himself, to say nothing of the taxes he had to pay or provision for his parents, wife, and children.

From May through September 1944 there were three typhoons in the coastal areas of Bac Viet. In normal times this kind of catastrophe would be enough to put the population in an impossible situation. But now the disaster fell upon them during wartime and during a time of economic disorder. Worst of all, the French colonizers were plotting to destroy the very vitality of the population, to increase starvation in every possible way so as to be able to neutralize the traditional unyielding spirit of the Vietnamese people, and thus to rule them more easily. For this reason, from September and October of 1944 onward, everybody realized that the tragedy of all times could not be avoided.

In normal times harvest season in the countryside was bustling with the activities of rice pounding and grinding. But during the seasonal harvest of the year 1944 things were completely different. The farmers went out into the fields, cried to the heavens, and moaned. People looked at each other with all hope drained from their eyes and uttered words that made it seem that they were saying farewells to one another: "There is no knowing whether we will still be alive to see each other by the time the next *chiem* harvest comes around."

The starvation began in early October. Earlier than any other year the weather was cuttingly cold. The north wind howled, and it pierced through the rags worn by the hungry and the poor. It penetrated their flesh and their bones and their weak insides. In the grey sky overhead there hung a damp layer of clouds that enveloped the hamlets and the villages. It rained continuously, day and night, and the dampness seeped into the very marrow of the hungry.

All through October and on through December the sun kept itself hidden behind the thick clouds, with but feeble rays making their way through to the tops of the drooping bamboo groves. The days and months dragged by slowly. Rain, wind, hunger, and cold seemed to slow down the wheels of time. It was so cold that people would lie in haystacks, covering themselves up with banana leaves. They were so hungry that they had to eat marsh pennywort, potato leaves, bran, banana roots, and the bark of trees. The villagers—fathers and sons, brothers and sisters, husbands and wives, ll of them alike—could no longer save one another. Regardless of the time of day or night, the hungry people, over and over again, would hug each other and would moan tragically.

Chapter 4 Giving birth to Communism

In a village of Thai Binh province, near the coast, there was a man named Ca Luong who knew earlier than anybody else about the violent and tragic consequences of the starvation.

One day early in October of 1944, after inspecting his crops in the coastal area, he came back very pensive and worried. He threw himself down on the ground and cried all night. The next morning his hair had turned gray. He had already prepared a relief plan. And he declared, "It is useless to be downcast. The important thing now is to have enough strength to carry out my plan until April of 1945. I swear that if I cannot accomplish this, I will kill myself."

He began giving relief aid from the tenth month of the lunar year of *than*.* And he kept his promise, since the last day he gave out relief aid was on the twenty-fifth of the fourth month of the lunar year of *dau*.† Following this there was a vegetarian feast and rites for those who had succumbed to the starvation.

The villagers were all moved by this, and they respected Ca Luong. There were, however, some former Communist political prisoners who never stopped propagandizing—that landowner Ca Luong had fed the hungry, not because of any human compassion, but only so that afterward he could still have laborers to work for him; that he had given relief because he planned on exploiting the field laborers later; and so on.

When these words reached Ca Luong's ears, he snickered, "Everybody knows who these Third International people are. They are the most downright tricky people under heaven. They

* 1944, the "year of the monkey."
† 1945, the "year of the chicken."

have dared to 'insult their father'* ever since the time of the Popular Front (*Mat Tran Binh Dan*).† They were still living in propitious times then with an advantageous situation going for them. But now we do not have even the time to pay sufficient attention to our own village inhabitants, so why should we waste words on these people?"

Having carried out his own private relief program, Ca Luong suddenly thought of the money and the rice owned by the village and the hamlets, which might also be taken out to provide relief and supplies for the population. If all the public resources and private resources were added together and if all aided one another conscientiously and with determination, then nobody would die from starvation. He suggested to the village council chairman and to the village chief administrator that they call a meeting to draw up a plan for saving the population.

On the day of the village meeting all the village elders were present. The poorer villagers also gathered around in front of the communal house (*dinh*) to hear the news. People paid the most attention to the village chief administrator, the canton chief, the "moneyed men,"‡ and the village council chairman. All decisions were in their hands, especially in those of the village council chairman.

These officials were sitting on an ironwood dais with a flower-design mat spread over it. When they saw Ca Luong appear, they slowly rose to welcome him. Ca Luong sat humbly at one corner of the dais, leaning his back on a pillar of the communal house. After a few minutes of routine inquiries, they began talking

---

* Swearword, here referring to the speaker himself.
† This refers to the Popular Front government formed by Léon Blum in France in 1936. During the brief duration of the Popular Front, French colonial policies in Vietnam had been temporarily relaxed to some extent.
‡ In Vietnamese, *ong ba* (literally, something like "man of wealth," or "rich sir"). This used to be an informal sort of designation of status by which the one or two wealthiest men in a village were known.

about hunger. Ca Luong went directly to the point, saying, "I suggest that the village officials release the rice that has been allocated to maintenance and repair of the communal house and pagodas, worth over seven thousand piasters, to use in providing relief for the population."

The village chief administrator cut him short, saying: "That won't do! If one should take it out to give it to the people, as you suggested, then if money is needed for maintenance, where can one get it?"

A certain "moneyed man" suggested, "Maybe it would be possible to lend it to them."

"That won't do either," said the canton chief. "If you lend it to them, then when they die, who is going to pay it back? If the village were to ask for reimbursement, then who would bear the responsibility?"

Ca Luong insisted, "It's the people's own money, and we are using it to save them. As long as there are still people, there will always be new resources forthcoming. Only as long as the people are alive can there be rites and sacrifices or any maintenance and repair of communal houses and pagodas. But if we let them die, who will there be to conduct all these things for, and what meaning will there be left in it?"

The village council chairman calmly turned the water pipe in one hand while stroking his graying beard with the other. His eyes, half shut, gave him a self-satisfied expression. He kept on rotating the water pipe without smoking it. Ca Luong, wanting to know the opinion of the village council chairman, lighted the pipe for him. The council chairman put out one hand to accept the light, saying: "Please!" With the other hand he opened his tobacco case and rolled some tobacco leaves. The light at the end of the green bamboo lighter stick went out, and some gray smoke rose from it. The council chairman tapped the cinder off and put the stick into a smoking lamp to relight it. But as he got it lighted, instead of smoking immediately, he laid the lighter stick down on top of the pipe, looked over to where Ca Luong was, and invited him to drink his tea. The light went out again. He slowly lighted the stick, playing it over the bowl of the pipe, and again the light went out. The council chairman dragged out the same game for several more minutes before he finally had his smoke. He inhaled the smoke three or four times. The last of these times he drew his breath in for a very long time and then released the smoke gradually through his nostrils and mouth. After smoking, he ordered his attendant to go and bring him some betel.

Ca Luong again asked, "What do you gentlemen think?"

"It is very difficult to decide," replied the village chief administrator.

The local "moneyed man" and the canton chief echoed, "Really difficult to decide."

Not until then did the village council chairman click his tongue and say, "It is already difficult for one to save himself. Right now we're already worried to the point that our knees are weak over the problem of meeting the rice quota we have to deliver to the government. If we don't, we'll have to go to jail ourselves. The village treasury still has to be worried about this, since the village has to pay the government for whatever rice it cannot deliver."

As if they had planned this as a signal, the village chief administrator, the local moneyed man, and the canton chief all agreed, "The instruction given by your honor is quite correct."

Ca Luong had long known that the village officials were rotten and corrupt, but he never thought that they could be so cruel. He took his leave of them, saying, "If by holding back public property you cause the inhabitants to die, then you will have to bear the responsibility."

The village council chairman was no longer standing on ceremony, and he said tersely, "To take public property to divide among the people is Communistic!"

Just then a thought that had been hidden within Ca Luong's mind for a long time came shooting out like an arrow, "It's people like you who give birth to Communism!"

Chapter 5 A haunting tale of a new year market session
At the end of the old year and the beginning of the lunar new year, I, too, went out to see what the market looked like when people were dying of starvation.

From early morning the buyers and sellers—and the hungry, of all ages and sizes, some coming empty-handed and others carrying things in their hands or on their shoulders—headed toward the market from all directions, in groups of threes and fives. At 500 meters or so from the market one could already hear its bustle and commotion. On the roads leading in, although there were a lot of people. very few of them laughed or talked or greeted each other as usual. They sky was still very low, and there was a desultory sort of drizzle.

As one stepped into the market area, one was at once struck by the gaudy-looking Chinese stalls with paintings of Chinese girls holding branches of cherry and willow trees, with the paintings by Van thien Tuong, Tien Tai, and Tien Loc, and with the parallel sentences* of poetry celebrating the new year, written in big Chinese characters. At these stalls the Chinese very carefully selected their customers. The majority of the customers were village officials or other well-known individuals. Otherwise the customers tended to be at least well dressed. As for all the rest of the people, they were barred right at the entrance.

As one proceeded inward from the marketplace entrance, in

* Parallel sentences are poetic verses that match each other word for word in rhythm and rhyme but are opposite in meaning.

addition to the stalls full of goods, one saw people displaying their goods in baskets all over the streets. The marketgoers vied with one another for every foot of ground to walk on.

The market was divided into many different sections. At the entrance was the section for wooden products. Mixed in with the moldy beds, the pillars, and the house beams (some of them partially burned) were numerous altars, incense stick holders, candle holders, and other articles connected with ancestral worship. A marketgoer offered a sharp opinion, "Who would ever think of buying someone else's ancestral altars to worship! They are getting absent-minded from hunger."

Next to the wood-products section was the section for fruit and sweets. The majority of the peddlers there were women. If they saw anybody who seemed to have money, they would greet him or her, saying, "Please buy a piece of cake from us, sir, madam!"

People who could buy things to eat threw the wrapping leaves, the banana peels, and the corncobs all over the walkways. The hungry would pick up the leaves and the peels to lick and chew on them. There were some who chewed the corncobs as if they were eating sugarcane.

Behind the sweetmeat stands, occupying the rooms of a new building with round hardwood pillars, was the wine shop. Because of the New Year festivities, the village council chairman had ordered this shop erected so that the village patrolmen could make some extra money and could at the same time have a convenient spot from which to watch over the market. The customers in the wine shop talked about the New Year market and about the starvation. To season their tales, they drank several cups of wine apiece to go with their ham, boiled chicken, roast pork, or hot bowls of noodle soup. As the wine went in, the words came out. They conversed in deep measured tones and laughed happily. Meanwhile, the hungry, who had risked their lives robbing food in the market, were being dragged back to this same area and were there tied up with their arms twisted behind them around the pillars of the shop. Now and then a customer would stand up and point a finger at them, yelling insults; "The best thing to do would be to have you bums beaten to death."

A certain customer who chanced to pass by likewise delivered a few kicks and insults to them: "Your fathers be damned, you thieves!"

That same morning the whole market was abuzz with the news that the village council chairman's eldest son had ordered the chief of the village patrolmen to sever the leg tendons of a certain boy named Lieu because he had dared to pick his pocket. People said that Lieu had met his deserved fate, since he had not paid enough attention to whom he was stealing from.

I fought my way through the confectionery section, the meat section, and then on to the bronzework and chinaware section. This section was less busy than the others. Besides the professionals in the business, there were a number of people selling their household articles. One could see that they had been propertied people just by looking at the things being sold: various types of tobacco pipes, intricately designed chinaware, large vases, censers and urns, tea sets, and, most abundant of all, the antique candle holders and joss stick holders.

At the end of the bronzework and china section was the ironware section. Besides the stoves and kitchen utensils, there were numerous types of knives and swords. Things seemed to be proceeding very solemnly here. The customers were either middle-aged men or physically well-built young men whose language was measured, whose gait was correct, and whose clothes fit nicely. They inspected the blades, fingered every bamboo joint of the handles, as if they were long accustomed to these special-ized products.

After I had thoroughly surveyed the ironware section, I jostled my way to the market's communal house, where the privileged had gathered to enjoy the New Year fun at gambling. At other times, such scenes of people matching wits with one another had been entertaining for me to watch. But this time the atmosphere within the communal house was somewhat lacking in vitality. Those who were engaged in their games, as well as the on-lookers, all seemed to sense that this playing while other people were dying was a contemptible, disgusting thing. Yet because of long-established custom and their "gambling blood," they still pretended to be enjoying it.

Standing in front of the communal house and looking at the village pond, I tried to recollect the scenes in which I had played at pitching coins and throwing dice when I was a kid. The rippled surface of the pond reflected a dreary sky. The New Year market scene seemed to be imprinted on the bottom of the pond, fuzzy under the drizzle.

As I was attempting to recall the past, a small skeleton stopped in front of me, opened up a dry and shrunken hand, and stared at me with wide-open eyes.

I looked at the ancient fig tree drooping down to the pond's surface, its foliage withering, and my heart was full of melan-choly at the thought that the fresh, green scenes of a young life were never to come back again. I shoved a piaster into the child's hand and unsteadily made my way homeward. I gazed upon all the many heartrending scenes, so I could be aware of and feel a deeper compassion for the hungry.

At the market gates things were different from the way they had been in the morning. Women and girls who had arrived late because their homes were far away had to lay out their bundles, baskets, and sacks on the side of the road. They were mostly food peddlers. People squatted next to their bundles, eating and talking. As I approached a certain meatball vendor who had the most customers, I saw behind her back, lying on the ground, the naked corpse of a thirteen- or fourteen-year-old girl. The skin and the shape of the body were still pretty and fair, completely different from the corpses of other hungry people. Some kind-hearted person had cut a banana leaf and covered the body. Flies and bluebottles clustered on top of it. The meatball vendor now and then would take a branch of bamboo and casually drive them away. The customers ate on as if nothing had happened.

I looked at the other people and then thought about myself. I was not moved as much as I wanted to be. I tried to take control of my mind, to kindle a flicker of humanity in my bronze-cold heart. I became extremely angry when, as my conscience was questioning me in this way, I heard the village council chairman's eldest son yell an order to the patrolmen: "Bury that girl immediately! The beauty and charm of the New Year market will be ruined if she's left like that."

A thought swirled about in my head: were not his heart, my own heart, and the hearts of everybody there perhaps all made of stone?

I removed my wooden clogs and walked barefoot in order to get home faster. In long strides I followed the interprovince road, which had been washed out by the several months' long rain, leaving only sharp jutting stones. After walking along part of this stone road, I turned into the village road. At the junction was the hamlet pond, a little larger than a paddy field. The water level, now lower than it had been, left the bamboo roots exposed. They fringed down the sides of the pond like beards. At the stone steps that led down to the pond there lay a dead woman still clutching a baby close to her breast. The baby, held tight against its mother's bosom, was still squirming and sucking at the nipple.

I dropped my head and pondered the words of Mencius: "People fear death yet enjoy inhuman deeds. This is like abhorring drunkenness, yet still continuing to drink wine."

Chapter 6 They prayed: let us die

Behind the green bamboo groves and next to families who every minute and every second wrestled with death, there were still people who led a life of velvet and silk with all the conveniences and pleasures of the time. These were the rich people who had connections with the bureaucrats and the colonizers. Among them was one named Han Tinh. Han was a man of poor origins who was completely ignorant of French and Chinese, as well as *quoc ngu*.* However, when one talked about the contracting business in connection with dikes and bridges (and public works in general), nobody knew as much about it as he. Any province or district chief who might be assigned to the area was obligated to cultivate the friendship of "Mandarin" Han. "Mandarin" Han was very close to the [French] Resident. Money could equalize all differences in social status.

During the years 1943 and 1944 "Mandarin" Han was given the responsibility of collecting rice from the local population. After the famine came, Han kept his gates closed. At night his houses were guarded even more strictly than the headquarters of the Inspector of the Army at the provincial capital. There were guard towers, warning drums and gongs, and guards on patrol. The hungry were obliged to look in at the bulging granaries of the "Mandarin," while resigning themselves to the fate of death.

* The national romanized script.

One night, like every other night [toward the end of 1944], the winds and the rain howled. Inside the "Mandarin's" house were several guests of good family, intent on playing cards. I, too, had been invited to take part. The officials and village elders sat on flower-pattern mats and velvet mattresses as they played. If they should wish to rest their backs, then there were divans, and there were opium pipes and a variety of fruits and other food. "Mandarin" Han's house was as merry as New Year's, with lamps and torches all brightly lit and the house attendants bustling about.

Late that night, the officials and the gentlemen decided to rest their hands and eat. At "Mandarin" Han's house there was a cook named Tich whose delicacies were always well suited to the taste of the good guests. Tich was always particularly congratulated on his duck gruel. So "Mandarin" Han ordered the duck gruel. The servants, however, were visibly ill at ease. It so happened that the "Mandarin's" buffalo boy, Ty, had taken the whole pot of gruel—nobody knew just when—and run away with it to his lodging. For he had heard that his father and brother were dying from hunger.

The province chief appeared sympathetic enough and smacked his thigh, smiling. "It's all right, as long as he took it back so his father could eat it."

At this point, I forgot about the other official guests, abandoned the feast, and ran over to Ty's lodging. When I arrived I saw him crying and wailing and calling out to "heaven."

"Why don't you feed him?" I asked.

"Sir, both my father and my brother just shut their mouths tight and won't eat."

I snatched the pot of gruel away from him, measured out a spoonful, and tried to persuade his father: "Please eat a little so you can gain back your strength."

The dying man shook his head. "Please, sir, spare us. Please let us die. Oh, what suffering! Now finally we will be able to die!"

I felt terribly disconcerted. But, pretending to keep my composure, I shook my head slightly and gave the pot of gruel and the spoon back to Ty.

Chapter 7 All inhuman

After receiving the summons from the provincial administrative headquarters to attend the meeting of the Relief Council, I took my umbrella and started out on foot early in the morning. In normal times the interprovince road was quite congested. Rickshas, motorcars, and people moved in unending streams. Now there were very few vehicles because there were fewer people using them and because the ricksha runners were mostly dead.

As I was occupying my mind with stray thoughts in order to kill time, from behind me there came the sound of a ricksha approaching and of a man calling out. I turned round and saw my friend Tam, a landowner, sitting in a ricksha with a Singer sewing machine.

Tam motioned to me. "Please come and get in. Are you on your way to the Relief Council meeting?"

"Yes. Where are you taking your sewing machine?"

"I am bringing it to the provincial capital to sell it to one of the board directors,* hoping that I can get ten more cans of rice for the relief program."

The ricksha stopped, and as the runner held firmly to the pull bars, I quietly stepped up to sit snugly beside Tam. The runner inclined his body forward to gain momentum. After having run

---

* In 1802, at the beginning of the Nguyen dynasty, the traditional system of court-appointed administrative "boards" (*bo*) was modified slightly to comprise the "Six Boards" of Finance, War, Rites, Appointments, Justice, and Public Works, each of which was headed by a "board director" (*thuong thu*). Since theoretically Tonkin was a French "protectorate," the same positions and the same nomenclature were maintained even after the French takeover, though the "board directors" were obliged to serve French interests.

about ten paces, he straightened his body, held the bars loosely in his hands, and ran swiftly along the stony road.

On the road we came across numerous hungry people and a few corpses, but nobody was paying any attention to them anymore. It took a really extraordinary case to stir people's hearts a bit.

Passing the corpse of a big strong man sprawled out on the roadside, Tam sighed, "It is so discouraging to think that a person of such fine build should have his hands tied up."*

As for myself, I had other feelings. Those who were half-alive and half-dead moved me the most. I was moved, too, on seeing a young girl digging for crabgrass nodules at the foot of an arjun tree. I thought that if one were reduced to digging for those scraggly weeds, then what else must there be left to eat! The mechanical, hopeless gestures of the hungry made my heart sad and imprinted the images of these people in my mind forever.

Every time someone reached out a hand to beg, Tam had the ricksha stop so he could give the person a dime. A ricksha that carried two persons and a machine was both heavy and bulky and so was difficult to pull. Each time it had to stop and let Tam get down and up again, it was very hard on the runner, but he at no time showed dissatisfaction. On the other hand, he was himself very sympathetic toward the hungry, and every time Tam would give something to one of them, the ricksha man, as if sharing in the enthusiasm, cheered up and tried to run all the faster.

I thought to myself: the ricksha hirer, the hitchhiker, and the runner—each with his own psychological outlook. How confusing!

The Relief Council meeting dragged on from morning until

* A Vietnamese expression that means being completely helpless.

noon. In the afternoon it met again from 3:00 until 5:30. Tam and I were to go to a certain inn to spend the night, before returning home the next morning.

The inns were more crowded than usual because there were so many officials, coming from all twelve districts to attend the relief meeting.

On the sidewalks outside the inns sat many hungry people waiting for handouts. Looking at their eyes one could see that they were as deep as the holes in the game of coin pitching.

Inside our inn, having exhausted all the old and new tales from hither and yon, we came back to the story of the starvation and of the interprovincial relief program.

Tam sat at the head of the table as quiet and solemn as an assembly chairman. Now and again he would nod his head as if to encourage a good idea. He sat there for about an hour and then suddenly stood up and, as he spoke, tapped the table lightly to emphasize every word: "People have been dying for several months already, but not until now has there been a relief meeting. It's really disgraceful!"

As he finished saying this, he stepped out the door and drew some money from his pockets to give to the hungry. The owner of the inn waited until Tam had come back in and then quickly asked his helpers to close the place for the night.

"In a little while," said the innkeeper, "they will be dragging their way here by the hundreds. It is so heartbreaking to watch them, but where could we get the resources to give them?"

Because we were not used to the place, that whole night Tam and I were unable to get to sleep. The next morning we got up early and went home. People were still sleeping, and there were only a handful of houses with open doors. On the streets there were only the municipal oxcarts rolling along in the process of collecting corpses. On one cart we saw that there were from five to seven corpses piled in a disorderly way on top of each other. The mat cover exposed pairs of legs that looked like dried and withered branches and also heads with straggly, tangled hair, like dry grass.

I asked one of the coolies, "How many corpses do you bury in a single morning?"

"There's no telling. From fifteen to thirty. But for the last few days the average has been about thirty. A lot of people have come up from the countryside."

"Look," Tam cut the coolie short. "That corpse down below there is moving its legs still!"

"No," replied the coolie, "it's the cart that is shaking. Anyway, even if there were somebody still moving, by the time we get to the graveyard, he will be completely dead. If we leave him behind, then for sure we'd just have to pick him up again the next morning. It's all the same."

This mater-of-fact reasoning surprised me. But Tam, not as hesitant as I, told the coolie with a determined voice, "It is a sin to bury people who are still alive. What makes you think there might not be somebody who would save them between now and nightfall?"

The coolie did not choose to answer. He beat the ox on the back with his rod, and the cart moved off quickly in the direction of the graveyard.

On the road home I said to Tam, "You are a really humane person."

"No!" replied Tam in the same voice he had used in speaking to the coolie a few minutes before. "I, too, am inhuman. I only give what I have in excess. I still have forty *mau* of paddy fields down by the coast, ten *mau* of paddy at home, and one *mau* of dry field land. If I sold it all and divided it up to the hungry, then nobody in my village would starve to death. But I would never go ahead and do a thing like that. That means I regard fields and land more highly than I do human lives. Just what sort of values, of human benevolence and kindness, do you imagine could be left in this soul of mine? All of us are inhuman, you see!"

Chapter 8 The meat that fell into the mouth of a tiger

The village council chairman was the son of the former village chief administrator, Hai, the grandson of a former canton chief, and the great-grandson of a sergeant of the imperial guards. The village council chairman had two sons. One had passed his baccalaureate first degree; the other was in his fourth year in Albert Sarraut High School.* The chairman's lineage had for generations been of superior standing in the village, and the members of the clan were all so famous for their wealth that their clan and personal names were known to everybody in the district.

The village council chairman was related to "Mandarin" Han Tinh by marriage: Han's daughter was married to the chairman's eldest son.

Since 1944 the chairman's sons had had to stop their studies temporarily and had gone back to the countryside to avoid the bombing. The eldest son, because of his wide circle of acquaintances, understood something of the activities of the *Viet Minh* and of the various *Quoc-gia* [Nationalist] parties. The chairman secretly let his eldest son enter the *Viet Minh* Party so as to protect the family. Meanwhile, the second son was working alongside Han Tinh's sons in various Nationalist movements, likewise to help make it easier for the family to adjust to changing conditions. The village council chairman and Han Tinh were quite satisfied with their plan, since they had their own people in every party. There were people with the French, the Japanese,

* A high school in Hanoi, named for a French Governor-General of Indochina, 1911–1914, and again 1917–1919.

the *Viet Minh*, and the Nationalist parties. There was no reason to fear!

The two gentlemen were on good terms with each other. Each was allied with the other in the consolidation of their "upward movement" positions, which their children would inherit.

During the Bac Ky [Tonkin] electoral campaign for representatives, when Han Tinh was elected [to the so-called "Council of Representatives" in Hanoi], the village council chairman at the same time gained a new foothold as a member of the provincial council. So they were both representatives. When the French collected rice, Mr. Han Tinh was given the responsibility of seeing that it was collected in his district. When the province organized its Relief Council, it was Mr. Han who was appointed as its chairman.

He was so busy collecting rice and money for the government that the relief business lagged behind. But it was better to let it lag behind than never to have it done at all. Finally, however, the Relief Council did start to function. That is to say, its officers collected an enormous amount of rice and money, albeit they gave out very little of it to the hungry—the rest going into their own and their children's pockets.

The eldest baccalaureate-holding son of the village council chairman, on hearing of the establishment of a provincial Relief Committee,* immediately founded a "ghost" village relief committee. And in the name of this "relief committee" he went to his father-in-law's house and got two tons of paddy rice "to give out to the population." But the people did not get even one grain of it. The baccalaureate-holding son gave the *Viet Minh* a part of the rice in order to buy them off. Another part was given to the village council chairman's household workers, and the last and

* In Vietnamese, *quy cuu te* (relief committee), presumably an outgrowth of meetings of the more widely based "relief councils" (*hoi dong cuu te*), as mentioned in Chapter 7.

greatest part he kept for himself. Causing a considerable disturbance, he transported the rice back to his own hamlet without making any attempt whatever to hide it from anyone's view. The people all knew about this but were all as tight-lipped as an oyster about it. If anyone should speak up, he would only invite trouble for himself. This eldest baccalaureate-holding son had a very hot temper.

Someone related this account to Ca Luong, and he only smiled stiffly. "The meat has already fallen into the hungry tiger's mouth, so how can anyone get it out again?"

Chapter 9 A father who abandoned his children

Although in normal times the Vuoc family was poor, they had always been comfortable. The husband and wife were around thirty years old, but they already had six children. Mr. Vuoc was strong, hardworking, and skillful at plowing, harvesting, and all the other farm activities. He was never known to miss a single day's work the year round. Mrs. Vuoc, too, was intelligent and hardworking, and whenever she went to the labor market, people wanted to hire her. Both husband and wife worked all day, while the household chores were left to the care of the eldest daughter, Suong. Suong had to look after her younger brothers and sisters, sweep the house, cook the meals, wash the dishes, and do all the other chores given to her by her parents. She worked very hard and never complained. Perhaps she did not consider her own life to be as hard as other people might think. She took it as a matter of course and continued innocently to lead her life of hardship.

When harvest times came round, they tended to be joyful days for the other children. They would roam all day in the fields picking lotuses, catching grasshoppers, watching people harvesting, listening to people singing, and so on, and in the evening, tired of rolling about in the soft and fragrant hay, they would go out to the river to swim and play. At night they would watch people threshing and grinding the rice under the moonlight. They were very happy. But Suong had never tasted that happy kind of life. At harvest times she would be seen carrying a water pipe and a piece of punk around the fields, greeting the harvest overseers and inviting them to have a smoke. They would then give her permission to go down into the fields to gather up the leftover grains. Whatever she could glean she would take home, husk it, and dry it, so that her mother could then sell it to buy material for her clothes.

The Vuocs loved their children very much. Every evening when Mrs. Vuoc came back from work she would lead her three daughters to the edge of the pond for a bath, while Mr. Vuoc would take their sons out to the river to teach them to swim and dive. The Vuoc children, before going to bed, were always given a bowl of cold rice with some sesame seeds or a small eggplant. They felt that their lives were easy.

Living in the country as they did, the Vuocs were accustomed to getting up very early to go to the rural labor market and stand there waiting for people to hire them as field laborers. Anyone who wanted to hire laborers also had to get up by at least the start of the "fifth watch"* and go down to the market to hire them. People shone their [kerosene] lamps on the laborers, examining them one by one, and when they came across someone who looked as if he would be a strong and steady worker, they would bargain for the price of hiring him. After the price was agreed upon, the laborer followed his employer home. After eating, each would be assigned to his job. By then the sun would be up. When the sun was overhead, the employer and the laborers would have their lunch. Then after resting for about an hour, they would start work again. In the evening, the employer would pay them their wage and give them an extra bowl of rice.

* About 4:00 A.M.

After the flood of the ninth month in the year of the monkey [1944], the Vuocs realized that famine was unavoidable, so the husband conferred with his wife: "From now on, if anybody hires us out to work, early in the morning we should have a light meal first before leaving home, so that in the evening we can bring back two bowls of rice instead of just one, saving the extra bowl for when the famine comes."

Before, Mr. Vuoc had seldom had to go down to the labor market. Since people knew that he was a good worker, they competed with each other in hiring him and would even go to his house to tell him the night before that he was hired for the next day. When the tenth month of the year of the monkey came, the husband and wife went out together to the market very early every morning, but they usually had to come home, shouldering their hoes and sickles, without any work. The eleventh and twelfth month passed, and there were many of the village inhabitants who died, but the Vuoc family was still intact.

In the early part of the year of the chicken [1945], the Vuocs lost their youngest daughter, who was two years old. The couple's grief seemed to cut them to the heart. Several days later, they lost another child. The boy was already five, and the husband and wife had loved him and cared for him most of all, but his body had just become too weak. After months of eating things that were fit only for the stomachs of pigs, like banana roots cooked with rice bran, he could survive no longer. Even though the death of his son had relieved the Vuoc family of a mouth to feed, by this time all the food they had stocked had been entirely used up. Even rice mould would die if it had to live on banana roots and pennywort all the time.

Whenever they could get a handful of rice, the Vuocs had to divide it into five or six portions, which was not enough to give each member of the family a mouthful.

The husband realized that, if such a situation continued, in only a few days he would have to follow his children into the grave. He said to his wife, "If we keep on dividing the food this way, we will all die, first of all myself. We will have to leave the four children to their fates. They will have to try to find food for themselves. Both of us are still young and strong, and even if heaven should cause them to die, after this famine is over, if we are still alive, we can still give birth."

Mrs. Vuoc shook her head and covered her face with her hands, crying. Looking at his wife, her hair tangled like a raven's nest and her legs exposed through the tattered, threadbare skirt that had been patched so many dozens of times, he wanted to cry, too, and take his chance with death.

But he gathered up his courage and tried to comfort her. "Of course, there is no one who does not love his children, after all the things gone through in bringing them into the world. But our family's situation right now is exactly like being in a rotted-out bamboo boat that meets with a big storm in the middle of a great river. If we try to save everybody, then all of us will surely die. If I should die, then you too will die, not to mention the children. If we insist on holding on to them, then we are all holding on to death."

Mrs. Vuoc was silent. From that day on, the couple ate alone and no longer divided the food up for the children.

The children, being so hungry, would charge in on their parents' table whenever the latter sat down to eat and would grab at the food. Mr. Vuoc would beat them off and drive them out into the streets, allowing them to come back only at night to sleep. Sometimes they would return home after having roamed around the village, so hungry and tired they could walk no further. However, even then, if there was any food around the house, their father would, to their dismay, have to tie them up at the house posts lest they cause any trouble.

About ten days later, Mr. Vuoc noticed that his daughter

Suong had not come home to sleep. He was, needless to say, worried about the fate of this girl who had had it so hard all her life. The next morning Mrs. Vuoc got up early and, as she stepped out of the house, screamed and cried out loudly. Her eldest daughter had fallen dead at the foot of the guava tree in front of the house. Mr. Vuoc saw his wife crying, then silently shouldered his hoe, and carried his daughter to her burial.

Several days later, two more children came back late at night and, with their arms wrapped tightly around each other, died on the front steps of the house. There was yet another daughter, but nobody knew where or when she died.

Chapter 10 Those who died early

Paddy fields need manure. Whether one grows melons, tobacco, or rice, one needs manure. For every *mau* of paddy field, the average yearly manure consumption is from fifteen to twenty loads. In a year's time, each village uses from several thousand to several tens of thousands of loads of manure. At the market price in 1943, each load of manure cost three piasters on the average.

Collecting excrement [primarily human excrement] had become a profitable industry in the countryside and required of the collectors just three things: the first was good health; the second was membership in a family that had traditionally collected excrement or belonged to an excrement-collecting guild; and the third was enough money to buy baskets, carrying poles, and a rake. The countryside was divided up into different "mining" regions. Each region corresponded to a specific guild that had the exclusive right to exploit it. Members of a guild could not go beyond the boundaries decided upon or trespass into areas that belonged to other guilds. Anybody who went against this arrangement would be severely punished in various ways (including the use of force) by excrement collectors in the other guilds. Yet if a certain guild could recruit several members who had "an excess of brains and courage" and could successfully extend the guild's boundaries, then the rest of the guild would all share in the benefits. This situation, however, seldom came about, and the world of the excrement collectors was usually peaceful. Early in the morning they would go out with their baskets and their rakes, collecting excrement left on the roads or the borders of the fields. With very unconcerned faces they would stand waiting alongside people who were doing their necessary business, and any dog who carelessly ran up to rob them of their goods would get a severe beating.

They would be finished with their collecting by about eight or nine o'clock. They gathered at the manure market each with a full, heavy load. There were always many customers.

The skin of the excrement collectors was usually pale or sickly yellow. It was said that if people in that profession did not eat and drink a lot, they would not be able to stand it. Since it was very easy to make money in this profession, the only people besides the rich men in the village who dared to spend money on drinking and gambling were the excrement collectors.

During the starvation period, however, nobody bought excrement anymore. Also, excrement for manure was becoming scarce because a lot of people had died; those who were still living had to cut down on their meals, or else, by consuming all manner of things as they did, they excreted a kind of green and runny substance that could not be collected for use as fertilizer.

Thus the manure collectors were all out of work. Because their bodies had been steeped for so long in the vapor of excrement and because they had been accustomed to eating their fill, the starvation fell on them hardest of all.

In my village, Mr. Phi was the one who fell first of all. The news quickly got about and spread terror among the poor.

I went to visit Phi's family one morning. The road was without any sign of life, the fields and paddies uninhabited. Trees, villages— all were drowned in the rain and the mud. There was so much mud that, even when I gripped my toes on the road, I could not feel hard ground. I thought of Phi as I walked along. Phi had tried to sell his house and his land, but nobody would buy it. Neither would anyone hire his wife or give jobs to his children. How shamed and angry he must have felt!

Phi lived in a thatched house with three rooms. When I arrived, I saw in the middle of the house four pieces of brick piled up over a bed of ashes. Next to them was a plank bed and above it was a bamboo bed covered with hay. There were three naked children lying on the plank bed, staring at me.

"Where is your father?" I asked.

One of the children pointed at the bamboo bed, "In that pile of hay. He died last night. Last night at the time when it rained and blew so hard, my father screamed a few times and then fell down, breathing heavily. When it was nearly morning, he went crazy and scratched his face open with his hands and then died. . . . We are very hungry, sir!"

"Where is your mother?"

"She is out asking for money to buy a mat to bury my father. There she is."

I turned around and looked out into the yard. Mrs. Phi staggered into the house. When I looked at her I became even more choked with tears. On the upper part of her body she had a piece of tattered matting wrapped about her; on the lower part she had on a worn-out skirt that must have been patched a hundred times. Mrs. Phi did not have enough strength or spirit left to think about her own nakedness. What was there left to be vigilant or bashful about? Nobody would bother to pay attention to a body that was not even comparable to the body of a dog. One could sell almost anything. But in her case, if she were for sale, people would not only have refused to buy her, but they would not even have taken her for free.

Mrs. Phi seemed to understand my thoughts. She cried out loud. And her brood of children cried, too. Their emaciated skeletons shook in rhythm with their moanings. I gave her three piasters and told her that in the evening when I came by, I would give her some bowls of rice.

I went home with a dark thought. In the village there were about fifty excrement collectors. Each family was composed on the average of four persons. The total number of people living by that profession was about 200 persons. All of them would die. . . .

[Chapter Eleven, here omitted, deals with various makeshift ways in which people tried to make the most of their insufficient diet in the hope of surviving the starvation period. Much of the chapter is little more than an enumeration of various edible greens, roots, and so on, along with special ways of preparing them, which does not lend itself to English translation without lengthy explanatory notes.]

Chapter 12 They only wanted to die . . . yet are still alive
The, one of the village patrolmen, and his wife had a special way of raising their children. Both boys and girls, on reaching the age of nine or ten, were ordered by their parents to go out and collect buffalo manure. At night it was up to them to find a place to rest their backs and sleep, for they were not allowed to come home. They would usually go to the tops of some of the brick tombs to spend the night. The sun, the rain, the dew, the wind, desolation, and darkness—none of these meant a thing to them.

But despite the fact that they led such a miserable life, the children also knew how to sing, to play, to think, and to judge a situation.

While the grown-ups did not know what to do to avoid starvation, two of the The children, one aged fourteen and the other eleven, displayed extraordinary resourcefulness.

The elder advised the younger, "The secret of begging is not to return only to those houses that give you things easily; you should not shy away from certain houses just because they throw insults at you. You must always be polite, smile when you should smile, and cry when you are supposed to cry. I will take you from one place to another, house to house. We'll play the game of 'circling the basket.'* Surely we'll manage to live."

Before going into a house to beg, they always sought out the children in the family to talk, joke, and sing with them. When they met the grown-ups, they introduced themselves and told their stories, "We pray you, sirs and madams, we are the children of patrolman The. During the day we have to collect buffalo manure, and at night we are driven by our parents out into the graveyards to sleep. Truly we are very hungry and cold. At night it is often as if somebody were pouring a can of cold water on our backs. We often wish that we could get a stomachache and die. Why is it that it is so easy for other people to die but not for us? Please give us a bit of rice. This is the first time, and it will also be the last time, we dare to come to your door to beg. . . ."

The two children kept their promise. All through the starvation period they came to my house only a few times. When the *chiem* harvest came, I was surprised to see them come back to visit me and play with my children.

* That is, make calculated rounds, not going to the same place twice within a short period.

The and his wife died during the starvation, and their children inherited their property, so they no longer had to sleep in the graveyards. The eldest took up his father's profession as an excrement collector.* From then on they lived a comfortable life.

Chapter 13 A dog that died . . . of starvation

I had a black dog whose hair was long and smooth, who had lustrous eyes, and who had a tail that looked like a reed blossom. Whenever I returned home, he greeted me happily, wagging his tail. When I slept, he used to lie under my bed to see to it that I had my sleep. Sometimes I got angry and beat him. His ears would droop down, and he would look at me trembling, as if asking for pardon. When my anger calmed down, he would then come slowly to my side, perceptibly happy. He was a faithful and lovable dog.

When the famine came, I felt that since there was not enough rice for people to eat, I dared not let the dog eat rice anymore. Once every day I called the dog into the room and let him eat a bowl of manioc gruel. I was afraid that if I let him eat outside, some hungry people might see and it would be too distressing for them.

After a little while my conscience again gnawed at me; the kind of gruel that I was letting the dog eat could be used to keep a man alive. What is more important than a human life?

I did not let the dog eat gruel anymore after that. I gave him the worst kind of rice bran with rice husk mixed in with it, and this was cooked with sweet potato vines. One day a patrolman

* The fact that Mr. The (the father) had been a patrolman did not mean that this was his principal or full-time occupation. Those whom the village council designated as "patrolmen" (*tuan*) did not receive regular salaries and had only part-time emergency duties, much in the same way as the volunteer firemen do in some parts of the United States and elsewhere.

came to my house to beg for food, and when he saw the bowl
of food for the dog, he picked up the potato vines and stuffed
them in his mouth, chewing with relish. After I gave him a bowl
of rice, the patrolman insisted on a little bran. My small child
ran off to get the bran, and he dropped a little bit of it on the
ground. The patrolman picked the bran up with his finger and,
along with it, some of the mud from the ground and put it into
his mouth. From that day on, I did not let the dog eat. Three
days later he was lying dead in a banana grove.

**Chapter 14 The hunger under heaven comes from the god of
agriculture**
It was about five kilometers from my house to the beach, an
area of fertile new hamlets. Most of the landlords came from
other districts, and the population consisted mainly of tenant
farmers. In the year of the monkey [1944], because of the flood,
the whole area suffered crop failures. The scenes of people
dying were beyond description.

One day at the beginning of the year of the chicken [1945], I
went to see Mr. Nhang, a relative in the coastal area.

Each bit of the road was a scene of tragedy. Houses, villages,
fields, rivers, roads, and bridges—all bore the mark of desolation.
Areas that a few months before had been bustling with the noise
of people working and trading were now empty and despoiled.

A number of rich people locked their gates tightly so that they
could lead a sheltered life. Some were afraid of thieves and
robbers, but there were those who had a higher regard for their
property than for human lives. They covered their ears, shut
their eyes, and did not care to know about anybody else at all. It
was none of their business whether other people survived or
died.

The poor had torn down their houses and had burned the

wood and straw to warm themselves and had sold whatever they could in order to get a bowl of rice or gruel.

At one place a group of houses could be seen with only their smoke-tinged earthen walls remaining, at another place a few partly burned pillars lying in the open. At still another place there were a few partially destroyed thatched roofs and a few bare foundations filled with grass, rubbish, and ashes.

On the vast paddy fields there were no people working.

When I passed the Dau-Phuong market, I saw a number of people—men, women, and young girls—who were still breathing lightly, rolled up in mats and lying on the side of the road. They were waiting for death and hoped that by lying there they would be seen by some kindhearted person who would bury them.

After walking another segment of the road, I arrived at the bank of the Tra River. The waves that gracefully rolled in and out carried two skulls onto the stone landing. Near the river there was a hut. I was told that in that hut there had been two sisters picking lice off each other. The ferryman told me: "They were just sitting there, and they died before they knew what had happened!"

On the other side of the ferry crossing was Duc Thinh village. The temple for the worship of Nguyen Cong Tru* was completely covered with moss. The village communal house was empty and stared blankly out at the river. The patches of grass on both sides of the road were sunk deep in the mud because of the months-long rain. I turned up a patch of grass with my feet. The upper part was a little green still, but the rest was already yellow and nearly all withered.

The rain became thicker and heavier. The sea wind blew the rain as if pouring it over my body and face. Leaning forward, I

* A famous general under Emperor Minh-mang (1820–1840).

plodded along, my right hand holding tightly to my umbrella and my left hand clutching my clothes to keep them out of the mud and to lessen the pull of the wind. Along a winding road of about a kilometer in length there was not a single human soul or a human voice.

It took a long time to get to Mr. Nhang's house. He had a wife and two children. He still had an aged father, a Confucian scholar who was about eighty years old that year. Mr. Nhang held senior status in the village. He knew both Chinese and *quoc ngu*. His property consisted of a buffalo and a few *mau* of paddy fields.

After the flood there was still a large basket of rice left in Mr. Nhang's house that should have been more than enough for his family's consumption until the seasonal harvest. But he did not calculate the situation correctly, and when he saw that people were selling their paddy fields cheaply, he became overly committed to getting rich. He exchanged most of his rice for fields, and only afterward did he realize that he had been foolish. Those who sold their fields had rice to eat, but Nhang's family, even though it had more land, now found itself in a very hard situation.

After greeting me, Nhang, without prompting, launched into a lengthy monologue: "Sir, down here we have more than a thousand field laborers, and if the whole population is included, there are about three to four thousand people; but there are only a few families that have rice. Even if they took all their rice to give as charity to the population, each person would still, if lucky, have only a few meals and then would starve just the same. Unbelievable hunger! People eat all kinds of edible roots. At first, they take the roots home, eat the bulbs, and plant the stems. But after a few days they become so hungry that they pull the stems up again and eat them, too. That is really 'tearing things up by the roots.'

"Now people eat both the bulbs and the stems of the wild irritating taro. They cut the taro into small pieces, dry it, then cook it mixed with some rice. They slice banana roots and boil them; then they pound them and shape them into small balls together with rice. There is less rice than banana roots; moreover, salt is extremely expensive, so people usually have to eat things unsalted. I do not know how they survive.

"Even on this diet they still have to go to work. Their clothes are all in rags or else have all been sold, with the result that they do not have anything left to cover themselves with. So they straighten out hay and use banana ropes to tie around their bodies. Over that they wear a worn-out mat, making a hole in the middle of it, putting their heads through it, and tying a banana rope around the waist as a belt. At night they leave it on as it is and crawl into a haystack to sleep.

"It is even harder on the children. They lie all day in the haystacks. Whenever there is a little sunshine they run out in swarms, like bees out of their hives, to beg. There are seven- or eight-month-old babies who are so hungry that their mothers do not know what to do other than to give them pieces of brick to suck on.

"During the day it is quiet in the hamlets and the villages, but when night comes, especially late at night, the hungry cannot sleep. So they shout at each other or fight with each other noisily. It is so cold that they have to pull down their houses bit by bit to burn in order to warm themselves. They burn everything except a small corner in which husband, wife, and children cluster.

"The most tragic is the situation of Hamlet Chief* Ban. His

* In Vietnamese, *truong ap*, chief administrative officer of the hamlet (*ap*), appointed by the "village council."

whole family died of starvation, and nobody knew about it. It was only long afterward that someone who passed by their house noticed the fetid smell and became suspicious. So he went inside to see, and a horrible scene was displayed before his eyes: Hamlet Chief Ban, his wife, and their child, who was three years old, had been gnawed to pieces by rats, and their insides strewn all over the floor."

At this, Mr. Nhang stopped for a second, rubbed his face, and then continued, "That's someone else's situation, but we don't know what's going to happen to us either. My wife's going to give birth to a child at the end of the month. If I cannot find a few cans of rice, then we will all die. Now I'm sitting here with you, but there is no knowing whether we'll ever meet each other again, and there also is no knowing what will become of us, you and me!

"Time may bring changes, but if things keep on this way, then it is an extremely dangerous situation! It is so heartbreaking, you know. We know that it will result in death and that the dead will be piled up like mountains, but there is nothing we can do about it. How frightening, how terrible! Whenever I think about it, my very guts and liver are jarred loose, and I get dizzy and unsure of my senses.

"My father, who is now over eighty years of age, also told me that there has never been a time when there was so much suffering as now. Perhaps in all the time from Ban-co* up to the present, this is the only suffering of its kind. In the Oracles† it says: 'After *ngo* [the year of the horse, that is, 1942] one will come to *mui* [the year of the goat, 1943], and then one will know

* Chinese equivalent to the biblical Adam.
† *Sam*, a collection of prophecies, written in verse and attributed to the famous writer Trang Trinh (1491–1587).

of *than* [the year of the monkey, 1944. As the word *than* also means fate or doom, this is an obvious *double entendre*].'

"Yes, we know our fate all right [in reference to the tragedies of the year of the monkey]! But now it is already the year of *dau* [the year of the chicken, 1945], and why are we still so miserable? It is really true: 'The hunger under heaven comes from the god of agriculture.' Only now do I understand the whole meaning of that saying."

A few days after I had come back from Duc Thinh, Mr. Nhang came to call on me. I asked my housekeeper to cook him two bowls of rice. But Mr. Nhang insisted, "Please give me three bowls."

Three bowls of rice meant about one kilogram, and when cooked it filled a two-person rice pot. Mr. Nhang cleaned up the whole pot, and after eating he sat there smoking, drinking some water, and talking with me, "People say that the French collect the rice to make us die of starvation. But I think the bureaucrats and dishonest merchants are also siding with the French in order to kill people off and take over their property. Also, it seems as if heaven, too, wants to harm our people. It is really true, for besides the famine, it is also extremely cold, colder than any other year. It is so cold and so damp that even animals cannot stand it. Even the strongest buffaloes now die easily. Though they may be eating and working normally, at night they cough a few times, then die. A peasant who has a buffalo can find work now and then and can also borrow. The whole family depends on it for survival. But once the buffalo dies, sooner or later the owners will die too. It is really true that, no sooner does one misfortune end, that it is followed by another. I think that only death can bring an end to it all."

Mr. Nhang let his arms drop loosely to his sides, his eyes fixed on nothing. His face became paler. After a moment of silence, without waiting for me to ask, he continued, "My buffalo has already died, you know; and perhaps this is the last time I shall be here to visit you."

The conversation had become so utterly tragic and we felt so exhausted that we put out the light and went to sleep.

The next morning Mr. Nhang had a heavy meal, then said good-bye and left for home.

Less than a week later Mrs. Nhang brought her children with her and came to stay at the midwife's place in my village. When she saw me, she begged, "Please, sir, help us. Otherwise, we will all be dead. My father-in-law died yesterday. My husband also will come up tonight."

Looking at Mrs. Nhang, I was moved but answered mechanically, "I will give you a can of rice to save until you give birth to the child. Now please bring along your children to my house to have dinner with us."

Mrs. Nhang came to my house with her children, and they all had their fill. When they went away, I gave her some potatoes so she could boil them for her husband that evening.

That night, Mr. Nhang came to see his wife and children but did not stop by my house. The next morning he went back again to Duc Thinh. A few days later I heard that he had died.

It was a pitiful story from beginning to end. Mrs. Nhang and her children were supposed to have taken the potatoes back to boil them for Mr. Nhang. It was a whole potful. The potatoes had already been cooked for a long time and Mrs. Nhang had waited and waited, but when her husband did not arrive, she opened the lid and tasted a potato. It was so good that she tried another. Her children imitated her, each one eating one of the potatoes. Mrs. Nhang's mother followed suit. When they had finished the pot, Mr. Nhang finally stumbled in from the gate, tired and hungry. When he found the pot was empty, he broke

out in a sweat, as if in a steam bath. He asked, "If you have anything left, please give me a bit."

The children looked at their grandmother and their mother
in bewilderment. The old woman silently went to bed. The two
children went along with her. Mrs. Nhang fondled the pot, tears
welling up out of control.

That night Mr. Nhang, very hungry, was not able to sleep, so he
went out into the garden and picked a ripe young eggplant to eat.
Next morning he said good-bye to his mother-in-law, his wife,
and his children and left for his hamlet directly. Mrs. Nhang
had tried to hold him back so she could beg for some food from
her relatives. But he had made up his mind and did not listen to
her.

Chapter 15 The humanitarian way
The famine had been going on for several months. I felt that
there was no other way of consoling the hungry than to pay them
a visit. Bringing along a few piasters or a handful of rice, I went
out into the rain and the northern wind.

First, I went to the Sinhs' house. Mr. Sinh himself had been
dead since the first month of the year of *than* [1944], leaving
behind a widow and three children, aged seven, ten, and twelve.

When I got near the Sinhs' place, which stood among fields
of paddy rice, I saw pale green smoke rising from under the
thatched roof. I felt relieved. If they were still cooking, then
they must have something left to eat still.

When I entered the house, I saw that Mrs. Sinh, her face
purplish-pale, was pounding some unripened rice in a stone
mortar that normally one would use for crabs and snails. One of
her children was boiling a pot of marsh pennywort. Another was
gathering things for the fire. When he saw me coming into the
house he ran after me, clutching an armful of twigs. The youn-

gest child, who was lying in a haystack, extended his hand out now and then to grasp a handful of the unripened rice [from the stalks] and put it in his mouth, chewing ecstatically like a child eating sweets.

When I handed Mrs. Sinh a piaster, she placed her hands together, bowed, and thanked me. I thought to myself: What good was a piaster, when a can of paddy rice was selling for 60 piasters?

After I left the Sinhs' house, I went to the Huus'. When I entered the house, the father and children were sitting around a dying fire. When they say me, they all stood up. The father asked the children to fetch the water pipe, and the elder brother asked the younger to get a mat.

I waited a few seconds, and when I did not see the pipe or the mat forthcoming, I leaned back against the bar of an old wooden bed and began to talk. "How many children do you have?" I asked.

"My wife died last year," Mr. Huu replied. "We are in mourning, you see. When the new year came, we could not do anything anymore. My two daughters used to be able to sell a little candy and food, and so we could earn a little that way. But for some time now, robbers and thieves have been as thick as sea worms. So one day when they took their goods to the market, it was all stolen. Thus we lost our capital, and now we have to stay at home hungry. I have five grown sons. We have always led an honest life and never had any sort of bad reputation in the village. But now, you see, we've become all hemmed in like this. We used to have a few patches of 'communal land' but had to dispose of them all. We have already eaten everything clean, so there is not a single grain of rice left in the house. We just don't know when we will die."

"Sir," one of the sons cut his father short, "the poor people are becoming more and more miserable because of the robbing and stealing from one another. Many families will starve because of this. For example, we planted a patch of potatoes, and the whole family was relying on it for our survival. We tried to guard it day and night, but even so people dug the potatoes up and ate them before they were ripe. Of that whole bed of potatoes we have only one small basket left, plus a few bundles of vines."

As he finished talking, he glanced over at the basket of potatoes on the bed and the few bundles of vines in the corner of the room.

The five sons just stood there with their hands on their hips and bitter expressions on their faces.

The powerlessness of these five sons in their prime and the hopelessness of an old father who could no longer fall back on his children for support made my heart contract.

After taking leave of Mr. Huu, I went to visit a succession of other families: the Ty family, husband and wife and eight children, of whom five had died; the Lai family, husband and wife and four naked children; the Duong family, a mother and two children; the Len family, husband and wife and three children; the Bang family; the Khon family; the Tai family; and so on. Most of their houses had lost their roofs and had only small fires or piles of ashes in the center of the dirt floors along with a few piles of hay.

Lastly, I went to the Chuc family's house, which had been built way back in the time of the Nguyen dynasty. Their thatched house had once been used by the Nguyen to house priests who conducted ancestral worship ceremonies for the clan, and it was still intact. When he saw me coming, Mr. Chuc ran out to meet me. His face was swollen and had a watery look to it, like a person with beriberi. When we entered the house he invited me to sit down on a divan on which an old mat was spread. He placed a water pipe on the divan and then ran out to get some kindling to light me a smoke.

I asked Chuc, "You look very pale. Don't they support you?"

"Sir, the officials did put aside two cans of rice for me, and the members of the clan [that is, the Nguyen imperial lineage] also gave me several piasters. It is very fortunate that our family can stand in the shadows of our ancestors. For a long time we have been used to eating little. We are suffering only because it rains and is damp all the time, and a lot of people have had their skin swell up like this. Sometimes the skin bursts on their legs and arms and faces, and blood runs out."

I was about to get up and leave for home when a voice echoed from inside a darkened room, "Sir, please help us keep alive through these difficult times."

"Who is that?" I asked Chuc.

"That is my brother-in-law and two other people from my native place. They are extremely hungry over in their village, so they came here looking for jobs."

I realized that Chuc had not wanted me to know that he and his wife had to divide their food and share their clothing with those three other persons. Out of compassion for them, Mr. and Mrs. Chuc were sacrificing in a genuine, though modest and quiet way.

Stepping out of Chuc's house, I thought to myself: when rich people give alms, that is considered a kind gesture, but when he who himself is poor and hungry and in a dangerous situation will share his food with other people, that is genuine compassion.

Chapter 16 Heaven is keeping close watch

Even if one had the resources, it was not an easy thing to be charitable. The hungry were numbered in the hundreds and thousands, and whenever they heard that relief was being distributed in a certain place, they would come rushing in to take their share. They stampeded and trampled and fought each other, and finally it was the strong who usually won out, while the weak sometimes were badly hurt or died without ever being able to get anything.

But this tragic scenario [of excess] never occurred throughout the six months of almsgiving at Mr. Ca Luong's house. Here the almsgiving was limited to the village boundaries, and there were set times and regulations.

The villagers who came for alms had to sit and wait according to the order of their family names. Those who bore the family name of Nguyen sat together with other Nguyen, the Pham sat with other Pham, the Do with other Do. There were ten patrolmen to enforce this order. They were absolutely forbidden to insult or to beat those who came to receive the alms. A few of the monitors were allowed to carry young bamboo branches, but these served merely to make a routine impression since, if someone were actually beaten with them, they would easily have broken into two or three pieces.

A list of those coming to receive alms had to be written up in advance. When the time came for giving out alms, whether it was cooked or uncooked rice, I would call the recipients up according to the list. Only those who were called could come up to receive their portions, and they had to leave immediately afterward through the gate. Ca Luong personally measured out the rice for the hungry. Each time alms were given it took the whole morning. Whenever we finished giving out things, our clothes and our bodies would be evenly covered with a layer of eczematous scales from the skins of the hungry, as white as the petals of *mai* flowers. The hungry always had a putrid burned smell that would induce dizziness and nausea in others. The smell of the hungry penetrated the clothes and the very skin of those standing near them. One had to bathe with soap, wash one's clothes, and smoke them before the smell would disappear. Strangely enough, however, when distributing rice to the hungry we were somehow, at the time, quite unable to perceive that putrid smell.

One day, as usual, I was sitting next to Ca Luong as we gave out alms, when Singh's wife, carrying a child piggyback, came up to receive her rice. Her two other children were missing. From the Huu family the sons came, carrying their father and putting him down beside the hedge next to my seat. Mr. Huu's skin had become purple-black, and his legs were swollen as in cases of elephantiasis. From the Bang family, only the wife came to receive aid. Mrs. Bang said to me, "Last night my husband had three stomach spasms, and then his breath left him."

As these pictures of starved people were reappearing in my mind, a young woman ran up close by me and was about to grab a handful of rice. A monitor next to me gently stopped her. The girl was about twenty years of age. Her hair was tangled like a frizzed hairdo left uncombed. Her sharp eyes brightened, and her mouth opened wide, displaying two rows of shiny black teeth* between blood-red lips. The young woman looked at me as if not comprehending why there was all that rice there and yet we did not give any to her, not understanding why the alms-giving here was so quiet and not as chaotic as it was at other places. She was an outsider, and according to the regulations she was not entitled to receive alms, yet in spite of the regulations I took a handful of rice and gave it to her. But what a calamitous miscalculation! As soon as the young woman had her rice, she went into a veritable frenzy. She pushed the monitor to one side,

* Blackened teeth were considered a mark of feminine beauty, at least by a considerable portion of the population. According to P. Huard and M. Durand, *Connaissance du Viet Nam* (Paris: Imprimerie Nationale, 1954), p. 110, as late as 1938, 80 percent of the peasant women still had blackened teeth.

squeezed herself next to the basket of rice, and thrust out her arms with the intention of carrying away the whole thing. Mr. Ca Luong sat quietly as if nothing had happened. Two monitors took her by the arms and gently led her out the gate. At that time a patrolman named Hap, who was a big, well-built man, dashed up and kicked the woman in the stomach. She fell to the ground. Mr. Ca Luong's face became pale, but he kept still. I felt sharp pains inside me and stood up. Luckily, after a while the young woman got up and walked away. We let out long sighs of relief. After the woman had walked about fifty paces, she turned around and looked at us, full of resentment.

After we finished giving out the alms, Mr. Ca Luong told me, "Heaven is keeping very close watch. Mark my word, before long you will see Patrolman Hap die of starvation. He may be hungry, but other people around him are also hungry, and yet he dares to beat them. Then what heaven is going to shelter him?"

Several days later, a Mr. Do in our hamlet also gave out rice gruel. Mr. Ca Luong and I were invited to direct it. Mr. Do was aware that he was unable to do it himself. We distributed the gruel at the gate of the hamlet. The hungry people sat inside the gate. A few huge pots were placed nearby. The hungry people, one by one, came up to receive a bowl of gruel apiece. Just as the last of the gruel was given out, the last of the hungry people finally had his share.

Mr. Ca Luong smiled and said to me, "See how closely I calculated it!"

I secretly envied Mr. Ca Luong for his ability always to think and work in a methodical way.

As we turned our backs and walked away, after about fifteen steps, we heard people crying and yelling, back where the pots were. When we looked back, we saw dozens of people sticking their heads into these pots, elbowing one another, climbing over one another. Those who had their heads inside were being pressed against the rims by the rest and could not have pulled their heads out again if they had wanted to. No sooner had some of the patrolmen successfully pulled one person out than two or three others squeezed in. Patrolman Hap became aroused and broke off a mature bamboo branch, which he swung heavily into the crowd of hungry people.

About a week later, on a rainy and windy morning, my family informed me that the previous night Patrolman Hap had passed by and had fallen dead on the path turning in toward my house.

Chapter 17 A ten-thousand-autumns' remorse

The river Tra flowed from the provincial capital to the village of Dong Nhan, and part of it formed a loop in the shape of a horseshoe. Dong Nhan village was situated right inside this loop like a small island. The sandy land here was extraordinarily fertile and produced famous grapefruit, four-season betel nuts, yellow betel leaves, and the like. Also, because the villagers lived next to the river, they could fish all year round and were thus self-sufficient, even though there was not much land—either private or communal—in the village. Around the bend in the river and southward up to the boundaries of the villages of Binh An and Huu Do, one could see, here and there, the fishing huts that guarded the dip nets belonging to the inhabitants of Dong Nhan and that, seen from afar, looked like small lake houses.

Mr. Kha, the holder of an honorary title of *nhieu*,* and his brother Mr. Ruan, a hamlet chief, had their houses on the riverbank near the home of a certain deceased hamlet chief, to whom both of them had previously been subordinates. Each family had a thatched three-room house with hardwood pillars,

* Bought from the village council and exempting the bearer from *corvée* labor, and miscellaneous village duties.

kitchen, two additions, and front yards between the houses and the river, surrounded by a bamboo fence. It was really as if the two houses were on a single lot, since they were separated only by a thin mulberry hedge.

Besides working together in the rice fields and planting areca-nut trees, grapefruit trees, betel, and tea, the two men had also gotten together to buy a boat that they used in transporting people's goods (for a fee) and for fishing.

Ever since the canton chief had died, his wife, his student son, Mr. Chuyen, and Chuyen's wife were becoming poorer and poorer every day. Thus the families of Mr. Kha and Mr. Ruan could no longer rely on them for special favors, even though they still went back and forth attending to them.

In the years of *than* and *dau* [1944 and 1945] this continuing master-and-servant relationship became closer still. The canton chief's family did not have enough to eat for several months on end. Mrs. Kha was moved by this and would sometimes cut down on her own food intake so that she could bring something over to give to the old widow. And how trying it was, since neither her family nor that of the Hamlet Chief Ruan had anything left themselves, except one meal of bran and one of greens daily. It was considered extremely fortunate if on a certain day they could have a bowl of rice or gruel.

At the end of the first month in the year of *dau*, the student son, Chuyen, was obliged to go back to his mother's native place to ask for help. He was allowed to buy a few dozen cans of paddy rice on credit. On the day he brought the rice home, he asked Mr. Kha and Mr. Ruan over and shared a few baskets with each of them. The situation of the canton chief's family was thus temporarily alleviated. During that period the prices of rice and bran shot up rapidly, worst of all in the coastal area. Chuyen consulted with Mr. Kha about taking four baskets of rice and two baskets of bran down to the coastal area to sell. This suggestion was agreed to by Mrs. Chuyen, Mr. Kha, and the canton chief's widow.

One day at the beginning of the second month of the year of *dau* [1945], Kha and Ruan and the student Chuyen transported the rice to the district of Tien Hai. The boat was away for two days, and then Kha and his brother, Hamlet Chief Ruan, returned. They told the old widow and Chuyen's wife that Chuyen had sold the rice and the bran at a very high price, that he had gone on to his mother's native place to buy more rice so he would not have to make an extra trip, and that he would come back to Dong Nhan in two or three days.

After she had waited for two or three days, the old widow became worried, and she said to her daughter-in-law, "Why don't you go over to the village and see why it is taking him so long?"

She replied, "Madam, it is now too late in the day, and moreover it is raining so hard. Let's wait until tomorrow or the day after. Then I'll beg leave to go."

Still, the old widow's mind was not at ease. She approached her husband's altar, lighted a few incense sticks, and prayed. Then she felt tired and again lay down in a hammock that hung from the house beams, next to the altar. As she dozed off, she imagined she saw her son walk in from outside. His face was swollen, his eyeballs were rolling upward, giving him a frightful appearance, and his clothes were all torn and covered with mud and blood.

"What happened, son!" she asked him.

He did not reply, only opened his eyes wide, and stared at her. She wanted to ask some more, but he had already disappeared. At that point, she woke up. Her son's wife was squatting on the floor by her side, asking, "What kind of nightmare did you have that you cried out so loud?"

"You mean you have been sitting here all this time?"

"I saw that you were dreaming, so I came to wake you."

The old widow, in a quivering voice and with tears streaming down her cheeks, told her daughter-in-law of the vision. The daughter's face became paler and paler. The old widow said, "This dream is an evil omen."

"Madam, since the two gentlemen came back, Mrs. Kha has been very sick. Perhaps she will die. When I went over to see her, she could only cry and could not speak. But I don't think she is starving, since I happened to see her daughter, Thin, washing a big basket of rice by the river. I'm a little suspicious about it all."

The next morning, as the first cock crowed, Chuyen's wife was already trudging through mud on her way to her mother-in-law's native village. When she arrived, she sought out the relatives and asked whether any of them had seen her husband. But none had. Disappointed and sad, she supposed that her husband probably had been harmed. The relatives asked her to remain for dinner, but she chose not to and so returned to Dong Nhan hungry. She dragged herself along like a lost soul and fell several times in the mud. Not until it was already dark did she finally recognize the fishing huts standing alone on the banks of the river. When she got home, she threw herself down and cried. The canton chief's old widow, who had been enduring hardships for a dozen years since the death of her husband, was now no longer able to stand the hard facts around her and more than once sobbed herself to sleep.

The old widow and Mrs. Chuyen were hurt most because Chuyen had not left a son. If Chuyen were dead, the lineage would be ended.

That night Mrs. Chuyen reported to the village chief administrator. The case went up to the province headquarters, and the two brothers, Kha and Hamlet Chief Ruan, were summoned for questioning.

The night that the two gentlemen, Kha and Ruan, had come back from Tien Hai, the children in the two families had already gone to bed. Mr. Kha went to the kitchen to find his wife and told her about everything that had happened.

"From now on our family's survival is guaranteed," he began the convervation, smiling naturally.

"The matter of life and death all depends on the will of heaven. Why are you saying that?"

"Just think, we have five children, brother Ruan has five children, that makes ten in all; with him and his wife, you and me, that makes fourteen persons."

"Who doesn't know that!"

"Brother Ruan and I thought it over and over. If our families could have Chuyen's cans of rice and the baskets of bran, then we would all survive. The only harm done would be to him alone. The night we arrived at the Lac Thanh waterfront we agreed to tell Chuyen about it, and then we fell upon him, hiding his remains in a brick kiln on the riverbank."

"How dreadful!"

"I agree with you, but Ruan forced me into it. He's the one who bent down over Chuyen's chest, choking him to death with his hands, and then stabbed him twice in the back."

"Murderers will pay with their own deaths. Haven't you heard that frequently enough from the old canton chief?"

"Don't worry. Now that people are starving like flies, no one will pay any attention to this matter."

"Where is the rice and the bran?"

"It's in the hull of the boat. Let's go together with Ruan and his wife and take it home. Surely we will survive now!"

"No! I will never accept things that are tainted in that way. I do not want my husband and children to have to eat that kind of thing. It's better to die! Brother Ruan and his wife can do whatever they like. Heaven, oh, heaven! How can you and your brother have forgotten the master-and-servant relationship? Who helped you both to take your wives and to build your houses? Who supported the two of you from childhood to manhood? How can you be so heartless and thankless? If your brother is cruel and inhuman, then you must counsel him and hold him back. Don't think you are without guilt. Who else but you are the murderers? You are the older brother, and you must bear your parents' responsibility. It is better to be hungry and clean, to be in rags and yet smell good. How could you have stooped so low? What a thing for me to have to suffer!"

From that night, Mrs. Kha was bedridden. About the middle of the second month she died, taking along with her a "ten-thousand-autumns' remorse."*

Mr. Kha was detained at the province headquarters, and when he heard that his wife had died, he threw himself down moaning and crying tragically. The more he missed his wife, the more he realized that he was guilty. "Who else but you are the murderers? You are the older brother, and you must bear your parents' responsibility!" These words preyed on his mind day and night. He became very repentant, and one day, in a questioning session, he confessed the whole crime.

Chapter 18 Too many dead

My village sank deeper and deeper into the morass of hunger and cold. Every day some two dozen people died. Some died digging up their potatoes in the fields; some died on the roads while out begging; some went down to the river to fish, fell into the water, and were not discovered by the village until three or four days afterward when they surfaced with bloated bellies; there were still others who had gone no further than their home gates when they had become so exhausted that they had no

* A Vietnamese expression suggesting an irredeemable burden of guilt that must be carried with one to the grave.

choice but to prop themselves up against the bamboos or the shrubbery fences to die there.

Those who had food or money left in the village hired the patrolmen to bury the unlucky. He who buried a corpse was given a cup of wine and a bowl of rice. At first, the patrolmen still wrapped the corpses up with mats when they buried them. But later on, since there were just too many dead, they put a rope around the necks and dragged the corpses out into the fields, scratched at the earth a little, and then left them there.

The countryside could no longer feed its population. People tried to persuade each other to migrate to other places. Some went to Yen Bai or Thanh Hoa; others to Lang Son, Thai Nguyen, and other places. Thousands of them went. Often the trains could not take all the passengers. Those passengers who could not go waited until they were out of supplies and then died at the railroad stops, trusting their remains to other people and to the rainwater.

Chapter 19 A statement, an indictment

In the midst of the famine I had to go up to Hanoi on personal business. By accident, I met a Frenchman who was an old classmate of mine. I told him of the rice collection, of the money [tax] payment, and of the miserable situation of the population.

"I know everything," replied my friend in a voice that revealed both anger and hopelessness. "I know that Va-Re [Varet] and his superiors . . . are all pigs. Don't tell me about it anymore. I'm terribly ashamed."

Books

Aubaret, G.
Histoire et Description de la Basse Cochinchine (an edited translation of Trinh Hoai Duc's 鄭懷德 *Gia Dinh Thong Chi* 嘉定通志). Paris: Imprimerie Imperiale, 1864.

Bayen, J. F.
Problèmes Medicaux et Sociaux de l'Indochine. Saigon: Centre d'Études Indochinoises des Forces Maritimes d'Extrême Orient, 1949.

Bernard, Paul.
Le Problème Économique Indochinois. Paris: Nouvelles Éditions Latines, 1934.

Boissière, Jules.
L'Indochine avec les Français. Paris: Société des Éditions, 1896.

Bonnafond, Louis.
Trente Ans de Tonkin. Paris: E. Figuière, 1924.

Borgstrom, George.
The Hungry Planet: The Modern World at the Edge of Famine. New York: Collier Books, 1967.

Borie, J.
Le Métayage et la Colonization Agricole au Tonkin. Paris: Giard et Biere, 1906.

Bouinais, Albert and Paulus, A.
L'Indochine Française Contemporaine. Paris: A. Challamel, 1885.

Bourbon, André.
Le Redressement Économique de l'Indochine 1934–1937. Lyon: Bosc frères, M. & L. Riou, 1938.

Buttinger, Joseph.
Vietnam: A Dragon Embattled. New York: Praeger Publishers, Inc., 1967.

Chaliand, Gerard.
The Peasants of North Vietnam. Baltimore: Penguin Books, Inc., 1969.

Chassigneux, E.
"L'Irrigation dans le Delta du Tonkin," Paris, *Revue de Geographie annuelle,* 1912, fasc. 1.

Chen Han-seng.
Agrarian Problems in Southernmost China. Shanghai: Kelly and Walsh Ltd., 1936.

Chesneaux, Jean.
Contribution à l'Histoire de la Nation Vietnamienne. Paris: Éditions Sociales, Librairie Générale de Droit, 1955.

Cultru, Prosper.
Histoire de la Cochinchine Française des Origines à 1883. Paris: A. Challamel, 1910.

Dao Duy Anh.
Viet Nam Van Hoa Su Cuong [A Cultural History of Vietnam]. Saigon: Xuat Ban Bon Phuong, 1951.

Decoux, Jean.
A la Barre de l'Indochine: Histoire de mon Gouvernement Général, 1940–1945. Paris: Plon, 1949.

Diep Lien Anh.
Mau Trang—Mau Dao: Doi song doa-day cua phu cao-su mien dat-do [Latex and Blood: The Wretched Life of the Rubber Plantation Workers in the Red-Earth Districts]. Saigon: Lao Dong Moi, 1965.

Dorgelès, Roland.
Sur la Route Mandarine. Paris: A. Michel, 1925.

Doumer, Paul.
Situation de l'Indochine, 1897–1901. Hanoi: F. H. Schneider, 1902.

Dubreuil, René.
De la Condition des Chinois et de leur Rôle Économique en Indochine. Bar-sur-Seine: Imprimerie C. Caillard, 1910.

Dumarest, André.
La Formation de Classes Sociales en Pays Annamite. Lyon: Imprimerie P. Ferreol, 1935.

Dumont, René.
Révolution dans les Campagnes Chinoises. Paris: Éditions du Seuil, 1957.

Durand, Maurice and Huard, Pierre.
Connaissance du Viet Nam. Hanoi: École Française d'Extrême-Orient, 1954.

Ennis, Thomas.
French Policy and Development in Indochina. Chicago: University of Chicago Press, 1936.

Estèbe, Paul.
Le Problème du Riz en Indochine. Toulouse: F. Boisseau, 1934.

Fairbank, John King, ed.
The Chinese World Order: Traditional China's Foreign Relations. Cambridge, Massachusetts: Harvard University Press, 1968.

Fei Hsiao-tung and Chang Chih-I.
Earthbound China: A Study of Rural Economy in Yunnan. Chicago: University of Chicago Press, 1945.

Gauthier, Julien.
L'Indochine au Travail dans la Paix Française. Paris: Eyrolles, Imp. de Laboureur, 1949.

Goudal, Jean.
Labour Conditions in Indochina. Geneva: International Labour Office, 1938.

Gourou, Pierre.
Les Payans du Delta Tonkinois. Paris: Éditions d'Art et d'Histoire, 1936.

Gourou, Pierre.
L'Utilisation du Sol en Indochine. Paris: Centre d'Études de Politique Étrangère, 1940.

Grandel, Auguste.
Le Développement Économique de l'Indochine Française. Saigon: Imprimerie C. Ardin, 1936.

Henry, Yves.
Économie Agricole de l'Indochine. Hanoi: Gouvernement Général, 1932.

Hoang Dao.
Bun Lay Nuoc Dong [Mud and Stagnant Water]. Saigon: Tu Do, 1959. First published in 1938 in Hanoi by Doi Nay.

Hoang ngoc Phach and Huynh Ly.
So Tuyen Van Tho Yeu Nuoc va Cach Mang, tap II, tu dau the ky XX den 1930 [A Collection of Patriotic and Revolutionary Literature, vol. 2, from the Beginning of the Twentieth Century to 1930]. Hanoi: Nha Xuat Ban Giao Duc, 1959.

Hoang Van Duc.
Comment la Révolution a triomphé de la Famine. Hanoi, 1946.

Isoart, Paul.
Le Phénomène National Vietnamien: de l'Independence Unitaire à l'Independence Fractionnée. Paris: Librairie générale de droit et de jurisprudence, 1961.

Jammes, Henri Ludovic.
Souvenirs du Pays d'Annam. Paris: A. Challamel, 1900.

Lafargue, Jean André.
L'Immigration Chinoise en Indochine, sa réglementation, ses conséquences économiques et politiques. Paris: Henri Jouve, 1909.

Le Kim Ngan.
To Chuc Chinh Quyen Trung Uong duoi Trieu Le Thanh Tong. 1460–1497 [The Organization of the Central Government under the Reign of Le Thanh Tong, 1460–1497]. Saigon: Bo Quoc Gia Giao Duc, 1963.

Le Thanh Khoi.
Le Viet Nam: Histoire et Civilisation. Paris: Éditions de Minuit, 1955.

Le Thuoc.
Nguyen Cong Tru [Biography of a Famous Court Official under Mingmang]. Hanoi: Le Van Tan, 1928.

Limbourg, Michel.
L'Économie Actuelle du Vietnam Démocratique. Hanoi: Éditions en Langues Étrangères, 1956.

Luong Duc Thiep.
Xa Hoi Viet Nam [Vietnamese Society]. Hanoi: Han Thuyen, 1944.

Ly Binh Hue.
Le Régime des Concessions Domaniales en Indochine. Paris: Les Éditions Domat-Montchrestien, 1931.

Marquet, Jean.
De la Rizière à la Montagne. Paris: Mœurs annamite, 1920.

Melin, Pierre.
L'Endettement Agraire et la Liquidation des Dettes Agricoles en Cochinchine. Paris: Librarie Sociale et Économique, 1939.

Monet, Paul.
Les Jauniers: Histoire Vraie. Paris: Gallimard, 1931.

Morel, J.
Les Concessions de Terres au Tonkin. Paris, 1912.

Ngo Tat To.
Tat Den [When the Light's Put Out]. 5th ed. Hanoi: Van Hoa, 1962. First published in 1938 in Hanoi by Mai Linh.

Nguyen Cong Hoan.
Buoc Duong Cung [Dead End]. Saigon, 1967. First published in 1938 in
Hanoi by Pho Thong Ban Nguyet San.

Nguyen Phuong.
Viet Nam thoi banh truong: Tay Son [Vietnam during the Expansion
Period: the Tay Son]. Saigon: Khai Tri, 1968.

Nguyen Tan Loi.
L'Économie Commerciale du Riz en Indochine. Paris: F. Loviton, 1930.

Nguyen Thanh Nha.
Tableau Économique du Vietnam au XVIIe et XVIIIe Siècles. Paris:
Éditions Cujas, 1970.

Nguyen The Anh.
Kinh-te va Xa-hoi Viet Nam duoi cac Vua trieu Nguyen [Vietnamese
Economy and Society under the Nguyen Rulers]. Saigon: Trinh Bay, 1968.

Nguyen Van Nghi.
Étude Économique sur la Cochinchine Française et l'Infiltration Chinoise.
Monpellier: Imprimerie Firmin et Montane, 1920.

Nguyen Van Trung.
Chu Nghia thuc dan Phap o Viet Nam: Thuc Chat va Huyen Thoai [The
French Colonial Policy in Vietnam: Myth and Reality]. Hue: Nam Son, 1963.

Nguyen Van Vinh.
Les Réformes Agraires au Vietnam. Louvain: Universitaire de Louvain,
Faculté des Sciences Économiques et Sociales, 1961.

Nguyen Vy.
Tuan Chang Trai Nuoc Viet [Tuan, a Young Man of Vietnam]. Saigon,
1970.

Nhat Linh.
Nguoi Quay To [The Reeler of Silk]. Saigon: Doi Nay, 1962. First published
in 1927 in Hanoi.

Osborne, Milton E.
The French Presence in Cochinchina and Cambodia. Ithaca, New York:
Cornell University Press, 1969.

Pasquier, Pierre.
L'Annam d'Autrefois. Paris: A. Challamel, 1907.

Pham Cao Duong.
Thuc Trang cua gioi Nong Dan Viet Nam duoi thoi Phap thuoc [The True Conditions of the Vietnamese Peasants during French Colonization]. Saigon: Khai Tri, 1966.

Pham Van Son.
Viet Su Tan Bien: Tu Tay-Son Mat-Diep den Nguyen-So [New Compilation of Vietnamese History (vol. 4): From the End of the Tay Son to the Early Period of the Nguyen]. Saigon: Tu Sach Su Hoc Viet Nam, 1961.

Pham Van Son.
Viet Su Tan Bien: Viet Nam Khang Phap Su [New Compilation of Vietnamese History (vol. 5): History of the Vietnamese Resistance against the French]. Saigon: Khai Tri, 1962.

Phan Du.
Hai Chau Lan To Tam [Two Pots of Orchids]. Saigon: Cao Thom, 1965.

Phan Huy Chu.
Lich-trieu Hien-chuong Loai-chi 歷朝憲章類誌 [A Reference Book on the Institutions of Successive (Vietnamese) Dynasties]. Presented to Minh-mang in 1821. Original text and translation into modern Vietnamese by Luong than Cao Nai Quang. Saigon: Saigon University, Faculty of Law, 1957.

Phi Van.
Dan Que [The Peasants]. Saigon: Nha Xuat Ban Tan Viet, 1949.

Phi Van.
Dong Que [The Countryside]. 2nd ed. Hanoi: Xuat Ban Tan Viet, 1948. First published in 1943.

Reischauer, Edwin O., and Fairbank, John K.
East Asia: The Great Tradition. Boston: Houghton Mifflin Company, 1960.

Robequain, Charles.
L'Évolution Économique de l'Indochine Française. Paris: Centre d'Études de Politique Étrangère, 1939.

Robequain, Charles.
The Economic Development of French Indochina. Translated and supplemented by I. A. Wood. Oxford: Oxford University Press, 1944.

Roubaud, Louis.
Viet Nam: La Tragédie Indo-chinoise. Paris: Librarie Valois, 1931.

Sansom, Robert L.
The Economics of Insurgency in the Mekong Delta of Vietnam. Cambridge,
Massachusetts: The M.I.T. Press, 1970.

Son Nam.
Hinh Bong Cu [Portraits of Times Past]. Saigon: Phu Sa, 1964.

Taboulet, Georges.
*La Geste Française en Indochine: Histoire par les Textes de la France en
Indochine des Origines à 1914.* Paris: Adrien-Maisonneuve, 1956.

Tawney, Richard Henry.
Land and Labour in China. London: George Allen and Unwin Ltd. 1932.

The Nguyen.
Phan Chu Trinh [Biography of a Famous Modernization Advocate].
Saigon: Tan Viet, 1956.

Touzet, André.
L'Économie Indochinoise et la Grande Crise Universelle. Paris: M. Giard,
1934.

Tran Huy Lieu.
Xa Hoi Viet Nam duoi thoi Phap-Nhat, 1939–1945 [Vietnamese Society
during the French-Japanese period, 1939–1945]. Vols. 1 & 2. Hanoi: Van
Su Dia, 1957.

Tran Trong Kim.
Viet Nam Su Luoc [A Short History of Vietnam]. Saigon: Tan Viet, 1964.
First published in Hanoi in 1951 by Tan Viet.

Tran Van Giau.
Giai Cap Cong Nhan Viet Nam [The Vietnamese Working Class]. Hanoi:
Van Su Dia, 1962.

Tran Van Mai.
Ai Gay Nen Toi? [Who Committed This Crime?]. Saigon, 1956.

Truc Chi.
Viet Nam Kinh-te luoc-khao [A Summary of the Vietnamese Economy].
Saigon: SAPI, 1949.

Truong Ba Can et al.
Ky Niem 100 nam ngay Phap chiem Nam Ky [In Memory of the 100th
Anniversary of the French Conquest of Cochinchina]. Saigon: Trinh Bay,
1967.

Twitchett, Dennis Crispin.
Financial Administration under the T'ang Dynasty. Cambridge: Cambridge University Press, 1963.

Vu Quoc Thuc.
L'Economie Communaliste du Viet Nam. Hanoi: Presses Universitaires du Vietnam, 1951.

Vu Van Hien.
La Propriété Communale au Tonkin. Paris: Presses Modernes, 1939.

Wang Wen-yuan.
Les Relations entre l'Indochine Française et la Chine. Paris: Éditions Pierre Bossuet, 1937.

Woodside, Alexander B.
Vietnam and the Chinese Model: A Comparative Study of Nguyen and Ch'ing Civil Government in the First Half of the Nineteenth Century. Cambridge, Massachusetts: Harvard University Press, 1971.

Documents and periodicals

Annuaire de la Cochinchine, Paris, 1884.

Annuaire Statistique de l'Indochine, 1942.

Annuaire Statistique de l'Union Française d'Outremer, 1929–1946.

Ban-Trieu Ban-Nghich Liet-Truyen 本朝叛逆列傳 [Biographies of Rebels against the National Realm]. Translated into modern Vietnamese by Tran Khai Van. Saigon, 1963.

Bulletin Économique de l'Indochine, no. 2 (August 1898); no. 17 (November 1899) ; vols. 3 & 4, 1944.

Bulletin de la Société des Études Indochinoises, n.s. 42, nos. 1 & 2, 1967.

Chau Ban Trieu Nguyen [Vermilion Books of The Nguyen Dynasty].

Dai Nam Thuc-Luc Chinh-bien 大南實錄正編 [Veritable Records of the Imperial Vietnamese Court]. Formal organization and compilation from 1821.

Dai Viet Tap Chi (magazine), no. 10 (March 1, 1943).

Dong Duong Tap Chi (magazine), no. 27 (November 13, 1937).

Études Vietnamiennes, no. 13: Problèmes Agricoles. Hanoi: Xunhasaba, 1967.

France-Asie, no. 125–127 (October-December, 1956).

Kham Dinh Dai Nam Hoi Dien Su Le 欽定大南會典事例 [Official Compendium of Institutions and Usages of Imperial Vietnam]. Compiled at Hue, 1842–1851.

Kham Dinh Viet Su Thong Giam Cuong Muc 欽定越史通鑑綱目 [Official General Summary of the Comprehensive Mirror of Vietnamese History]. Hue, 1885

Muc Luc Chau Ban Trieu Nguyen 目錄硃本朝阮 [Catalogue of Nguyen Dynasty Imperial Archives].

Nam Phong Tap Chi [The Vietnamese Ethos], no. 44 (November 1920); no. 104 (April 1926); no. 173 (June 1932).

Revue Indochinoise vol. 1 (Hanoi, 1925); vol. 3 (French language edition of *Dong Duong Tap Chi*, 1938).

La Revue Indochinoise, no. 33 (Hanoi, December 25, 1937).

Revue Indochinoise Juridique et Économique, vol. 1, 1937.

Su Dia [History and Geography] no. 6 (Saigon, 1967).

Témoignages et Documents Français Relatifs à la Colonisation Française au Viet Nam. Hanoi: Association Culturelle pour le Salut du Viet Nam, 1945.

Thanh Nghi (magazine), no. 12 (May 1, 1942); no. 47 (October 16, 1943); no. 55 (February 26, 1944); no. 57 (March 11, 1944); no. 59 (March 25, 1944); no. 63 (April 29, 1944); no. 107 (May 5, 1945); no. 110 (May 26, 1945).

Trung Bac Chu Nhat (magazine), no. 172 (August 29, 1943); no. 251 (July 1, 1945).

Viet Nam Tan Bao (magazine), April 8, 1945.

Vietnamese
mau = 3,600 square meters, or slightly less than an acre
sao = 360 square meters, or one-tenth of a *mau*
hoc = 60 liters of rice, or about 44 kilograms
gia = 40 liters of rice, or about 30 kilograms
noi = 20 to 25 kilograms, depending on the locality
thang = 1/47 of a *hoc*, or about 3 pounds

French
kilometer = 0.62 miles
square kilometer = 0.3861 square miles
hectare = 2.47 acres
meter = 39.37 inches
metric ton = 1,000 kilograms, or about 1.1 U.S. tons
kilogram = 2.2 pounds
liter = 0.908 dry quarts, or 1.057 liquid quarts.
gram = 0.035 ounces

Chinese
mow = one-sixth of an acre
kung = one-sixteenth of an acre

GLOSSARY OF WEIGHTS AND MEASURES

Note: Vietnamese names have not been inverted.

INDEX